Imaginization

For Karen
Evan and Heather

Imaginization

the art of
c*reat*ive
management

GARETH MORGAN

SAGE Publications
International Educational and Professional Publisher
Newbury Park   London   New Delhi

Significant discounts are available to individuals and organizations who wish to order quantities of *IMAGINIZATION*. For more information, please call Sage Publications' Customer Service Department at 805-499-9774 between 7:00 AM and 5:00 PM, Pacific Standard Time. Quantity discounts only apply to customers in the USA and Canada.

For information address:

SAGE Publications, Inc.
2455 Teller Road
Newbury Park, California 91320

SAGE Publications Ltd.
6 Bonhill Street
London EC2A 4PU
United Kingdom

SAGE Publications India Pvt. Ltd.
M-32 Market
Greater Kailash I
New Delhi 110 048 India

Printed in the United States of America

Library of Congress Cataloging-in-Publication Data

Morgan, Gareth, 1943-
    Imaginization: the art of creative management / Gareth Morgan.
      p.   cm.
    Includes bibliographical references and index.
    ISBN 0-8039-5299-6.
    1. Industrial management. 2. Organizational behavior.
  2. Organizational change. I. Title.
  HD38.M612   1993
  658—dc20   93-12148

          95 96 10 9 8 7 6 5

Sage Production Editor: Diane S. Foster

Imagination is more important than knowledge.

To raise new questions, new possibilities, to regard old problems from a new angle, requires creative imagination and marks real advance in science.

Albert Einstein

Imaginization

. . . an invitation to
develop new ways
of thinking about
organization and
management.

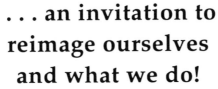

. . . an invitation to
reimage ourselves
and what we do!

This is a book about new management practice.

But it's also a book about new management theory . . . theory that can self-organize, evolve, twist and turn . . . perhaps change at the speed of light?

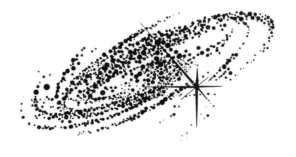

Organization *is* imaginization!

We are leaving the age of organized organizations and moving into an era where the ability to understand, facilitate, and encourage processes of self-organization will become a key competence.

It's impossible to develop new styles of organization and management while continuing to think in old ways.

An organization has no presence beyond that of the people who bring it to life.

You can't create a learning organization. . .
But you can enhance people's capacities to learn and align their activities in creative ways—

Ideas about organization are always based on implicit images or metaphors that persuade us to see, understand, and manage situations in a particular way.

Metaphors create insight.
But they also distort.
They have strengths.
But they also have limitations.

In creating ways of seeing, they create ways of not seeing.

There can be no single theory or metaphor that gives an all-purpose point of view, and there can be no simple "correct theory" for structuring everything we do.

The challenge facing modern managers is to become accomplished in the art of using metaphor to find new ways of seeing, understanding, and shaping their actions.

Contents

flourish, while respecting the need for integration and accountability within the organization as a whole.

Preface

Many people are struggling in their attempts to deal with the new world realities, particularly as they affect the domain of organization and management. Everywhere we look, traditional structures are being reshaped or falling down. Powerful nation-states are fragmenting. Once-successful companies are finding that sure-hit formulas no longer work. People, and even whole communities, are finding the world moving beneath their feet as traditional markets, industries, and sources of employment disappear under the impact of new information technologies and a restructuring of the world economy.

As a result, many once-successful managers find themselves out of work or floundering as bureaucratic hierarchies and familiar career plans disappear. Those fortunate enough to retain their jobs face major challenges and readjustments. Rather than continuing in their old style, they have to find new ways of managing in flat, decentralized organizations where a capacity to flow with change is becoming a key requirement.

If one reads the popular management literature, there's no shortage of advice as to what people and their organizations need to do to be successful in this fast changing world. The messages are forceful ones:

"Become flexible."
"Adapt."
"Self-organize."
"Thrive on chaos."
"Develop a learning orientation."
"Become more creative."
"Be market driven!"
"Foster entrepreneurship."
"Empower your staff."
"Decentralize."

One may want to debate the buzzwords and the precise directions given, but there's a consistent theme here. In the new global environment, old styles of organization and management no longer work. We have to find alternatives.

But *how* is this to be achieved? How can one encourage the new organizational styles in practice? How can people develop the modes of thinking and styles of management needed to make the new approaches a reality?

That's what this book is all about.

It's a book about the new management and new styles of organization. But, more fundamentally, it's a book about the kind of thinking that managers and people working in organizations need to develop if they are to be successful in dealing with a turbulent world.

I have called the book *Imaginization* to capture the fundamental challenge.

As a society, we have become preoccupied with the idea of finding ways of fixing and controlling the world around us. "Getting organized" has meant finding that structure or solution for a situation that's going to last—hence the typical organization chart, with its concern to shape everything into neat and tidy parts. In more stable times, the process worked. But, in times of change, organizations that are organized in this way run into trouble because they can't adjust to the new challenges being faced. That's why fresh ways of thinking about this problem are so necessary.

The challenge now is to *imaginize*: to infuse the process of organizing with a spirit of imagination that takes us beyond bureaucratic boxes. We need to find creative ways of organizing and managing that allow us to "go with the flow," using new images and ideas as a means of creating shared understandings among those seeking to align their activities in organized ways.

Imaginization is a way of thinking. It's a way of organizing. It's a key managerial skill. It provides a way of helping people understand and develop their creative potential. It offers a means of finding innovative solutions to difficult problems. And, last but not least, it provides a means of empowering people to trust themselves and find new roles in a world characterized by flux and change.

In writing this book, I have chosen to speak to multiple audiences. The first includes practicing managers, organizational consultants, and executives in business, government, education, labor unions, and not-for-profit organizations who wish to tap their creative abilities in dealing with problems of change. Hence every chapter demonstrates imaginization in action, showing how we can mobilize our capacities for creative thought to rethink our roles as managers and develop fresh approaches to organizational design, planning, and the management of change.

In this sense, *Imaginization* is designed and written as a practical book on management with the practitioner in mind. But it's also relevant to a more academic audience and to students of management who want to take organization and management theory out of the straitjacket created by conventional academic discourse. Readers familiar with my earlier book *Images of Organization* will find that the following chapters extend the scope and implications of that work in a way that seeks to develop a new kind of organization theory: one that can evolve, develop, and change in a fluid, self-organizing way.

Imaginization offers a means whereby people in everyday situations can explore and challenge their taken-for-granted assumptions while opening new avenues for understanding and action. I believe that it offers an approach to organization and management that demystifies the process of theory building and shows how it's possible for *everyone* to become their own theorists, developing penetrating insights about the organizations in which they work and their roles within them.

ACKNOWLEDGMENTS

As everyone knows, the writing of a book such as this can be a long and demanding task. It starts with a neat idea that grows, then grows and grows. It's only years later that we see the final result. So, as I write these final words and bring this project to a close, I feel a sense of both relief and accomplishment and an enormous sense of gratitude to those who have helped me along the way.

First, I want to offer my sincere thanks to the individuals and organizations involved in the projects and change interventions discussed in the following chapters and to the thousands of people who have participated in my seminars and workshops on the new management. I have learned so much from their insights and ideas as we've explored and developed the implications of imaginization in practice. As you will see, the following chapters present a mixture of cases and experiences involving a variety of people working in many different kinds of organizations, some large, some small. Some are well-known, but I have chosen to use pseudonyms throughout, so that we can focus on the issues rather than the names involved. I am immensely grateful for their contributions and thank them for helping to make the learning and writing connected with this book such a challenging and rewarding task. I also owe much to the writers featured in the bibliography and to my academic and professional colleagues in Europe and North America. Though it's not possible to mention them all by name, they've made an enormous contribution.

I owe a special word of thanks to Rhea Copeland for the wonderful secretarial support provided throughout the project. She has organized the production of the manuscript with great skill and enthusiasm, and her cheerful and unfailing help has made the whole process thoroughly enjoyable. In many respects, this is as much her book as mine.

I also owe a great debt to my artist-illustrator, Sacha Warunkiw. Together we've enjoyed developing the process of "fax art," whereby we convert the results of my research into a visual form. His artistry and our shared sense of humor have proved crucial in my attempt to break the constraints of words and writing in communicating ideas about the new management. I thank him for his unending patience and creativity.

My colleagues Joe Arbuckle, Robert Burns, Alan Engelstad, Lin Ward, and Asaf Zohar have also contributed to aspects of the research for this book, and I am grateful for their help and insights. Both Joe and Robert were involved at an early stage of development and have played a key role in helping me shape the basic ideas. My friends at Sage Publications have also proved wonderful partners in converting the manuscript into a published reality. This is the fourth book that we've done together and, as always, it has proved a great experience.

I am a lucky man to be able to say thank you to so many people, but luckier still to have the love and support of a family who have nurtured the growth of the ideas and provided a creative context in which to work. My wife Karen has provided a constant source of inspiration and support as both a friend and a colleague. Her influence is enfolded in everything I do, and I value our partnership in more ways than I can say. It is to her and our children, Evan and Heather, that I dedicate this book, with love and thanks, and in the knowledge that without them life wouldn't be half as full or nearly as much fun.

GARETH MORGAN

1 Introduction

Imaginization: The art of creative management.

In this chapter, I explore the concept, showing how we can mobilize images and ideas to organize and manage in new ways.

When asked to give a "short" summary of what imaginization entails, I like to emphasize the following five points.

1. Imaginization is about improving our abilities to see and understand situations in new ways.

To illustrate, consider the drawing on page 3. It presents a pig surrounded by a butcher, an artist, a wolf, a farmer, a veterinarian, a philosopher, a Muslim, and a small child.

My question: What is the pig?

It's a simple question, but the answer is quite difficult because the pig is many things at once. This is why I've surrounded it with the different characters. For the wolf, the pig is food; for the Muslim, it's an unclean animal; the butcher and farmer are eyeing commercial quality and value; the veterinarian is considering the pig's state of health; the child is thinking about the story of the three little pigs; and so on. The precise meaning and significance of the pig will vary according to the frame of reference through which it is viewed. Each frame opens or closes a horizon of understanding by directing attention in a particular way.

The same is true when it comes to understanding the world of organization and management. Our understanding of what we are seeing changes according to the frame or image that shapes our viewpoint.

Consider, for example, a manager who is dealing with what she perceives to be a "problem of communication" with her staff. The message she is trying to get across has not taken root. She feels that she needs to do more work on her personal communication style.

But what is this problem of communication?

WHAT IS THE PIG?

Is it the result of how jobs are designed?

Are people not hearing what is being said because priorities are elsewhere?

Is the problem arising because different people are on different "wavelengths" and are hearing different things?

Or is there a political dimension to the problem, with people not hearing because they do not *want* to hear?

It's a problem of communication all right. But what *is* the problem?

It's a simple example, but it cuts to the heart of many organizational issues because the manager cannot resolve the problem in the frame in which it is defined. If she persists in seeing her difficulties as a communication problem, she may never penetrate to the level of understanding that will allow the underlying factors to be addressed.

The same is true in our attempts to understand, design, and manage organizations more generally.

Many concepts of organization and management have a mechanistic flavor. For the last 200 years, managers have learned to see and understand organizations as being equivalent to human machines and have tried to design and run them as such. Hence complex tasks and activities are fragmented into separate parts, allocated to separate departments, and then fragmented again as detailed jobs are defined and allocated to groups and individuals coordinated and controlled through job descriptions, hierarchy, and all manner of sophisticated systems for monitoring performance. But organizations are not machines. They employ living beings who often refuse to act like cogs in wheels or to pursue formal organizational objectives. People working in machinelike organizations have needs,

interests, and inclinations of their own and rarely entirely submit to the requirements imposed on them. This is why this kind of organization often ends up as a battlefield, with one group pitted against another, or as a place where people withdraw into states of apathy or play an elaborate bureaucratic game where little of substance is achieved.

In an earlier book, *Images of Organization,* I explored the limitations of this kind of mechanical thinking, showing how organizations, like the pig discussed earlier, can be many things at once and how different images of organization can provide frameworks for understanding, designing, and managing organizations in many different ways.

For example, think about an organization as a living organism with specific sets of needs that *must* be satisfied if it is to survive. Think about it as a culture, as a political system, as a psychic prison, as an instrument of domination.

Different images generate different insights. For example, if we learn to view organizations as cultures, we begin to understand how they are held together through patterns of shared meaning, shared values, ideologies, rituals, and belief systems. If we view them as political systems, attention is drawn to the conflicting interests and power plays shaping everyday reality. If we see them as psychic prisons, we begin to understand how individuals and groups become trapped by their belief systems. If we view them as instruments of domination, we highlight their inhumane and socially destructive qualities. And so on.

In reality, organizations may combine all these different characteristics, but our limited ways of seeing filter and block a lot of the different dimensions. As a result, we rarely grasp the full nature of the problems with which we are dealing, and that's why the problems are often so difficult to resolve.

Images, assumptions, and frames of reference can act as different lenses, allowing us to see what we otherwise cannot see. Or, to change the metaphor, they act like radar systems allowing us to pick up significant messages from a situation that would otherwise escape attention.

Subsequent chapters provide numerous illustrations of how we can use this insight to improve our ability to "read" and grasp the different dimensions of organizational life, and to make sense of problematic situations. They invite us to learn how to recognize when we're dealing with a highly mechanized organization, with one that is dominated by aspects of its culture, with situations that are highly politicized, or whatever. They encourage us to recognize when we're going to be swallowed by "gulfs of inactivity," when we're being handed a "political football" or are dealing with a situation that's in danger of "boiling dry."

In effect, the aim is to encourage us to do in relation to the world of organization what we are already doing in the rest of our lives! In everyday situations, we are all accomplished readers of the circumstances in which we find ourselves. We open ourselves to nuance. We learn to pick up key signals. We "see the angles." We develop the knack of finding resonant images or metaphors that help us to make sense of things. We use all these readings to shape appropriate actions.

Imaginization builds on this skill, and seeks to bring it to life as a basic competence for effective management.

2. Imaginization is about finding new images for new ways of organizing.

If we see things in old ways, it's very difficult to act in new ways. That's one of the main problems with organization and management today. Old ways of thinking are so ingrained that they're difficult to shake off.

Consider, for example, how charts and diagrams tend to dominate thinking about organizational design. They're a product of the static understandings generated by a mechanical view of organization. This almost always forces managers to

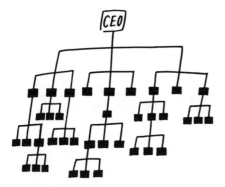

look for the equivalent of an engineering blueprint to capture what they're doing.

Hence we develop an organization chart to describe the structure of our organization. We turn it upside down if we feel that we are getting too hierarchical or remote from our customers. We "delayer" and cut out the middle to streamline decision making. We "downsize" and amputate parts of the hierarchy to reduce costs and overhead. We move to a matrix of columns and rows when we want to balance the needs of projects with those of functional departments. We move to group or "team-based" structures when we want to create more participative, "employee-driven" organizations. Any reorganization involves redrawing the organization chart or reshaping the hierarchy, replacing solid lines with dotted lines, and so on.

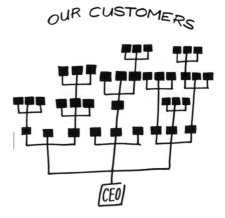

Organization charts are useful tools, but they can also be extremely limiting because they entrench the idea that one's organization is a structure that can be engineered and reengineered to produce appropriate results. A new organization chart

is often seen as a solution to an organization's problems. But, more often than not, it can leave the basic problems unchanged. For example, when you reshape or "downsize" a bureaucracy, you usually just end up with a smaller bureaucracy!

When you move to a matrix, you often end up with

bureaucratic management in another form. You don't necessarily create an organization that can flow and self-organize
along with the changes being faced.

Organizations used to be places. They used to be things.
They could be regarded as having clear-cut goals and objectives that would endure over time and they could be designed and
managed in a mechanical way. Organization charts, clearly defined systems, flow diagrams, and other engineered blueprints, provided effective models for systematizing organizational activity. They still do if one is organizing a routine,
predictable task.

But, as information technology catapults us into the reality
of an Einsteinian world where old structures and forms of
organization dissolve and at times become almost invisible, the
old approach no longer works. Through the use of telephone,
fax, electronic mail, computers, video, and other information
technology, people and their organizations are becoming dis-
embodied. They can act as if they are completely connected
while remaining far apart. They can have an instantaneous
global presence. They can transcend traditional barriers of
space and time, continually creating and re-creating themselves through changing networks of interconnection based on
"real time" communication. As one network comes into being,
others dissolve. Temporary alliances can replace fixed structures. The reality of our Einsteinian world is that, often, organizations don't have to be organizations any more!

In this world, mechanistic thinking breaks down and managers have to find fresh images for understanding and shaping what they're doing.

Thus, in the following chapters, I'll be giving a lot of attention to how it's possible to design organizations as if they were "spider plants" or like dandelion seeds blowing in the wind. I'll show how the image of termites building a nest can provide fresh perspectives on planning and the management of change. I'll show how an image of Einstein's theory of relativity can create interesting insights for the redesign of products and services. I'll show how all kinds of ad hoc imagery can be used to create breakthroughs on organizational problems and find new initiatives in difficult situations.

The process of imaginization invites creativity. Just as it encourages us to see and "read" organizational situations with fresh perspective, it also invites us to "write" our organizations in new ways.

To give a brief illustration of what's possible, have you ever thought about trying to design or manage your organization holographically? The hologram is one of the marvels of laser technology. Common examples are now found in those shining images on credit cards and on the covers of glossy magazines that change color and shape when viewed from different angles. More sophisticated holograms, such as those found in contemporary art galleries, present multidimensional images that look like sculptures in light. As you change position and walk around the "sculpture," it changes before your very eyes!

These holographic images are created with lasers that scatter beams of light so that information relating to the whole image is contained *in each and every part*. It sounds crazy, but it's true. The holographic plate on which an image is encoded, the equivalent of a negative in photography, can be broken into hundreds of different pieces. Any one of those pieces can then be used to re-create an approximation of the whole, because the whole image is contained in *all* the parts! Everything is enfolded in everything else. It's just as if one were able to throw a pebble into a pond and see the whole pond and surrounding scenery in each and every one of the drops of water produced by the splash.

One of the challenges of this holographic image is to find ways of building wholes *into* parts. It seems paradoxical, especially in organizational contexts where the traditional logic is to build wholes out of separate parts. But it is an eminently workable idea.

For example, culture is basically holographic. It's a system of attitudes, inclinations, capacities, values, beliefs, and social practices where characteristics of "the whole" are latent within the parts. Culture is something that unfolds: It emerges and "comes alive" as people enact its characteristics.

Information technology also has holographic characteristics in that it has the capacity to spread information and intelligence throughout a system, so that people can be completely integrated even though they are far apart, because they possess the knowledge and intelligence to act on behalf of the whole.

Bring these two ideas together and we have a novel way of thinking about how we can create and manage decentralized organizations that are completely unified, because people are on the same "wavelength" and have the capacity to reproduce the character and style of their organization naturally and spontaneously. Organizations designed and managed in this way may have much more in common with dandelion seeds and spider plants than with the bureaucracies of old.

My point is that we can't hope to create new organizational forms in old ways. We have to get beyond tinkering with existing organization structures. We have to imaginize and explore creative possibilities that can add new chapters to the history of how we organize and manage.

3. Imaginization is about the creation of shared understandings.

Organization *always* hinges on the creation of shared meanings and shared understandings, because there have to be common reference points if people are to shape and align their activities in an organized way.

One can see the process in all kinds of organizing activity. For example, one of the important functions of leadership is to generate a sense of shared vision and shared values that will help people mobilize efforts in a common direction. The same is true of corporate culture. Even organization charts are powerful creators of meaning. They help people define and know their place and are of immense symbolic value in communicating a sense of order. Bureaucratic structures, rules, regulations, job descriptions, reward systems, and other controls pursue the same objective: this time by defining clear frameworks within which people are expected to operate. Even the process of organizing by holding a gun to a person's head is ultimately about the creation of a shared understanding: that, if one does not act appropriately, the consequences will be fatal.

The challenge in times of change is to find shared meanings that are themselves in flux, so that people are encouraged to find an intelligent place in the world around them. Consider, for example, how the president of a large and very successful company is shaping a major transition in the way it does business. In formal terms, the company is changing from a centrally controlled style of management to one giving much more autonomy to business units. Powerful functional departments will eventually be replaced by decentralized decision-making units linked by new information flows. But the change cannot occur over-night, and, as the company changes, it cannot undermine the viability of its existing business. The new structure and style has to be invented as the company goes along, but in a way that allows the existing business to continue to be successful.

To communicate the challenge, the president encourages his staff to think about their situation as one where "we're rebuilding our house *while still continuing to live in it.*" He is at pains to emphasize that the change is not just a renovation but a complete rebuilding in which *everything* will eventually be transformed. The image allows him to talk with staff about the necessity of identifying "the bearing walls" of the existing business. They have to be sure that these are not knocked out too early, or else the whole business will come tumbling down. They thus have to check existing supports as they go along and have to think about developing the walls that will be needed in the future organiza-tion. Eventually, all the old walls will be knocked out, but, for the moment, staff are engaged in a process of cautious demolition and simultaneous rebuilding. The image helps them find mean-ing and convenient reference points in a world that's in danger of falling all around them. The metaphor helps them find ways of coping with the discomfort and potential dangers of their current situation while looking forward to the new "home" that they will eventually produce.

This ability to invent evocative images or stories that can resonate with the challenges at hand and help motivate and mobilize people to achieve desired goals, or to cope with the unknown, is becoming a key managerial skill. It is central to the process of imaginization, and in the following chapters I will be giving many more examples.

Over the last 20 years or so, most senior managers have become very aware of the importance of developing a strong sense of vision and the corporate values that can help guide their staff in an appropriate direction. They are aware of the importance of developing a strong corporate culture and of controls and systems that can support it in practice. But strong leaders, strong visions, and the strong signals sent by corporate controls can also create traps. They can create shared under-standings of the wrong kind, fostering conformity and compli-ance rather than a willingness and ability to flow with change.

Ambiguity, uncertainty, questioning, instability, risk, chance encounter, crisis, openness, quest, challenge: These seem to be the characteristics of situations in which innovation thrives, and which systems of shared meaning need to support. To create learning-oriented organizations, one needs to evolve visions that invite continuous questioning; one needs to foster values that can open the organization to new insights and encourage staff to develop understandings and practices appropriate to the challenges at hand. One needs, in short, to encourage understandings that generate capacities for learning and continuous self-organization and an ability to deal with crisis and opportunity positively. Our capacities for imaginization can serve us well here, helping us to mobilize the power of shared understanding in fluid, creative ways.

4. Imaginization is about personal empowerment.

People are reluctant to relax their hold on existing reality unless they feel that they have somewhere to turn.

That's why so many organizational change programs are so threatening. When a person's role is being challenged, the person also feels challenged and, unless he or she can find a way of grasping new possibilities, there's no space in which to respond.

The process of imaginization can make an enormous contribution here by helping people grasp new perspectives on their situations and by opening new possibilities for development.

This will be discussed in more detail in Chapter 2. But, to illustrate the challenge, I'd like you to imagine a battle in olden times. A Roman general is fighting his arch rival. He and his troops have arrived at the battle scene first. The general has taken command of the highest hill. He is able to survey the whole battle scene and issue appropriate commands to his troops. In return, he receives detailed information from the front line.

In contemporary language, he has super vision and can act as an excellent supervisor.

Unfortunately, this military model of top-down control, which may be perfectly appropriate for fighting a battle from the top of a hill, has been transferred willy-nilly into organizational contexts and is now causing problems for many managers because they are charged with being supervisors when the reality of the situation is that their staff have far more knowledge and insights on what's being managed than they do. They try to supervise because they're "in charge" but they end up making a nuisance of themselves. To overcome their problem, they need to recognize that their formal role is an anachronism and find new ways of imaginizing themselves as "resources" to their staff, as "troubleshooters" who will have to tackle specific problems, as "boundary spanners" whose main task is to integrate their units with the rest of their organization, or through some other resonant image that grasps what they need to do.

It's a simple example but it cuts to the core of what imaginization is all about. As individuals, we frequently get trapped by images of ourselves and our role and, as a result, lock ourselves into inappropriate modes of behavior.

By becoming aware of this, and learning to challenge our images when appropriate, we can find a way out. Indeed, we see the process at work in the history of management thought as successive images of management give way to others. Consider, for example, the concept of management itself. If you trace its history, you'll be led back to the art of horsemanship. *To manage* originally meant putting a horse through its paces.

Now, we freely talk about managing people. What an act of imaginization!

In the early history of people management, you'll find there's a lot of horsemanship. It's no accident, for example, that we talk about the "reins of power." Early managers specialized in putting their employees through their paces. Now, of course, management has become much more sophisticated. We've imaginized new forms, talking about participation, motivation, collaboration, empowerment, partnership, and the like. The search for these new forms began when the human "horses" began to unionize. It received a further boost in affluent, democratic Western societies employing an educated work force and still continues as we wrestle with problems of managing situations where we can't be physically present or have no chance of knowing what's going on. Consider, for example, some of the popular management advice of recent years: manage by walking around; become a "one-minute manager"; become a visionary; become a "servant-leader"; and so on. In essence, the images invite us to imaginize ourselves in new ways.

By grasping the central relationship between images of ourselves, our situations, and the behaviors in which we engage, we can marshall the power of imaginization in a fluid manner. We can learn to be critical analysts of the ideas and assumptions that are locking us into inappropriate behaviors and learn how to mobilize new insights and develop new capacities.

The power of the basic idea is vividly illustrated in a story related by Karl Weick about a group of people who got lost in a severe snowstorm in the Swiss Alps. They were stranded and on the verge of giving up hope, when one of the party found a map in one of his pockets. Mobilized by the new possibilities, they mustered their energy and eventually found their way back to civilization. Imagine their surprise, when, after their return home, it was pointed out that it was a map of the Pyrenees, not the Alps!

The adventure illustrates how a new image and new understanding of a situation can create space in which new initiatives and new actions can emerge. Without the map, the group would have probably perished. But it was not the map, so much as the image that they had a map, that enabled them to create the self-organizing initiative that allowed a new outcome. As noted earlier, people and their behaviors tend to be confined by the images that they hold of themselves and their situations. By opening oneself to new images, and the new sense of identity they create, one can reach beyond the limitations of the status quo and allow new possibilities to emerge.

In the most basic sense, imaginization invites a way of thinking. It encourages us to become our own theorists and to feel comfortable about acting on the basis of our insights. It invites us to develop a skill that I believe we all have, even though we may not realize that this is the case. By recognizing this, and thinking creatively and intelligently about ourselves and our situations, we can "push the envelope" on our realities and reshape them positively.

5. Imaginization is about developing capacities for continuous self-organization.

If the challenge of the past has been to "get organized," the challenge of the future is to find ways in which we can remain open to continuous self-organization: so that we can adapt and evolve as we go along. This is what imaginization ultimately helps us to do, because it involves a constant process of interpreting and reinterpreting where we are and where we want to be. It opens the way to a mode of personal theorizing that can create a self-organizing reservoir of new insights that can be modified or replaced as better ones emerge.

I have an image of the modern manager as someone who is equipped with a sophisticated radar system that allows her to "sense" or "read" what is happening and to use this reading to shape or "write" an appropriate response. It is an image of a creative manager who is always able to develop novel insights, understandings, and actions to meet the challenges at hand. It provides a powerful means of breaking the constraints of bureaucratic thinking and for launching our organizations into the reality of an Einsteinian world where capacities for continuous learning and self-organization are likely to become the norm.

Bureaucratic organizations tend to be variety-reducing systems. They take complex and uncertain patterns of information and, through rules, programs, and standardized frames of interpretation, try to filter the variance and create conformity. They try to fix and structure the world outside and inside the enterprise, creating rigidities and an artificial stability that then act as barriers to change. They encourage organization as a disciplined activity.

Self-organizing systems, on the other hand, try to remain open to novelty. They thrive on randomness, ambiguity, and contradiction, using the dilemmas and problems thus created to generate innovative responses. The process of imaginization enhances this process by mobilizing individual and collective imaginations to generate new insights, pose new questions, and generate innovative actions. It provides the basis for *increasing* the variety within a system, to keep it fresh and alive in view of the challenges being faced. It improves a system's capacity for learning, dialogue, and change because it's based on an interpretive process that's fluid and dynamic. In contrast with more bureaucratic systems that seek organized closure on issues and problems, it embraces openness as a source of vitality and life. Imaginization taps and provides a source of creative energy, enhancing and sustaining capacities for self-organization in ways that can help people, as individuals and in groups, renew and vitalize themselves in a free-flowing way.

This is the promise of the approach, and in the following chapters I want to illustrate it in practice. Clearly, from what has been said, the process of imaginization cannot be reduced to a simple recipe, for that would regiment and destroy the variety on which it thrives. Imaginization extends an invitation: an invitation to a way of thinking, a way of seeing, a way of doing. It's more of a mind-set and a capacity than a technique.

Most of the chapters draw on my own personal experience in using the approach, in effect inviting you to join me on my projects. The aim is to take you right inside the process, so that you can experience it as directly as possible, and find ways of making it your own. In offering the accounts described in these chapters, I must emphasize that I am not trying to create an authoritative "this is the way it is" point of view. Thus as you read, you may find yourself challenging what I am seeing and the interpretations being made. You may find that you have your own insights or special angle. You may wish to identify with the standpoint of specific people in some of my cases and imaginize from *their* point of view. If so, please join in and create your own "reading" and dialogue with the situation at hand. For this is what imaginization is all about.

In this spirit, I discuss a mixture of cases involving many different kinds of organizations. Most are based on fairly brief encounters, because I specialize in short, strategic interventions, designed to create new momentum in stuck situations. I have deliberately included a mix of successful and less successful projects, because not all interventions have Hollywood endings. This mix helps to show the strengths and limitations of imaginization in practice, allowing us to derive maximum learning from the experiences.

Because I have chosen to write a book that demonstrates imaginization in practice, I have delayed discussion of theoretical and methodological issues until the appendixes. As you will see, the approach builds on interesting theories about how people create and enact their realities and on the role of image and identity in processes of self-organization and change. Readers are invited to turn to this material whenever the need arises. Like the other chapters in this book, I have written them as freestanding essays that can communicate their message at almost any point in the text.

So, without further ado, join me on a journey of imaginization. Feel free to roam as you will.

2 Looking in the Mirror

As organizations are flattened, decentralized, and turned upside down, managers often have to rethink themselves and their roles in fundamental ways. Yet this can be an extremely challenging task. For how can we learn to see ourselves anew? How can we find fresh ways of thinking, behaving, and communicating with those with whom we work?

This is the challenge addressed in this chapter. It offers a method for imaging and reimaging managerial roles. The approach is playful, inviting you to engage in some personal reflection on your managerial style to promote better self-understanding and open new possibilities for future behavior.

IMAGING AND REIMAGING
YOUR MANAGERIAL STYLE

A View of the Boss

Martha: My boss?

As an animal or storybook character?

Well . . . I guess I'd describe him as a fox . . .

The fox in *The Tale of Jemima Puddle-Duck* by Beatrix
Potter . . .

You know the story?

Jemima is looking for a place to build her nest and meets
this smooth, well-groomed fox. He's very polite and
helpful, and offers Jemima a place in his woodshed. They
become good friends—at least Jemima thinks so—until
his plan to eat her and her eggs is discovered. He was so
smooth—even asked Jemima to bring back some sage
and onions on her next visit to her farm!

That's what my boss is like.

Mr. Impeccable.

So smooth. Completely in charge.

Always helpful.

Always gives the impression that he has your
interests in mind.

But he's not to be trusted. I have a sneaky feeling that,
despite all the velvety talk, he's really out for himself.

I've never thought about him that way before. But
that's who he is . . . the fox in *Jemima Puddle-Duck*!

*   *   *   *   *

A View of the Managers in Head Office

Jack: They are cuckoos who lay their eggs in other birds'
nests. . . . They watch all the toil that goes into the

nest-building. Then they fly in, knock all the eggs out, and lay their own. . . . We are the other birds. We are just trying to build and live in our nests, but head office keeps coming in and laying its eggs!

George: They act *as if* they're city dwellers with cottages in the country. . . .

We're the contractors who maintain the cottages.

But we do so much work on them, we fall in love with them . . . just like architects fall in love with their buildings.

But the city dwellers *think* they are the owners and want to direct and be involved in all the work. They call all the budgets, decide on everything that needs to be done, and set the standards.

But, at the same time, they try to give us the impression that *we* are the owners!

Mario: They're kennel dogs . . . pampered poodles living in a make-believe world. . . . We are more like field dogs familiar with the challenge of the wilderness. We know how to survive. . . . The poodles run around in their yard and think that they know what it's like to be out here in the field. But, in reality, they can't cope.

Bert: The managers at head office are cunning and sly—like foxes. We are German shepherds . . . hardworking, very territorial, loyal dogs. We are intelligent but, compared with the foxes, we're naive. Unfortunately, they usually outsmart us!

* * * * *

The Managers That We Have to Deal With in Product Development

They're like mules . . . very stubborn; they push if they're pulled, and pull if they're pushed . . . they're very closed-minded.

They're like camels . . . they have a very narrow focus; they think they're always going the right way;

they're not very willing to explore alternative
creative routes.

They're owls . . . very wise. They have all the
information and data; but they don't do anything in
particular except sit and look wise!

The Managers That We Have
to Deal With in Marketing

They're peacocks . . . all show; no real substance.
They look good; people like to watch; but they serve
no useful purpose.

Penguins. . . . they look good; they're always well
dressed. . . . But they're not very intelligent.

Irish setters . . . very good looking dogs. But not very
intelligent at all. They've no real knowledge.

* * * * *

I have chosen these three vignettes to raise important issues
with regard to management style. They all feature people talking
about their bosses or other managers with whom they work.

In the vignette featuring *The Tale of Jemima Puddle-Duck*,
Martha was asked to describe her boss in terms of some animal
or storybook character or whatever image came to mind. She
came up with a vivid description of what she was feeling about
her boss and why she was feeling uncomfortable with aspects
of his style.

In the second example, regional plant managers were asked
to talk about their bosses at head office. Note the commonali-
ties between their descriptions of the insensitive city dwellers,
the cuckoo, the pampered poodles, and the smart fox. Note the
consistency between the experience of the rural contractors,
the displaced birds, and the hardworking but undervalued
field dogs. The images cut to some core feelings about working
for remote, absentee managers who override local experience,
insight, and knowledge.

In the third example, we have a set of highly divergent
images, one group generated by marketing managers to describe managers in product development, the other generated

by product development managers to describe their counter-parts in marketing. Note the consistency. The product development managers are "mules," "camels," and smart but immobile "owls." The marketing managers are "peacocks," "penguins," and "Irish setters"—"all show."

We could spend a lot of time talking about all three sets of images, what they mean, and whether they do justice to the people on the other side of the descriptions. But my main purpose here is to use them as a springboard for launching a more general discussion about the nature and impact of managers and managerial styles.

The Tale of Jemima Puddle-Duck cuts to the heart of one person's sense of discomfort with her manager. The other two sets of images capture core experiences in the other two organizations. The views are inherently subjective and, no doubt, biased. They probably overplay the importance of certain aspects of the managers' styles and downplay others. But, despite all this, they grasp essentials that can provide an enormous and constructive influence on managers interested in improving their impact.

To bring the point home, how would you feel if *your* staff had described *you* in these terms?

Would you be happy with the result?

Shocked?

Focus on rationalizing or explaining the unfair characterization?

Or what?

What would you do?

Suppose that you received the information by chance—as the result of overhearing a conversation or through the invited comments of a well-meaning friend?

Would you carry on as normal?

Or look seriously at aspects of your behavior to find the basis of the perceptions and what can be done about them?

The three vignettes I have presented all give fairly negative views of the people to whom the imaging process was applied. I have selected them with this in mind, because it's the negative comments in an evaluation that often help us to look most seriously at what's going on.

And that's the fundamental aim that I have for this chapter. All of us operate out of some kind of image of who and what we are. All of us project images, most of which have both negative and positive consequences. If we can come to understand these images, and how they coincide and collide, we have an enormous resource for improving the impact of what we do.

Hence the title of this chapter: By "looking in the mirror" and seeing ourselves both as *we* see ourselves, and as *others* see us, we have an opportunity to imaginize powerful new possibilities.

To emphasize the point further, try thinking about your boss or some other significant manager or colleague.

Do you have someone in mind?

If so, think about them in terms of *any* image that occurs to you—whether bird, plant, animal, TV or storybook character, or whatever. The collage presented on the following page may stimulate some ideas.

Please take a few moments and see what comes to mind . . .

Then, reflect on the image or images that you've chosen.

Why have you selected them?

What is it about the personality, style, or behavior of the person selected that brings these images to mind?

Are they positive images?

Do they carry negative connotations?

What are their strengths?

What are their weaknesses?

Do they capture the essence of the person's impact and behavior?

Or is it necessary to use different images to capture the person's approach in different circumstances? If so, what would these be?

Now, consider how your reflections could be of help to the person in question. If you had an opportunity to affirm, change, or strengthen aspects of how he or she manages in practice, what would you say? Can you formulate three or four key ideas or statements that would provide valuable feedback to the person concerned?

Unless I'm mistaken, you probably have some very interesting insights to share.

So, with this in mind, let's return to the point I made earlier about the benefits to be derived from "looking in the mirror" and understanding more about our own personal impacts.

If we are able to find ways of helping our boss or some other significant person gain a better appreciation of their presence and style, isn't it also likely that there's scope for generating interesting insights about our own?

The trouble is that it's often easier to see and understand the character, impacts, strengths, and weaknesses of others.

One way to address this problem is to find a safe way of exploring the issues with colleagues and others who are able to provide insights on your management style. For example, consider consulting a friend or assembling a small group of people who would be comfortable with the exercise and then create a supportive environment in which they feel free to give you the feedback you need. Perhaps you'll get more accurate feedback if you're absent. Perhaps relations are sufficiently open to allow you to be present and hear what's said directly. Perhaps you will need a third party to facilitate the process and synthesize results.

To illustrate the kinds of insights that can emerge from this process, the following example features the experience of a manager who solicited feedback from a key member of his staff. He was responsible for a number of diverse, decentralized projects, relying on the expertise of employees and co-workers for detailed implementation. He and his coworker were each asked to characterize the nature and impact of the manager's style using the images in the collage presented earlier or through any others that came to mind. After selecting and describing their images, they were then invited to examine the "key messages," the similarities, differences, strengths, weaknesses, and lessons to be learned.

The manager selected a giraffe, a tornado, spice, and Sherlock Holmes.

His colleague selected an ant, a lion, a whirlpool, a blender, Robin Hood, and the "third little pig."

The Manager's Images

The giraffe was chosen to represent, in his words, "how I try to gain an overall view of things. How I try to look a long way in all directions to see what's coming before others see it. . . . The giraffe is strong and can really move when necessary. But it gets into a lot of difficulty if it sits down or gets into an awkward situation."

The tornado was selected to represent how he "spotted problems" and moved in on them "as quickly as possible." How he "shifted from issue to issue and place to place," and how he represented "a very strong force—sometimes with the downside of demolishing all that stood before."

The spice, stimulated by the collage image of pepper and salt, was chosen to represent how he tried "to add character and interest" to the activities that he was involved with. "I try to be something that makes a difference. . . . I can add a lot of flavor, but if I add too much I have too forceful a presence—I destroy the other ingredients."

The image of Sherlock Holmes was selected to capture his interest "in getting to the bottom of things . . . how I tend to have a take-charge mentality, yet also need to rely on the likes of a loyal Watson. . . . It also shows how I have an interest in the unexpected, the mystery, the challenge."

His Coworker's Images

The ant was chosen to represent the industrious way the manager went about his work and how he was able "to carry enormous burdens . . . much bigger than his size would indicate." The image also symbolized "the great need for collaborative activity in building anthills and how he depended on the support of others." The image was also chosen for other reasons: because of the image of "a bug"—"he bugs people as he pesters them to get results" and because, while the ants go off in all directions, "they always have to end up at *his* own personal anthill!"

The image of a lion was selected to capture the manager's "daunting presence; he intimidates; he's noticeable; and he often creates discomfort."

The whirlpool was selected to represent "power in the middle, and because of its constancy. It is powerful . . . it sweeps everything into itself. . . . It can be impressive, and great to watch. But if you get too close you get sucked in."

The kitchen blender was selected because it's an object with "power at the center, blending all the ingredients into a single product."

The image of Robin Hood, selected directly from the collage, was used to conjure the image of someone who was "generous, bright, trustworthy, a leader . . . but someone on his own track, getting others to join *his* cause . . . demanding and impatient."

The "third little pig" was selected as another storybook character, representing how the manager "was clever, building his house out of bricks, and outsmarting the wolf," but as someone who "didn't invite the other little pigs to join in. He

just let them go their way and build their houses of straw and sticks. . . . [He was] smart, capable and successful, and not afraid to challenge the wolves . . . but at times, insensitive to the needs of others."

THE MANAGER'S IMAGES OF HIMSELF

 I take an overall view of things. I try to look a long way in all directions But I get into awkward situations

 I move quickly in tackling emerging problems But I have a tendency to demolish everything in my path

 I am able to add spice and flavor But I can overwhelm other ingredients

I'm ingenious and like to get to the bottom of things But I tend to take my Watsons for granted

HIS COLLEAGUE'S VIEW

 you're incredibly industrious BUT you bug people and want everything your own way

you're strong and impressive BUT you intimidate and create discomfort

 you're powerful BUT you overwhelm

 you are a generous and trustworthy leader BUT It's always YOUR cause

 you are clever, resourceful and bold BUT you're insensitive to the needs of others

METAPHORS CAN SEND HONEST, CLEAR MESSAGES!

Reflection and Evaluation

The two sets of images converge on many important points and highlight both strengths and weaknesses in the manager's style. Some of the key ideas are illustrated in the adjacent table.

When asked to identify the key themes in *his* set of images, the manager focused on how they illustrated his desire and ability "to take an overall view of things" (the giraffe and tornado) and his "interest and ingenuity in tackling emerging problems" (the tornado and Sherlock Holmes).

His coworker reflected on how *her* images focused on how the manager tended to be a very strong force that always succeeded in getting his own way, *but often at the expense of others.* She saw this as the basic characteristic uniting her interpretation of the ants and the anthill, the intimidating lion, the all-consuming power of the whirlpool and the blender, and the forceful and single-minded aspects of Robin Hood and the "third little pig."

One of the interesting aspects of their analysis is found in the way the different images converge on similar strengths and weaknesses. Note, for example, the incredible parallels between the tornado, whirlpool, and blender and how they capture the idea of a forceful presence that tends to "suck everything up" and dominate situations. Note how all the images tend to convey a sense of power, industriousness, and determination, often accompanied by an excessive degree of single-mindedness.

The exchange created a powerful experience for the manager. He saw that his sheer confidence and competence were becoming a liability and that he needed to do something about this to restore a more genuine and open collaborative environment in which he and his staff could *all* work to the best of their abilities. In summarizing his key learning, he said, "I have to recognize that everyone doesn't want to get sucked into my vortex and that a lot of creative opportunities, as well as the energies of other people, are being diluted and repressed because of my tendency to move so fast and to overcontrol processes and outcomes."

The exercise created a safe, constructive environment in which the manager could explore and find ways of improving his personal impact.

The consistency between the images, each of which seemed to be sending the same message in a slightly different manner, had enormous evocative power. They captured the essence of his situation and delivered their message in a way that was difficult to ignore. No doubt, the exercise would have been even more impactful if the manager had been prepared to involve a wider group of people in the process, because other perspectives could have added great richness. But, even so, the manager was able to tap into a key aspect of his behavior and take valuable lessons from the process.

Using the Exercise in Other Settings

On a purely technical point, there are a variety of ways in which you can use the basic exercise. For example, people can work in pairs or small groups, developing their own images and then sharing them with the larger gathering. The "safety factor" for people who are concerned about disclosing their personal images and views of their boss, or other significant person, can be increased by using a group imaging format so that group rather than individual images are presented. (See Chapter 9 for an example of a group imaging process.)

The collage of images presented earlier can be used in a variety of ways. It can be used to "seed" the imaging in a very general manner, as was done in the above example, helping people find a place to start. It can also be used as a kind of visual checklist to help people get at different types of images: animals, household objects, storybook characters, and so on. At first glance, this "seeding" of the process may seem to introduce a degree of bias, suggesting the images that people may find relevant. But, in my experience, the process has a kind of "Rorschach" quality. People "read" into the images what they want to see and say. If the image is going to fit, they make it fit in a particular way. Hence images of cows, birds, or Robin Hood assume a special significance and meaning according to their resonance with the task being faced.

The important point in using the exercise is to find ways of ensuring that people feel safe in exploring and expressing their feelings and views about the matters at hand. If this can be achieved, then the process will acquire a momentum of its own, and the insights, experience, and creative capacities of those involved will usually produce fascinating results.

IMAGING NEW MANAGERIAL STYLES

In presenting the above examples, I have focused on showing how imaging processes can be used to pinpoint the strengths and weaknesses of a manager's existing behaviors. But the basic approach can also be used to identify new images for shaping one's role.

To a degree, this is implicit in what has already been said, because, in understanding one's strengths and weaknesses, one is given some indication as to how one can become effective. Hence the "tornado" needs to have more sensitivity for the needs and contributions of others. The mules, camels, and immobile owls need to become more open and flexible. The peacocks, penguins, and Irish setters need to compensate for the fact that they seem "all show." And so on.

But there is more that can be done.

To illustrate, let's return to the dilemma of the "supervisor" who tries to supervise even though he doesn't have "super vision," discussed in Chapter 1. This is a common problem facing managers nowadays. In stabler times, "supervisors" could command their staff from a role within a bureaucratic hierarchy that was clear and well understood by all. Their elevated position often allowed them to see better than anyone else and, provided that they established clear lines of communication, they could supervise the work of others to their hearts' content. But, in times of change, bureaucracy breaks down. Problems arise that no one is mandated to solve. It becomes impossible to keep personal control of all the information needed to do one's work. If one relies on commands and rigid controls, bottlenecks appear. The supervisor-manager who was once a source of stability and strength becomes a part of the problem. That's why so many are now being removed as hierarchies are flattened and decentralized and work turned over to self-organizing teams that are able to operate with a minimum of direct "hands on" control.

The trouble in such situations is that the managers who perpetuate inappropriate styles of behavior are probably doing what they feel and believe they are supposed to do. They usually have a view of themselves as "supervisors," "decision makers," or "links" in an established chain of command and translate this self-image into the corresponding form of behavior. In their hearts, they may know that they're perceived as being ineffective and a part of the organization's problems, but they have nowhere to turn. For what are they to do? Unless they can reimage their role in a fundamental way, they are likely to remain well and truly stuck in the old mold until removed through some kind of reorganization, "delayering," "downsizing," or whatever.

Yet it's in these and other difficult situations that a creative "look in the mirror" can be of great help. Consider, for example, the sequence of images presented on pages 36-38, which I often use to help people gain fresh perspective on their potential as managers or to generate new ways of thinking about approaches to managing change. Each image captures an aspect of what a manager's role might mean in practice and has implications for how managers can shape their basic behaviors. Some of the images can be seen as conveying negative qualities; others, positive; some, both. They provide excellent springboards for creating dialogue about what managers and change agents can do to be more effective in their roles.

Thus, using this approach, our would-be supervisor may find that his or her real value and potential contribution rest in being the equivalent of the construction worker on page 36. Or perhaps they rest in performing bridgelike functions, as in the image below. Perhaps they rest in creating an entirely new image of what could or should be done to add value to the organization.

My central point is that, by rethinking basic aspects of one's role in this way, one may be able to imaginize a completely new approach to management.

This, I believe, is one of the major challenges facing managers today. As their organizations are restructured and adopt

more flexible, decentralized styles of operation, old styles of management no longer suffice. To be effective, the people involved have to find ways of reimaging their styles so that they are appropriate for the new context that's emerging.

My work with managers and change agents interested in finding a new place in their organizations usually generates numerous images through which they can do so. The range is staggering. Some become designers and managers of "umbilical cords" or "organizational bumblebees," as discussed in Chapter 4. Others adopt the role of "strategic termites" (Chapter 3). Some decide to become ferrets or lighthouses. Yet others choose to see themselves as facilitative window cleaners, helping other people in their organization gain a clearer view of what's happening in the world outside.

In the following chapters, many more possibilities will emerge.

The important point, for now, is to recognize that, as discussed in Chapter 1, managers have a tendency to get trapped by their *images* of their role. Indeed, even the image of being a manager may no longer be relevant and prove a liability, especially if the aim is to promote capacities for self-organization and change.

Such is the challenge facing management in turbulent times. It's a challenge that requires an ability to develop completely new ways of thinking and acting: by breaking free of the taken-for-granted images, assumptions, and blind spots that don't serve us well and by developing alternatives.

The ideas and methods discussed in this chapter provide us with a powerful means of doing so. By "looking in the mirror" and confronting our impacts, we have a means of seeing our strengths and understanding our weaknesses. By using the same methods to imaginize new roles and new possibilities, we also have an opportunity to reimage and remake ourselves and our behaviors so that our personal and organizational effectiveness can be enhanced on an ongoing basis.

That's the promise of the approach. So, if you're intrigued by the possibilities, why not give this aspect of imaginization a try?

3 Strategic Termites

Let's get right in-
side the process of
managing
change!

In times of change, plans and planning often prove ineffective because they create rigidities. In highly politicized contexts, they often serve as magnets for political opposition, catalyzing and crystallizing the views of those who do not want to travel in the planned direction. This creates an enormous dilemma for would-be leaders or managers, because they have to find ways of planning without plans or, at least, of creating some kind of visionary framework that can evolve and adapt as circumstances require.

This chapter explores some ideas that I've found particularly powerful in helping managers reimage their leadership role in such circumstances. They're based on the image of a "strategic termite." It's a humble metaphor and, for many people, a distinctly unflattering one. Who, after all, wants to be seen as a termite? But the image has enormous power for would-be leaders who wish to generate major change in difficult situations, safely, yet effectively. It provides a way of tapping many of the insights emerging from the new disciplines of cybernetics and chaos theory in an evocative, practical manner.

TERMITES AND EMERGENT SELF-ORGANIZATION

Termites! Small, blind creatures related to the cockroach.

Creepy, crawly things that eat wood and make houses crumble.

Whenever I mention the possibility of becoming a "strategic termite," most managers seize on negative interpretations.

"You want us to eat away at the bureaucracy?"

"You're inviting us to become subversive?"

The metaphor, at first sight, does have these negative associations. But they're not the ones that I want to emphasize here. Subversive behavior in an organization tends to attract the exterminator. The person who seeks to create change by directly undermining existing policies and structures often runs into trouble. Create a hole in bureaucratic functioning one week, and chances are that next week the basic structure will be twice as strong as before.

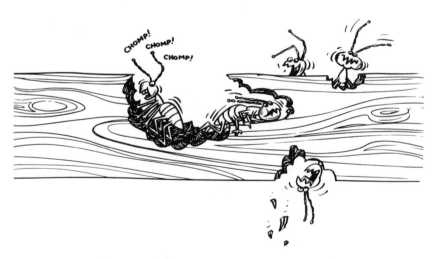

So let's redirect attention to some of the more positive aspects of termite behavior, especially those exemplified in the processes through which termites build their nests and engage in mutually supporting activities.

Imagine a termite colony somewhere in the tropics. There are thousands of termites milling around.

The ground on which they start to build their nest is quite flat. The termites begin their work by moving earth in a random

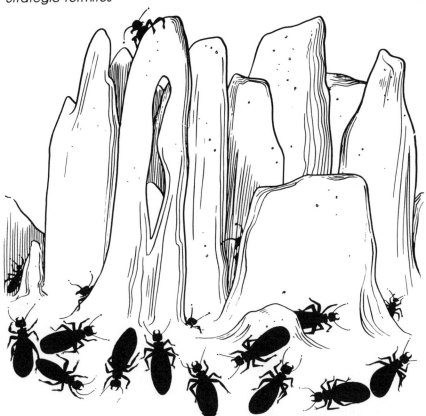

TERMITES ARE MASTER BUILDERS!

Termite nests are products of random, self-organizing activity where structures emerge and unfold in a piecemeal, unplanned way. They provide inspiration for developing coherent approaches to strategic management and change, without the straitjackets and problems imposed by trying to follow predetermined plans.

fashion. Gradually, distinct piles of earth begin to emerge. These then become the focus of sustained building activity, resulting in columns located *in more or less random positions*. These are built to a certain height, then construction stops. When columns emerge that are sufficiently close together, building resumes until they are joined at the top to form a rounded arch. In this way, the termite nest evolves as an increasingly complex structure, with the arch as the basic unit. The approach eventually results in a kind of free-form

architecture, comprised of interlocking caverns and tunnels
that are ventilated, humidity controlled, and beautifully formed.
African termite nests may rise 12 feet high and measure 100
feet across. They can house millions of termites. In terms of
scale, they're equivalent to human beings creating a building
more than a mile high.

Needless to say, the accomplishment has attracted the attention of many scientists. How do these blind creatures manage to
produce such architectural masterpieces? No one knows for sure.

A queen termite occupies a royal cell in the center of the
mound. It's suspected that she plays a crucial role in processes
of communication within the colony. But, if there's a plan or
blueprint, where does it come from?

How do the termites direct and control their activity?

How do they coordinate their work?

How do they acquire the ability to repair parts of nests when
they are destroyed, returning them to states that are as good as
new?

There are lots of unresolved issues here. Instinct, habit, and
various forms of communication play an important role. For
example, the termites' deposits of saliva are believed to form
important parts of their communication system. But one thing is
clear. Termites don't build their nests like humans build houses
and office towers. They don't follow predetermined plans.

One exciting theory emerging from the study of termite
behavior is that work in the termite colony reflects a self-
organizing process where order emerges "out of chaos." While
the nest always has a familiar pattern, it is infinitely variable
in terms of detailed form. It is impossible to predict the detailed
structure in advance, because it emerges as a result of the
scattered pattern of droppings. This is what makes the construction process so different than that of human beings. The
"masterpiece" evolves from random, chaotic activities guided
by what seems to be an *overall* sense of purpose and direction,
but in an open-ended manner.

We have in this view of termite behavior a splendid image
for rethinking many aspects of the leadership process in human
organizations. For example, it suggests that effective leadership or change management may not have to be based on a
detailed strategic plan. It may not be something that has to be

imposed. It may be something that can emerge and take form in a self-organizing, evolutionary way.

In my research on the management of change, I encounter many successful "strategic termites." They are managers who have clear aspirations about what they would like to achieve. But, instead of trying to force-fit their vision, or direct and control a situation to achieve the results they would like to see, they manage in a much more open-ended way, encouraging and allowing desirable initiatives to emerge from the evolving situations being faced. "Strategic termites" are incremental and opportunistic in their approach to change. They build on ideas, actions, and events that they initiate or that spontaneously come their way. They are *strategic* in the sense that, while their activity is open to the influence of random opportunity, decisions and actions are always informed and guided by a strong sense of what they are ultimately trying to achieve. They have "plans," but they don't implement plans and are not constrained by plans. They are people who know where they would like to go. But they do not always know the route by which they're going to get there!

In this positive, expansive, and free-ranging interpretation of termitelike behavior, I believe there's an important message for people who wish to undertake leadership roles in turbulent times. Here are some stories illustrating different aspects of the metaphor in practice.

WHEN YOU CAN'T BUILD A BONFIRE . . .

George Terry is the director of training and development in a highly decentralized $8 billion company operating in the natural resources industry. His mission is to help managers and employees at all levels of the company develop the competencies and skills needed to meet the challenges of a changing world. For the most part, interest in human resource management is not high. The industry is renowned for its hard-nosed, "bottom line" approach. Its cyclical nature, which can generate years of plenty followed by rapid and deep cutbacks, makes the systematic development of human resources an incredibly difficult task. George, however, has made major progress against the odds. His approach is based on the idea of anticipating and spotting opportunities for meeting specific training and development needs and on building a record of success that makes him an indispensable and highly valued contributor to his organization.

In evolving his approach, he has made a number of very important decisions. First, he has chosen not to build a training department. Sharing an assistant and secretary with other managers, he conducts his work with the help of a network of about 20 trainers and consultants, hired on a task-by-task basis. This keeps his overhead costs to a minimum and allows him to expand and pace his work with the flow of the business cycle. His access to this network allows him to use exactly the right person for the task at hand and to deliver service very economically. Most of the expenses are charged directly to the line managers using the services, so George's budget is minimal, given the scale of his operations. Hence, when it comes to budget cuts, there is nothing to cut as far as his services are concerned. There is no real slack or waste, so the value that he adds is clear for all to see.

To develop his general strategy and approach, and to inject new information and fresh ideas into his work, he networks outside the organization a great deal. Over the span of a year or two, he relies on the help of a small group of five or six carefully chosen consultants he feels will be able to expand his thinking and range of options in approaching specific problems. The consultants are used on an individual basis, a day or so at a time, according to need. His "department" is thus a flexible external network containing the best available talent, where the ability to add real value to operations is the basic condition for continued membership.

Internally, George targets the plant and line managers who can make use of his services and lets his approach evolve from there. The lack of formal interest in human resource development within the company means that he can't force his ideas and programs onto the organization, even if he wanted to. He thus has to take a gradual, incremental approach, allowing success to build on success.

As he puts it: "You have to find that spark of enthusiasm and fan it, because you know that you can't build a bonfire.

You look for every seed of enthusiasm, and try to build pockets of success. . . . If you can get four or five managers to buy into an idea and deliver a success, they will tell others, and off it goes. . . . The process can be like pushing a piece of rope across the top of a table; it's slow and difficult and you need patience. You'd love to run to the other side and pull it, but you can't do that."

His patience and persistence have paid off. Many of his programs have expanded as the need has grown in the light of demonstrated success and value. For example, an initiative originally aimed at influencing the skills and competencies of the top 100 managers within the company has been extended to include more than 300, as participants encouraged their colleagues and staff to get involved. Projects originally designed to solve managerial problems in specific plants have proliferated throughout the company. The process has also generated numerous demands for other services and activities from managers who see the benefits of George's activities. His approach is thus completely "customer driven." Nothing happens unless it can meet the needs of a specific manager who is prepared to pay the bill. George has his own ideas, and the managers have theirs. The service that is provided is usually a product of the two.

All this happens without any strategic plan. George's vision is to make a contribution to human resource management within the organization by adding value wherever he can. He knows the kinds of results that he wants to see. But, at any given time, he has no idea of the detailed way in which they will eventually be achieved. As he says, you can't build a bonfire and expect everyone to join in. The culture of the organization demands a more informal approach. He knows that the only way he can be effective is to proceed incrementally in a way that earns and builds respect among the line managers, supervisors, and hourly workers who benefit from his initiatives.

He knows that the results he delivers are "soft results" in a hard-nosed industry and that, if pressed, he would find it hard to demonstrate the concrete financial returns on human resource expenditures. Rather than build up the costly infrastructure needed to monitor and evaluate the effects of his activities, he thus stays away from the whole issue of evaluation. He doesn't develop grand plans or costly proposals that would require discussion and approval from hosts of corporate staff. Instead, he relies on his proven method of serving the needs of internal clients who *know* that his programs deliver results and are prepared to pay the monies needed for their staff to attend. His strategic contribution to the company builds from there!

George is not altogether comfortable using the termite image as a way of capturing his basic style of management. As he says, "It *is* rather unflattering."

But it captures the essence of what he does. He knows that a human resource management plan or large department would attract all kinds of opposition. He has very little support from the top of the organization and knows that any change has to be driven from the middle. He thus burrows away in a persistent, yet flexible and creative fashion within the context of his overall vision.

He builds on whatever initiatives attract the interest of potential clients.

He "floats" his own ideas. He spots resonant needs.

He takes every opportunity to build activity wherever he can.

When he is successful, his "termite columns" get higher and higher as they attract the attention of other managers interested in his services. The line managers talk and spread the word. He goes with the flow, putting most of his efforts into serving the managers who really want to do something.

He doesn't sap his energy by trying to sell his ideas and programs to managers who will never buy.

Gradually, yet very effectively, the edifice that he is building takes shape. As he puts it, "We try something, and if it doesn't work we bury it. If it does work, we hoist it up the flag pole, and give others a chance to see what can be done. . . . Many senior managers want to see change, but they don't know how to drive it, or how to behave. . . . They find it threatening. But if we do good stuff for them and for the line managers, and people *say that it is good,* they support it. . . . If you ask for permission to do something within the context of a formal plan, you find yourself having to go higher and higher in the organization. But if you can find a line manager who has an interest, and give him a modest proposal, he'll usually say 'yes.' . . . It's just a process of involving people in change. Lots of human resource managers are not prepared to take first risks. They like to get permission. They like the security of reports. . . . I don't write memos and I don't write proposals. I do it by word of mouth. I get a manager to send ten people to a workshop. If it's good, they'll tell you. If it isn't, you have to try something else. Gradually it takes off."

George lives and models so much of what it takes to be a successful manager in a turbulent world. He is achieving great success against the odds and making a major contribution to his organization. If he waited for change on human resource management issues to be driven from the top, he'd "wait forever." Instead, he takes the initiative and, by building trust and credibility through modest yet significant steps, he is achieving as much as one could ever expect from any formal strategy or grand design.

JUST DO THE SMALL STUFF

Here's another short story of a successful manager, steering change from a middle management position in a manner consistent with the termite strategy.

Peter Fulgoni is the director of the Financial Planning and Administration Division of a large government department with a budget of $3 billion. The division employs more than 500 staff; 400 are located in dispersed regional offices. He has been in the director's position for just over two years. During this time, he and his colleagues have worked to create major changes in how the division does business. Staffing has been significantly reduced through natural retirement, and the division's work has been invigorated by a strong customer orientation. Morale among staff is at an all-time high.

The platform for change was set by a conference involving key divisional staff, held a week before Peter formally started in the division. He was invited to attend because it provided a great opportunity for him to gain information about the department and his future role. It was a regular conference at which the usual administrative issues were discussed, prominence being given to the need to develop more of a customer orientation in the execution of work. The message: The division needs to shift from "a red tape" to a "green tape" mentality, to help rather than block people, to encourage them to take more risks and be forward looking.

As Peter puts it, "It was the usual stuff . . . the sort of stuff you read in the management books. . . . But it got the adrenalin going. . . . There was a real good feeling that we had to change. . . . The trouble is . . . after this kind of conference everybody goes back and it's business as usual. You fill out your checks, and you apply your processes, and no one keeps that momentum going."

So Peter decided to take action and, in his words, to "do some good follow-up." Shortly after starting in the division, he got a group of people together and developed "a hit list" as to what could be done to start cutting red tape.

As he puts it: "The red tape, green tape idea sort of caught on. . . . Red tape means you're telling someone you can't do that. That's what the rules are. Sorry. Go back and rethink your program.

"Green tape means helping someone to go forward . . . [saying]: 'If you want to get there, here's how you can interpret the rules to meet our needs.' . . .

"It's about helping the customer to get where he wants."

As the questioning around the "hit list" developed, the group started to talk about the basic values governing their work and how they could begin to operate differently. They began setting realistic aims for themselves as to what could be achieved, and the change process gained momentum from there. One thing led to another, and the process spread as other groups were set up to look at issues in their areas.

Throughout, Peter encouraged people to "green tape" what they were doing. He provided them with information about the broader context in which they were operating. He encouraged them to see where their work "fit into the big picture."

Gradually, the process of asking questions began to acquire a momentum of its own.

With the downsizing of the organization as a backdrop, people began addressing fundamental issues relating to their work and where they and the department were heading. They started to question processes and procedures that had been in place for years, and whether they made sense. For example, "Why did the most senior manager in the department have to sign travel expense claims? . . . Why couldn't the whole process be delegated to the managers who were directly accountable for the expenses?" It was felt that, if these managers didn't know whether they had enough funding, or whether the expenditure was appropriate, they didn't deserve to be managers anyway!

As existing processes of accountability and control were questioned in this way, those working at lower levels of the organization became empowered to do new things. The effects rippled unexpectedly as people began to address issues relating to the organization of their own work. They requested training in skills that were underdeveloped. They forged new partnerships with each other and with the clients they served.

Peter's main role was just "to get the ball rolling" and to "provide support throughout the process." There were no glossy brochures announcing the division's empowerment program; no fanfare around the direction that Peter and his colleagues wished the division to take; no big events or large-scale courses or programs to improve customer service or decision making. They simply got on with the process of making the "green tape environment" a reality, letting the detailed courses of action and tactics unfold.

In talking about the process, Peter uses many metaphors. His favorite is that he focused on doing "small stuff . . . not rocket science stuff." He also likes to talk about "making a stew," with lots of ingredients being thrown in along the way but with no one ingredient being allowed to dominate. By focusing on doing simple things that would get staff asking questions about their work, he helped to get the organization on a new path.

Throughout the process, he had no *specific* view of where the path would lead or of the detailed milestones that would be passed. Rather, he put his energy behind the vision of creating a green tape environment, allowing and encouraging his staff to forge the detailed way. The emphasis was on creating small changes that would have a cumulative impact: "on making 1% improvements all over the place, to get that 1,000% improvement." As Peter puts it, "When you try to do one thing to get a 1,000% improvement, you're doing a major project, which you're thrusting on the organization. The staff don't learn through that. There's no ownership. . . . But when you get people to do a 1% improvement all over the place, you change the mind-set. That's a powerful ingredient for the change process. . . . You get a thousand people out there that have a different way of looking at things . . . To me, that's the stuff that makes things happen."

Peter and his colleagues have created substantial change by making small, significant changes that attracted the interest and attention of those immediately involved, allowing the "columns" and character of their new organization to emerge. They're strategic termites operating out of a strong sense of strategic vision, backed by the energy, persistence, patience, and creativity needed to make the vision reality.

"TRY IT AND SEE . . ."

My third strategic termite story involves *Speedy*, a very successful small firm operating in the fresh foods industry. After almost 20 years as a family enterprise, it was acquired 2 years ago by a food conglomerate wishing to obtain a stake in the "fresh" side of the business. As part of the agreement, key family members agreed to stay on in senior managerial roles. Management changes at the top of the conglomerate, however, created an unexpected drift in commitment to the fresh food initiative, resulting in the early retirement of Speedy's head in favor of Rick, a younger and very able member of the family. He recruited John, a like-minded individual, to join him in the management of the business, and over the last 18 months they've done an excellent job consolidating and developing Speedy's success.

Speedy has always had an action focus, adopting a "try it and see" philosophy. Short time horizons and tight deadlines, driven by the "sell it or smell it" nature of products, have encouraged an action orientation. People see the opportunity for a new product or process innovation and try it out. If it works, the innovation is built into standard practice. If it fails, it is discarded, and attention is focused elsewhere. For the most part, innovation is based on a philosophy of constant improvement. There is not a great deal of room for the introduction of completely new products and, when such innovations are achieved, competitors can be expected to follow suit very quickly. Rick and John thus place great emphasis on speed, quality, service, and adding value in every possible way as key means of developing the business. This allows them to attract the best suppliers and to provide a superior service to customers in every aspect of their operations. While there are strong operational procedures and systems for managing the day-to-day business, they are applied within a context that is always open to experiment and innovation.

Rick and John are both "strategic termites" in their basic mode of operation. They have a clear understanding of their business and its priorities and refuse to be shifted from their focus on speed and adding value wherever they can. Their approach is ideally suited for the fast-moving fresh food environment.

But it causes all kinds of problems in dealing with their parent company. In contrast with the perishable fish, meat, vegetables, pasta, and other fresh products with which Speedy deals, the parent's focus is on high-investment products with a long shelf life and pay-back period. The parent is a strong, well-managed, and highly professional company. Consistent with the nature of its core business, it places emphasis on developing new product proposals requiring careful research, test marketing, and planning. The corporate culture tends to be dominated by highly formalized processes of control.

Speedy, on the other hand, is all action, *now.* Memos, plans, controls, and formal strategy rationalizations follow on the heels of what is already happening.

The differences cause many problems because the parent is keen to impose its approach on Speedy whenever it can. Rick and John have to resist this, doing whatever they can to "create a shield" that will protect Speedy's priorities and mode of operation. More often than not, the parent's well-intentioned requests for more structure and advance planning divert Speedy's staff from core priorities. They break the value-added focus and tight coupling with the changing environment that underpins Speedy's success.

John's reflections on some of the differences between Speedy and its parent highlight the basic problems: "It's absolutely amazing, the rate at which things can happen in [our] environment. It's dramatically different from how it happens at the corporate level. . . . We've been involved in some areas where we want to develop new business that typically takes corporate five to six weeks; it takes us just two days!

"It creates a little bit of nervousness at head office, because it's an unusual feeling to be presented with a proposition and 'Take it or leave it.'

"If they take it, then in two days it happens."

Rick adds: "Actually . . . everything will be in place before we write, say, a strategy document about it. We basically put a footnote saying, 'By the way, points x, y and z have already been done. Thank you very much. We're now moving on.' . . . This is the kind of stuff that gives us a tremendous edge in competing against companies that require a lot of approval levels."

From the parent's point of view, Speedy looks rather chaotic. But, from Rick and John's perspective, everything is fine and dandy. They have done an enormous amount of work building the day-to-day capacities of their staff, so that they know the business inside out: knowing who they are dealing with, how to buy and sell, and how to resolve issues as they arise.

As John puts it, "The principles and processes [through which we operate] are instilled in the people and the way they work, not in the controls. . . . We expose them to what's happening in the company. . . . Instead of giving them the odd tree to look at, we give them the whole forest. . . . But it makes [our parent] very nervous."

The action focus within Speedy leads to a constant search for action opportunities. Plans, proposals, and the exploration of alternatives are not priorities. The focus is on understanding and *living* the business, relying on insight and instinct as to what is likely to work. Rational searches for alternative courses of action, as encouraged by a more planning-based approach, don't fit the style. Speedy doesn't have time for planning in a formal sense. The constant concern is *to act*, because, as Rick points out, "In this business, if you don't move, you're dead. Period! . . . You have to do it on the fly."

The relations between Speedy and its parent highlight important differences between a "termite" approach to strategic development and that encouraged by more formal, "planned," approaches to change. In Speedy, the strategy has evolved naturally as a means of building the business around key opportunities. In a context characterized by rapid change, it's a highly effective strategy because no one has the crystal ball that allows one to predict precisely where one wants to be in a year's time. Speedy's solution to this problem is to remain "incredibly focused" on what it takes to develop the business and to minimize the influence of anything likely to get in the way. As a result, the "columns" for building the enterprise emerge almost unconsciously, as staff go about the day-to-day process of adding value wherever they can.

THE TERMITE STRATEGY IN PERSPECTIVE

If you're a manager charged with opening a new factory in a year's time, or a marketing executive responsible for the national launch of a major new product next spring, the termite strategy is definitely not the way to go. Complex operational issues require careful planning and well-organized "critical paths." But, if you're trying to keep pace with a rapidly changing environment, trying to unlock a new strategic initiative, or trying to energize a sluggish corporate culture in an organization that really doesn't want to move, a termite approach may well prove very appropriate.

Plans and critical paths, though valuable operational tools, are far less effective for managing in the midst of flux or for steering major strategic change. The evidence on this is mounting as major organizations struggle with the implementation of carefully designed "across the board change." The plans for such change often take years to develop and quickly become outdated. They often become straitjackets because of the political and other alignments that are created. They are often inflexible, and their implementation often mobilizes cynicism and resistance from many quarters. All too often, they become ends in themselves, saluted in annual reports, and launched with great fanfare, but fizzling in implementation because all the real energy has been put into the creation of the plan itself.

   This may seem a rather cynical view, but the experience is all too true, especially for large, highly professionalized organizations that pride themselves on the quality of their organizationwide systems and controls. Many organizations that have built solid competence in planning as the route to change often find that they have done little more than add an extra layer or division to their bureaucracy. They find that planning itself becomes an arena for politicking and control. Despite the best of intentions, it can interfere with business success. This is part of the message of the Speedy story.

   In these circumstances, the "termite strategy" becomes an interesting option both for top managers wishing to engage in innovative change and for middle managers surrounded by resistance to change.

   Look at the pattern manifested in my three termite stories. On the surface, the activities of the various managers seem opportunistic, disjointed, nonstrategic. But, on closer examination, it's possible to see a clear philosophy and approach at work.

   Look at what George Terry does as human resource director in the difficult context presented by his organization:

- He has a very strong sense of what he wants to accomplish in terms of building new managerial competencies.

- He has a keen value-added focus. This drives the detailed work; he focuses on adding value whenever he can.

- Managers tell each other about the successes. Word spreads. Systematic programs begin to emerge.

- George's strategy emerges and takes form as he goes along.

- He looks for pockets of interest and enthusiasm and builds on them.

- He builds on success; he doesn't get immobilized by modest failures. When things work, he does them again.

- The company's "human resource strategy" is built from the ground up. Organizationally, George is almost invisible. He is opportunistic, incremental, goes with the flow, and doesn't fight against the odds.

- He knows where he is going. But he never knows the path by which he is going to get there!

Look at what Peter Fulgoni does in the traditionally staid and change-resistant environment of government financial services:

- He has hooked into a strong vision about the possibility of replacing "red tape" with "green tape," of generating a corporate culture geared to customer service.

- He's interested in creating a thousand 1% changes, not a single 1,000% change.

- One thing leads to another. Small issues lead to larger ones. "Green tape" questioning unfolds in its consequences.

- As the process gets more diffused, the momentum grows. Success leads to success.

- He believes in doing "small stuff, not rocket science stuff."

- He develops a short "hit list" of green tape issues with realistic aims and mobilizes a group effort to tackle them.

- The signing of travel authorizations raises more general problems relating to the management, accountability, and empowerment of staff generally.

- Peter remains fairly invisible. He relies on mobilizing a group effort. The detailed ideas and tactics as to what needs to be done unfold as he goes along.

Look at how John and Rick are coping with Speedy's fast changing environment:

- They have a strong vision of adding value to key business activities wherever they can.

- If it works, they do it again; if it fails, they rapidly shift focus elsewhere.

- Their constant focus on adding value through speed, quality, and service provides the key through which they sustain and build the business.

- They have a focus on action, experiment, innovation, and doing it "now" rather than on producing plans.

- Success builds on cumulative, small gains.

- By doing the small things right, they create big breakthroughs in attracting the best suppliers and the best customers.

- They refuse to get diverted from addressing the key tasks facing the business.

- There are no plans, no formal proposals, no systematic searches for alternatives. Strategy emerges from successful action.

- They try to shield themselves from the diversions created by head office.

- John and Rick know where they are going. But they don't know how they are going to get there!

The parallels between what's happening in these three cases and what happens in the building of a termite nest are strong. None of the key players actually sees himself as a strategic termite. They don't explicitly see themselves as building the organizational equivalent of nests, columns, or arches or as mobilizing a colony. But this is one useful way of thinking about what they are doing.

Consciously or unconsciously, each of the key players has a strong grasp on how to foster and develop the self-organizing capacities of the systems in which they work. As in my image of a strategic termite, they are driven by a strong sense of what they are trying to achieve, and they use their energies to nudge and push the system in an appropriate direction.

ORDER CAN EMERGE FROM CHAOS

Management theory has long been held in the grip of a highly rational view of what good managers do. It is a view that reflects a linear pattern of thought, based on the importance of careful planning, coordination, and control.

But, as Henry Mintzberg has shown us through his observation of managers at work, this is not what managers actually do. Managerial behavior is often much more random, contingent, and unplanned. Typical managerial situations in today's world are buffeted and shaped by all kinds of unexpected influences that upset the best laid plans.

Effective managers have to learn to cope with the flux. They have to find creative ways of going with the flow. They have to help coherent, relevant initiatives emerge from the dynamic and unpredictable events that surround them. They have to be skilled in managing disorder and in helping their organizations self-organize and evolve in a relevant, open-ended way.

This new context challenges much of the old rhetoric of rational planning and control.

Many successful organizations look rational, especially when hindsight is used to impose 20-20 vision on events and to create a straight line from where the firm started and where it has ended up. But, if one looks closely, the path has often had many starting points, many detours and false turns, and has depended on a lot of chance encounters and changes in direction along the way.

The famous example is found in the way Honda achieved its impact on the North American motorcycle industry. As Richard Pascale relates the story, in 1959, Honda sent three people to the United States to "capture" the U.S. motorcycle market. This was the strategic vision.

They had $100,000 in cash and $150,000 worth of inventories. By 1966, they had a 63% market share! They went to sell large bikes but ended up selling small bikes instead.

Their success was guided by a form of action learning that built on successful aspects of their experience. They found that the small 50 cc bikes that they had brought to the United States for their own use attracted the attention of the public wherever they went. They were faced with a cash-flow problem and some quality problems in the production of the larger bikes. They thus started to sell the small bikes. This course of action built on some chance meetings with a buyer from Sears, who also saw an opportunity for his organization. The overwhelming impact on the motorcycle market built from there.

The story illustrates how detailed strategy can emerge by building on fairly random events: just like a termite column! Success doesn't have to be imposed through the straitjacket of a predetermined plan.

The image of "strategic termites" operating through processes where a sense of order is allowed to emerge from chaos has a lot to teach us about management in a turbulent world. That's the spirit in which I evoke the metaphor and invite you to think about the messages conveyed by my three short case studies.

The invitation of this chapter is to consider the situations in which it may be appropriate to become a "strategic termite" and to consider the tactics for mobilizing a termite colony!

If you've been pushing and struggling to implement a strategic plan without success, or struggling to mobilize action across your whole organization, "think termite!"

You'll need to be strategic and develop a clear sense of the broad direction and results to be achieved.

But you'll have to avoid force-fitting or imposing a firm plan.

Strategic termites are always driven by a broad sense of vision. But they're careful not to get trapped by the vision. They operate on a piecemeal basis, keeping in close touch with what is happening in their organization. They initiate, encourage, and support activities and ideas consistent with their general aspirations and allow themselves to enrich and reform these aspirations so they can evolve with the dynamic nature of the challenges being faced.

They look for opportunities to create "mounds" of activity consistent with the direction in which they want to go: a project or alliance here, a project "over there."

They hope that these "mounds" will attract the attention of others and provide a focus for further development.

They encourage people to build mounds of their own. They support them in whatever way they can, to build momentum over a wide area.

They are always watching for new opportunities: nudging, pushing, and catalyzing activities in ways that can help the organization build activities supporting the desired change.

But they never force or try to overcontrol the process.

They recognize that they are just a part of the emerging self-organization: players who are strategic, opportunistic, open to learning and innovation, and guided by a strong political sensibility as to what may or may not be smart or feasible.

They recognize that there are many paths toward a desirable future and work hard to allow an appropriate path to emerge. Theirs is an evolving journey, not a forced march.

The termite metaphor provides a way of thinking about how to mobilize large-scale change through small, incremental initiatives. So, if you're blocked in your current change initiatives, consider incorporating elements of the "termite strategy" into your current practice. You may have little to lose! Whether you are a chief executive or middle manager, working in a business corporation or for a labor union, in a voluntary organization or in a government bureaucracy, it's usually possible to find many ways of building momentum toward achievement of your aims.

You may start alone, but, as you begin the journey, you'll probably find that other termites join you. Termites attract termites. The "mounds" of activity that you initiate or support will often energize, focus, and mobilize others of similar mind. They will help yet others create new perspective and leverage on their situations, thus adding to the momentum. In this way, small changes can result in large changes as the process develops the "critical mass" and momentum needed to produce a significant transformation.

4 On Spider Plants

It's impossible to develop new styles of organization and management while continuing to think in old ways.

As I have suggested, numerous organizations are now facing the challenge of finding more flexible, adaptive forms. Decentralization and a flattening of hierarchies are key priorities. But the influence of old thinking often constrains what can occur.

In this chapter, I offer the image of a spider plant as a way of rethinking organizational design and managerial styles to promote flexible, decentralized modes of operation. I have structured my discussion around an exercise inviting you to think about your organization in these terms. See it as just one example of how we can imaginize alternatives to the mechanical "blueprints" shaping so much organizational design and find ways of managing multiple decentralized teams, projects, and other organizational units in a controlled yet self-organizing manner.

For many of us, the process of designing a new organizational initiative usually involves reaching for a blank piece of paper and sketching an organization chart. Before we know it, we find ourselves drawing boxes and lines linking people and the activities they are expected to perform. This mapping can prove very useful. But it can also be incredibly limiting, as the lines and boxes become constraints, locking us into linear and rather reductive patterns of thought. As we sketch, we split and shape complex activities into neat and tidy parts, tying the process of organization to a variation of the mechanistic-bureaucratic mode.

To break free, we need to develop new images of organization that can help us imaginize new forms. This is especially important in an era of rapid change, where free-flowing, organic images that have more in common with brains, webs, cells, balloons, bubbles, and umbilical cords are more likely to be relevant than the static blueprints found in typical organization charts.

To illustrate, have you ever thought about your organization as a spider plant (Exhibit 4.1)? If not, you may find it

EXHIBIT 4.1 THE SPIDER PLANT

instructive to do so. On the following pages, I invite you to engage in a short exercise using this metaphor. This is followed by a discussion of some of the insights that emerge when managers use the metaphor to gain fresh perspective on the management and design of their organizations. If you are going to do the exercise, I suggest that you do so *before* reading the account that follows. It will be much more meaningful that way!

The Spider-Plant Exercise

Part I

(a) Select an organization for the purpose of this exercise, preferably the one with which you are most involved at this time. If you wish, you can focus on a subunit or department within a larger organization or network of organizations.

_____

(b) Now, describe the organization or unit as a spider plant. Feel free to let your imagination run wild! What parallels can you find with the image presented in Exhibit 4.1? List them below.

Characteristics of the Spider-Plant	Parallels in my organization
_____	_____
_____	_____
_____	_____
_____	_____
_____	_____

(c) How well does the image fit? Does it grasp the nature of your organization? Does it create any new insights?

_____

Part II

(a) Now, use the spider plant to think about how your organization or unit *could* be.

In other words, use the image—interpreted in whatever way you wish—as the basis for a new organizational design. If you had the opportunity to design your organization (or subunit) as a spider plant, how would it be? Use the method of drawing parallels between the spider-plant image and characteristics of the new organization as a means of developing your design.

Spider-Plant Characteristics	Parallels in the New Design
_____	_____
_____	_____
_____	_____
_____	_____
_____	_____
_____	_____

(b) What are the differences between the new organization and the one you described in Part I of this exercise?

Do any new insights for shaping the management process emerge?

I have used variations of this exercise on organizational change projects and in numerous management seminars.

The "graffiti boards" on pages 68-71 present some typical responses and some creative adaptations of the image that emerge when the possibilities are explored.

Responses to the exercise vary according to the organization or situation one has in mind. If one's managing in a tight, centralized bureaucracy, the image of the spider plant may seem to have little relevance. One may "push" one's imagination and see that one is working in a large "pot," reinterpret the spider plant as a form of hierarchy where the stems or tentacles define lines of control and resource flows, see how the whole system is dependent on power "in the pot." But, all in all, the exercise often seems hollow or contrived. It does little more than reinterpret the existing hierarchy.

If, on the other hand, one is working in a more decentralized situation, or in a centralized organization that is trying to launch new initiatives in a more decentralized style, the metaphor resonates much more readily. As reflected in the "graffiti board" images and quotes, many interesting questions come to mind:

What is the role of the central pot?

How large should it be?

How should "offshoot" businesses or departments be linked to the pot?

How should the stems or "umbilical cords" be defined?

How can one use these umbilical cords to create autonomy for decentralized, self-managing units (the offshoots) while securing integration and accountability in the system as a whole?

How can one use the spider plant as a model for managing multiple projects or decentralized teams in a "hands off" way?

And so on!

If you examine the images and quotations presented on following pages, I think you'll find a storehouse of ideas about how the spider plant can create fresh dialogue and insight about the problems of designing and managing decentralized initiatives.

Here are four key ideas that frequently emerge with managers interested in pursuing the implications of the metaphor:

Idea 1. We must break the constraints set by large "central pots."

Spider plants begin to spin off tentacles and new offshoots when they outgrow their pots: It's part of the attempt to find new ground in which to grow.

OUR PRESENT ORGANIZATION . . .

"THE POT IS CENTRAL OFFICE."

" THE OFFSHOOTS ARE SUBSIDIARY DEPARTMENTS AND BUSINESS UNITS. THE POT FEEDS THESE UNITS. THE LINKING STEMS CHANNEL THE FLOW OF RESOURCES."

" MOST OF THE GROWTH IN OUR ORGANIZATION IS INSIDE THE POT. THERE'S VERY LITTLE OUTSIDE."

"SOME OF THE SUBUNITS ARE FEEDING THE POT !!!... THEIR LIFE IS DRAINING AWAY."

GROW DAMN YOU!

"SOME OF THE LEAVES ARE WITHERING AND BROWN. THEY'RE THE INEFFICIENT PARTS OF THE ORGANIZATION; THE DEPARTMENTS AND PEOPLE THAT ARE DEAD OR DYING."

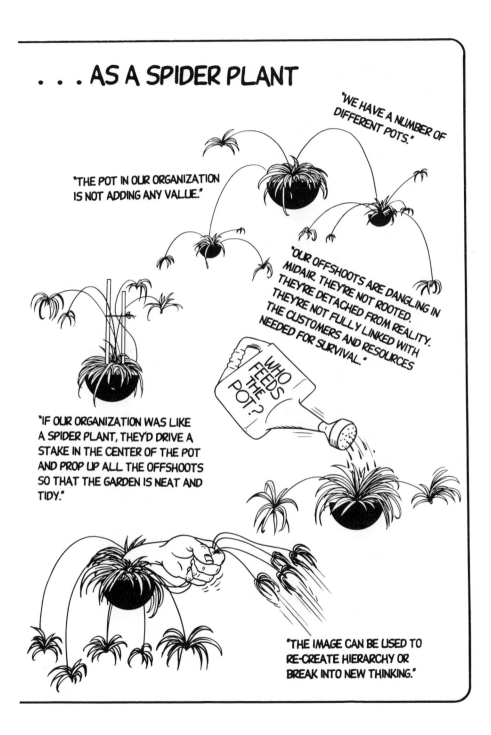

. . . AS A SPIDER PLANT

"WE HAVE A NUMBER OF DIFFERENT POTS."

"THE POT IN OUR ORGANIZATION IS NOT ADDING ANY VALUE."

"OUR OFFSHOOTS ARE DANGLING IN MIDAIR. THEY'RE NOT ROOTED. THEY'RE DETACHED FROM REALITY. THEY'RE NOT FULLY LINKED WITH THE CUSTOMERS AND RESOURCES NEEDED FOR SURVIVAL."

WHO FEEDS THE POT?

"IF OUR ORGANIZATION WAS LIKE A SPIDER PLANT, THEY'D DRIVE A STAKE IN THE CENTER OF THE POT AND PROP UP ALL THE OFFSHOOTS SO THAT THE GARDEN IS NEAT AND TIDY."

"THE IMAGE CAN BE USED TO RE-CREATE HIERARCHY OR BREAK INTO NEW THINKING."

DESIGNING OUR ORGANIZATION . . .

"IT'S A MODEL FOR GROWING LARGE WHILE STAYING SMALL."

"GREAT FOR ORGANIZING SPIN-OFF BUSINESSES."

"A GOOD MODEL FOR ORGANIZING IN THE GLOBAL ECONOMY. WE CAN RE-CREATE OURSELVES IN MANY DIFFERENT CONTEXTS."

"WE DON'T HAVE TO BE IN A MONOLITHIC CENTRALIZED ORGANIZATION."

"IT SHOWS HOW WE CAN SHRINK THE SIZE OF OUR CURRENT POT."

"THE STEMS ARE UMBILICAL CORDS. THEY REPRESENT THE FLOW OF RESOURCES AND VALUES AND CAN BE USED TO INTEGRATE THE WHOLE ORGANIZATION."

"I'M A MANAGER IN THE POT. THE OFFSHOOTS ARE PROJECTS AND TEAMS THAT I'M MANAGING. ALL I'VE GOT TO DO IS DEFINE THE STEMS LINKING ME TO THE PROJECTS, AND I'LL HAVE A WAY OF MANAGING AT A DISTANCE THAT STILL GIVES A LOT OF ACCOUNTABILITY AND CONTROL."

. . . AS A SPIDER PLANT

"A GREAT IMAGE FOR DESCRIBING AND DESIGNING FRANCHISING SYSTEMS WITH OUTLETS LIKE MCDONALDS, BUT MOST ORGANIZATIONS HAVE TO BE MUCH MORE DIVERSIFIED."

"YOU HAVE TO BUILD PAIN AND PLEASURE INTO THE SPIDER PLANT - THE PAIN OF ACCOUNTABILITY AND THE PLEASURE OF REWARDS AND SUCCESS."

"LET'S GET MORE TEAMS AND PROJECTS OUTSIDE THE POT SO THEY HAVE SPACE TO DEVELOP."

"WE NEED TO THROW MORE FUNCTIONS AND BUSINESSES OUT OF THE POT."

"WHEN THE TIME IS RIGHT, WE CAN SNIP THE STEMS AND LET SELECTED UNITS DEVELOP ON NEW GROUND."

"IT'S DIFFICULT TO KNOW HOW MUCH LATITUDE TO GIVE THE NEW OFFSHOOTS. HOW DEPENDENT SHOULD THEY BE ON THE POT? HOW LONG SHOULD YOU HELP THEM TO SURVIVE OUT THERE BEFORE CUTTING THEM OFF, OR BRINGING THEM BACK IN?"

71

But what do our organizations do when they want to grow? They usually find a bigger pot!

This is the core dilemma facing so many organizations. They want to grow, but they can't shake free of the idea that they are an integrated organization. Hence the small office grows into a series of offices occupying the whole floor of a building. Eventually, they spread onto three floors. Then the company takes over the whole building. Eventually, the building gets too small, so they move to a larger one. Then growth spills into neighboring offices. The company eventually occupies an "industrial park," and so on.

Organizations grow. Then size becomes a barrier to flexibility.

The message of the spider plant is this: Why grow in this way?

Because you can grow large while staying small!

You can grow by replicating yourself in a decentralized fashion. Franchising and retailing systems have mastered the art. But the principle can be applied in other contexts as well.

In times of rapid change, large "central pots" can be a liability. They tend to be expensive, slow and inflexible. Perhaps there are ways of "shrinking the pot" by spinning off different elements of one's business, so that they stand as quasi-autonomous units.

FROM THIS:

TO THIS:

Perhaps one can "spin off" HRD, MIS, and other functional departments into separate businesses with the mandate of generating 75% of their revenues from outside the established organization in five years' time.

Perhaps there are ways of building one's activities around a large number of small, highly differentiated pots, in different regions or different businesses, or of pursuing some of the other ideas presented in the mosaic of images and ideas presented on the graffiti boards.

Try thinking about them and see!

Idea 2. Successful decentralization depends on the development of good "umbilical cords."

Umbilical cords are lifelines. As the spider plant reaches out and searches for new ground, it receives nourishment from the mother plant. When it "roots," and is able to sustain itself, the cord is no longer necessary.

There is a message for our organizations here.

Many are struggling with processes of decentralization or of spawning new entrepreneurial initiatives. They desperately want to create more flexible, innovative units, but they get hamstrung by traditional patterns of thinking about control and accountability. As a result, the new units get enmeshed in report-writing and rule-following requirements and other hierarchical requirements that make them extensions of the central bureaucracy.

Yet, if those in the central bureaucratic "pot" could think in terms of "umbilical cords," like those of a "spider plant," they'd have a means of reconciling the contradictory demands of creating decentralization while sustaining control and accountability.

Decentralization is basically an umbilical cord activity.

Why do organizations want to decentralize? Because they cannot manage from the center. Because they want to create a local presence. Because they want to give local units the power, control, and autonomy that will allow them to flourish in their local niches. Because they want to give space for some kind of self-organizing activity. The whole thrust behind decentralization is to create local nodes of activity that can flourish by tapping local resources, by meeting the needs of customers, by adapting to the variations of local environments, and so on.

The problem is to do this while retaining a measure of central control that prevents the decentralization from becoming an anarchic process. The local units have to be accountable to the center in some way. If you're a franchise producing identical pizzas or hamburgers, or replacing mufflers in cars, this can be achieved bureaucratically, using rules, manuals, and controls to define the "umbilical cord" in almost every detail. But, if you're in a business or other activity that demands more local initiative and creativity, then the umbilical cords need to be defined more flexibly.

Try thinking about some different situations. For example: You are a factory manager responsible for a manufacturing unit employing autonomous work groups. You want to give the groups autonomy and space to move. You recognize that you can't be a "hands on" manager exercising close control. How should you design the umbilical cords between you and the work groups? Are you going to impose a degree of uniformity? Or are you going to have a different "cord" for each group?

You are a project manager responsible for seven separate project teams. How do you define your relationship with each team?

You are the head of a business unit producing and marketing multiple products. What umbilical cords should you develop with the managers responsible for the different units?

You are chief executive of a company with five different business divisions. How do you define the umbilical cord with each division?

I've witnessed many situations where this kind of umbilical cord thinking has created instant transformations in a manager's ability to focus on key tasks and key relationships. For what could be easier than thinking about management as a "cord" concept. Typically, managers get overwhelmed by detail and ideas about what they should or should not be delegating and controlling. As a result, it's difficult to see the forest for the trees.

In these circumstances, it is useful to:

Step back and see the spider plant.

See oneself or one's office as the pot.

See one's projects, one's teams, or one's business as the offshoots.

Think about the connecting "umbilical cords" and what they should look like.

Think about their different dimensions.

Are the cords one thick, solid strand: a well-defined control system?

Or do they comprise many strands, as illustrated in Exhibit 4.2?

Reflect on why you are defining the cord and on what you are trying to do.

Are you trying to achieve a "tight rein" where you can control and stay on top of everything?

Or do you want to define a set of principles and parameters that will create a controlled space that allows people in the decentralized units to self-organize on their own initiative?

How is each cord going to be defined?

Are you going to define it yourself?

Or are you going to do so by creating dialogue between both ends?

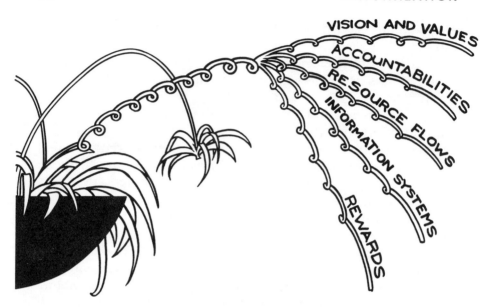

EXHIBIT 4.2 "UMBILICAL CORDS" MAY HAVE MANY STRANDS

There are many questions, and the answers depend on the details of the situation one is managing. They can result in the re-creation of a bureaucratic style of tight control or a more open-ended style of collaborative management. They can result in a cord with fixed characteristics or in one that evolves and changes over time.

If one is dealing with a tight franchising situation where one knows *exactly* what one wants to do, and how to do it, cords can usually be predesigned. But, when one is dealing with more open-ended situations, dialogue and learning are the key priorities.

My favored approach in such situations is to get "both ends" of the cord together, to arrive at a definition of mutual needs. What is the manager "in the pot" trying to realize through the project, autonomous work group, or business representing the offshoot? What help does the offshoot need to flourish? What are the mutual requirements for sustaining and developing the health and growth of the whole plant?

The dimensions of the "cord" illustrated in Exhibit 4.2 were the outcome of a "designing the umbilical cord session" involving a manager and a new business initiative. The session resulted in a "cord agreement" defining five strands:

Strand a. A shared sense of overall vision and values.

What is it that we are ultimately trying to achieve?

What are the philosophies and values shaping basic do's and don'ts?

What is the territory within which a new business unit can feel free to roam, *knowing* that it has the support of "the pot"?

Agreement on these issues serves to create space within which the unit can move without detailed control or encumbrance. With a shared understanding of the vision and direction in which the overall system is trying to move, the various parties can self-organize their activities autonomously, yet in an integrated way. They know when they are working within agreed-upon parameters. They know when they are stepping outside. They know when further discussion and consultation will be necessary. The offshoots remain autonomous yet connected!

Strand b. Agreement on accountabilities.

Autonomy requires accountability. So what are the responsibilities on both sides?

The unit is being given space. What is it going to deliver?

How are results going to be assessed?

How is "the pot" going to be responsive to local needs?

A broad sense of agreement on these issues helps to clarify the operational parameters and general obligations through which activities are discharged on a daily basis.

Strand c. Resource flows in both directions.

What are the key resources that will be exchanged?

What financial and other support will the offshoot receive from the pot?

What will it provide in return?

What are the time frames in which these arrangements will operate?

What contingencies will require a fresh agreement?

Shared understandings here create a sense of the financial and other resource realities shaping the project.

Strand d. Information systems.

What information and information systems can "the pot" provide the offshoot?

What information does "the pot" need from the offshoot?

How is it going to be made available?

Agreements here help to ensure that the new unit receives all the information it requires to be effective and that the pot will develop "early warning systems" and other indications of when further dialogue or intervention may be appropriate or necessary. Such information systems are crucial for developing "hands off" styles of management that still lend a measure of control.

Strand e. Rewards.

There's the "pain" of accountability, and there should be the pleasure of appropriate rewards.

How will the offshoot and the pot share the success of new ventures?

Will the new unit be able to retain a substantial share of its profits, or, as is often the case, will it be "drained" by the pot?

Also, how can members of the new unit be rewarded at a personal or team level?

How can accomplishments be recognized and celebrated?

How can rewards be used to sustain the vitality of the new enterprise?

The understandings and agreements struck through this kind of "cord dialogue" are crucial in creating a shared frame of reference through which "the pot" and "offshoots" can operate in harmony *without direct control*. Whenever one engages in decentralized activity, there is always a danger of the decentralized units lurching in directions that violate the spirit or principles of the enterprise as a whole. The bureaucrat tries to protect against this by minimizing the space for maneuver through the creation of hierarchy, rules, and top-down management. The umbilical cord manager looks to shared understandings as a means of creating integration while *maximizing* the space, autonomy, and self-organizing capacities of the units being controlled. Minimum, rather than maximum, specifications and controls are the order of the day.

EXHIBIT 4.3 "CORD DIALOGUE"

I can't overemphasize the importance of this point, because the familiar pathology in most organizations is that of over-control. The managers at the center tend to define too much and impose too many requirements. The focus is on maximum specification rather than "minimum specs"! The challenge in developing innovative self-organizing initiatives is to have minimal yet highly effective control, to give as much space as possible. The idea of managing through umbilical cords pro-vides an excellent means of doing this.

Clearly, the attitude that shapes the definition of an umbil-ical cord is crucial. If one is trying to create a decentralized yet controlled pattern of self-organization, umbilical cords need to be approached flexibly, with learning in mind. Cord dialogue sessions should not be seen as negotiating sessions with bind-ing results or as attempts to push the other party into a fixed position. They should be based on a process of genuine dialogue designed to explore and meet mutual needs. The aim should be to develop shared understandings rather than blueprints and to create a process that will help to manage conflicts and produce linkages that can evolve with experience.

With an initial "cord agreement" in place, the managers in "the pot" and in the decentralized offshoots are in a position to operate with maximum space and autonomy. So long as they watch for the warnings and anomalies that suggest the cord agreement may be becoming inappropriate, and needs to be reshaped in some way, they can create a context in which the overall system can evolve with a minimum of direct control and intervention. Anomalies in this context are not problems; they create opportunities for genuine dialogue and learning.

Idea 3. Develop different "cords" for managing different situations.

One frequent reaction to the spider-plant image is that "it's too uniform"; it's a "system of clones"; "OK for describing McDonalds . . . but our organization is much more diversified!" The point is an excellent one, because most organizations are highly diversified. They don't always have the uniformity of a franchising or retailing chain.

Why, therefore, be constrained by the metaphor?

Imaginize! Develop a hybrid (Exhibit 4.4)!

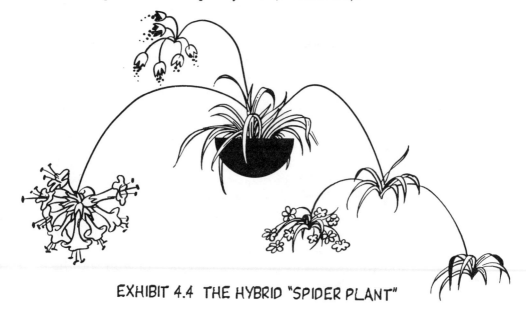

EXHIBIT 4.4 THE HYBRID "SPIDER PLANT"

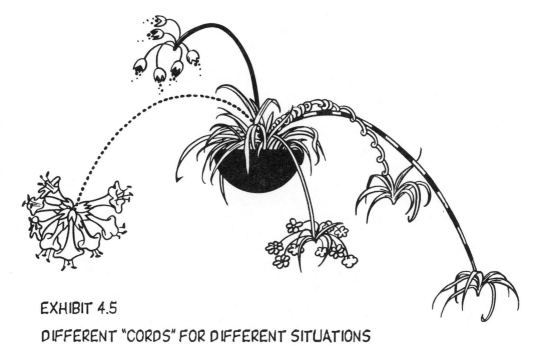

EXHIBIT 4.5

DIFFERENT "CORDS" FOR DIFFERENT SITUATIONS

The image has important implications. The different "flowers" have different requirements. They thrive under different circumstances. Some are fast growing. Others take longer to develop.

The same is true in our organizations. Though the typical bureaucratic "pot" tends to have a cloning influence, propagating rules, controls, and a dominant culture in a way that remakes the offshoots in the image of "the pot," the different offshoots may need to be highly differentiated to survive in their local environments.

The "hybrid" image has important design implications, because it highlights how the umbilical cords linking each offshoot to "the pot" may need to be different (Exhibit 4.5). This underscores the point made above about the importance of "cord dialogue" in arriving at an umbilical cord agreement that meets the specific needs of the offshoot as well as those of the central pot.

I find the hybrid spider plant a powerful image for capturing the need for organizational differentiation. So many organizations get caught in a "uniformity syndrome," trying to impose the same style of management on diverse situations, even when it's not entirely relevant. That's what "big pots" tend to do!

The "hybrid" spider plant sends the clear message that different umbilical cords need to be adapted to the contingencies of local situations.

I also find the "hybrid" image useful in helping organizations understand the role and need for different models of organization, as discussed in Chapter 7. For example, the "six models" approach discussed there can be used to create a new "hybrid" spider plant, as illustrated in Exhibit 4.6. This speaks to the challenge faced in so many organizations. They need to adopt different styles of organization and have to find ways of keeping the differences alive under the subtle but ever present cloning influence of the culture of the dominant model in the central pot.

Umbilical cords to the rescue! If the managers in the central pot are able to appreciate and use the umbilical cord concept, they have a new means of defining parameters and controls in a way that will help to manage the relations between internal and external environments (see Exhibit 7.6) and give new initiatives the space needed for success.

EXHIBIT 4.6 A "SIX MODEL" SPIDER PLANT

Idea 4. Encourage bumblebees.

The "hybrid" overcomes the uniformity or "cloning" problems of the spider plant.

But there is another problem that's frequently raised.

Doesn't the spider plant imply a system that's too decentralized?

What about lost synergies and potential coordination between the offshoots?

The umbilical cords tie the offshoots to the pot. But they're not integrated with anything else.

These are important issues, for the problem in many decentralized organizations is that, as each part works in isolation, each occupies a world of its own and doesn't learn anything from the others.

The difficulty, however, is to find a way of coordinating and integrating potential benefits while avoiding the pitfalls of further bureaucratization, because initiatives from "the pot" often undermine required autonomy in the offshoots. The traditional response is to find ways of drawing lines of communication and coordination between the offshoots. But, as illustrated in Exhibit 4.7, this runs the danger of tying the whole system in knots. The drawing reflects the first attempt of a group of senior managers in dealing with the coordination problem!

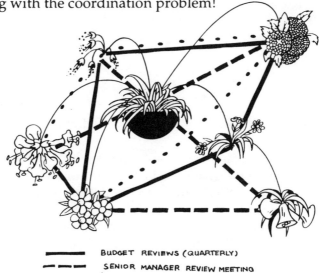

BUDGET REVIEWS (QUARTERLY)

SENIOR MANAGER REVIEW MEETING

"DOTTED LINE" REPORTS ; FOR INFORMATION

EXHIBIT 4.7 BEWARE OF KNOTS!

Another approach rests in building requirements for coordination into the umbilical cords. For example, managers in the offshoots could be mandated to collaborate and coordinate across the whole system and be encouraged to disseminate information, ideas, and innovations on a regular basis. "The pot" could facilitate the process and to fund and "resource" meetings that will help to achieve the desired results.

But, if we stretch our imagination, there is another way in which synergies and integration can be achieved: by introducing "organizational bumblebees" that fly around and create the required cross-pollination (Exhibit 4.8)!

EXHIBIT 4.8 ORGANIZATIONAL BUMBLEBEES

There's a new role here for managers who used to be located in the pot. Every decentralized organization needs a few good bumblebees flying "from plant to plant," keeping in touch with what's going on, spotting synergies, highlighting needs and linking them with resources, identifying "best practice," making connections, and disseminating what's learned. Many HRD, MIS, and other organizational development functions can probably be served much more effectively in this free-floating mode than from departments in the central pot.

Of course, the style of the bumblebee is crucial. As one executive expressed the problem, "We have lots of bumblebees in our organization. The trouble is, they're killer bees." And, as another executive put it, "They're also swarming!"

The bees needed to pollinate a spider-plant organization must be facilitators, orchestrators, and coordinators who are at the service of the offshoots. They need to be welcome and "invited in." They should not be making forced entries!

THE SPIDER PLANT AS IMAGINIZATION

In the foregoing pages, I have tried to push the spider plant to its limits.

At first glance, there may seem absolutely no parallels between one's organization and a spider plant. The metaphor seems almost absurd. But, as we "push" and explore, it's amazing how our minds can *create* meaningful linkages and how we can merrily end our discussion on the role of "bumblebees" in managing decentralized organizations.

For the process to work, one must feel free to play with the metaphor's strengths and limitations, letting links and ideas unfold in whatever way they will. When I introduce the spider-plant image in change interventions or in workshops on the new management skills, especially when I move from the ordinary representation in Exhibit 4.1 to the hybrid in Exhibit 4.4, many managers see an instant relevance. They're immediately thinking about the "umbilical cords" and how they can use them for managing their teams, projects, or businesses in new ways. But for other people the process is more strained. They may see the spider plant as just another way of thinking about hierarchy or, perhaps, remark on how the image presented in Exhibit 4.1 is too perfect: "Spider plants often have dry, brown, withered leaves!"

Yet it's amazing what this kind of comment can evoke. People start thinking about brown, withered leaves and find themselves seeing them in their organization. Smiles go around the group. Everyone knows who or where the brown leaves are. They know why they're withering!

This is the power of imaginization. It creates space for new thinking, free of the usual patterns of dialogue. We start by talking about a spider plant and, before we know it, we are talking about "withering leaves" in Department X or Y. The process can have a powerful impact!

It is difficult to overemphasize the evocative role of metaphor. When it resonates and "flies," it really flies and can develop in many unexpected ways. Sometimes it goes nowhere. But, more often than not, it unleashes a flood of ideas, some of which eventually will be forgotten while others stick.

Sometimes it will just result in the identification of one key issue. For example, in one "spider-plant session" with the top management team of a growing and highly diversified company, the relevance of the metaphor was immediately recognized:

"That's us."

"That's what we're doing."

"We're the spider plant!"

But the core discussion returned to one basic question: "How can we find the right people to manage the offshoots?"

That was the critical business problem: finding the right people! As one of the executives went on to say: "We interview hundreds of highly qualified candidates, and still have difficulty getting the right one. . . . The spider plant is fine in theory. But it only works if you can find the right people to manage the offshoots!"

As a result of this observation, which basically questioned the utility of the model, discussion focused on current recruitment practices for top management and on stories of recent successes and failures. The system, professionally, was impeccable. Everything was being done as it should be.

"But do you know what's missing?" asked one of the senior vice presidents. "We don't play poker with them."

The new metaphor placed the selection problem in a new frame. The potential new managers were subject to all the usual recruitment tests for aptitude, personality, and other skills. But they were never tested with their sleeves rolled up in the thick of battle.

The problem: How does one create a surrogate of "playing poker" in the selection process?

The progress from spider plant to poker is probably a one of a kind event. But it serves to illustrate a central point that I observe time and again. A powerful new image can set people thinking on a new track—creating new insights or reinforcing or rejuvenating older ones. The point is that we must let the process go. Encourage, but don't force. Let it lead where it will. Even when people focus on the limitations and weaknesses of a metaphor, this doesn't necessarily lead to dead ends.

In writing this chapter, I have tried to illustrate and model the same process. Witness, for example, the way we have jumped from the spider plant in Exhibit 4.1 to the "hybrid" in Exhibit 4.4, to the variation in organizational styles illustrated in Exhibit 4.6. The potential *weakness* of the uniform or clonelike nature of the original image, which created insights for franchising but not for diversified organizations, was used as a springboard for elaborating the image in completely new ways. Note how the "stems" or "tentacles" became "umbilical cords" and how the "cords" were then elaborated in a completely new way to generate new insights, for example, through the multiple strands illustrated in Exhibit 4.2. This is a distortion of the umbilical cord concept but one that leads to new developments. Note how the lack of synergy between the offshoots of a spider plant, another potential limitation of the metaphor from a management standpoint, was used to generate the idea of bumblebees. And so on.

This, for me, is what the process of imaginization is all about. It's about pursuing the implications of a resonant image or metaphor to develop new insights that can help us organize in new ways. It is a process that allows us to break free of the constraints of traditional thinking and to create the opportunity for new behaviors rooted in a new image of what one is doing.

The development of new images through which one can see, rationalize, and understand new actions and behaviors is crucial for establishing genuine change. One of the reasons bureaucratic thinking is so robust and enduring in situations where it doesn't produce desired effects rests in the fact that the managers do not have alternative models for rethinking and reshaping their behaviors. The calls to be faster, more flexible, more innovative, and more creative just don't cut the ice, because you can't be all these things if you're stuck in old ways. It's through new resonant images, like the spider plant, that we can create a new conception of what we need to do.

As I have tried to show, it provides us with a completely new way of thinking about organizational issues, encouraging us to see how we are often "hooked" by the concept of a large central pot and the hierarchical forms of management to which it gives rise. It shows how it's possible to grow large while staying small, that one can control and create accountability while giving space through well-designed umbilical cords, that one can unleash organic growth through local processes of self-organization while avoiding anarchic development, that one can be a large organization that still keeps in touch with the demands of many local environments. It provides a lifeline for managers who want to delegate authority to teams and project groups by combining a "hands on" and "hands off" style of management.

The metaphor has great relevance for decentralization in business and government. It provides a way of reshaping the management of education and other social services, so that they are "driven" and managed at local as well as more centralized levels. It provides a way of mobilizing "grass-roots" activity on environmental and social problems, building around the needs of families, neighborhoods, and communities. The model can serve the needs of the chief executive who is thinking about the structure of her total organization. It can help the factory manager who wishes to use umbilical cords to sustain the self-organizing capacities of autonomous work teams.

But, when all is said and done, we have to remember that the spider plant is just a metaphor. As such, it will resonate in certain circumstances more than others. Like all metaphors, it has strengths, and, as we have seen, it also has limitations.

The important point to remember, and this cuts to the core of imaginization as an approach to management, is that it provides just *one* example of the many ways in which we can use metaphor to create new insights about organization and management.

As demonstrated through the other chapters in this book, there are virtually no limits on the process. Hence the aim of this chapter is not to get *everyone* going back to their offices and managing their projects or designing their organizations like a spider plant, though this may be appropriate. Rather, the purpose is to model and illustrate the basic and potential elements of a process that can help us to reshape old thinking, old managerial styles, and old organizational designs in many different ways. Often, it's a question of finding an appropriate metaphor for reshaping what we do.

Organizations are never changed just by changing structures. They're changed by changing thinking, and this is where imaginization can be of help. Our organizations have been dominated by the mechanical thinking underpinning bureaucracy. Perhaps it's now time to open ourselves to thinking based on spider plants or other organic, growthful imagery that will provide the basis for more innovative, flexible, and humane modes of practice.

So, open yourselves to new images of organization.

Don't worry too much about finding "the right one" or "the wrong one."

Don't feel constrained by your starting point.

Just let the process unfold. Feel free to grasp, elaborate, and shape resonant insights. Use them to create a basis for new dialogue about the needs at hand. Feel free to change, modify, develop, and distort metaphors when appropriate. Openness and receptivity to the creative process count! Ultimately, imaginization is about finding creative ways of dealing with the problems, challenges, and difficulties we face. Maybe your spider-plant thinking will only lead to "poker." But, if poker is the critical problem, you may be on a new path to an all-important solution.

The following chapters provide further illustrations of the approach in practice.

5 "Political Football"

In previous chapters, I have shown how imaginization can be used to rethink organizational design, management styles, and approaches to the management of change. Now, I want to illustrate its use as a diagnostic process through which managers, change agents, and consultants can "read" and help to "rewrite" what is happening in organizational settings. This chapter is a long one because my aim is to take you right inside my practice as a change agent by giving you a detailed account of the method in operation.

The story involves Teleserve, a bureaucratic organization wishing to experiment with a self-organizing approach to workplace management. The desired change was spurred by a highly politicized context involving increasingly difficult relations between labor and management. The chapter illustrates how the organization wrestled with its difficulties and how the change process was able to proceed to a successful conclusion when management reframed its understanding of basic problems and created space in which new initiatives could emerge.

As an illustration of imaginization in practice, the story is particularly powerful in showing how key reframings can be achieved through "metaphors of the moment" that present resilient problems in fresh light. It also shows how successful change strategies can be encouraged to self-organize and evolve with minimal external help.

It was a sunny day in June. I was leaving my office for a meeting when the phone rang. Graham Thompson, human resource consultant at Teleserve, was on the line. He introduced himself, saying that he wanted to know if I'd be interested in running a seminar for a group of managers in his organization.

I explained my predicament. We could speak briefly or arrange for a longer conversation at another time.

"Well, the situation is this," he replied.

"I've been reading *Images of Organization*. Our company is described in Chapter 2 [the mechanistic bureaucracy], and we need to become more like Chapter 4 [a self-organizing brain]. We were hoping you'd be able to help."

I was struck by the humor and brevity with which Graham captured the situation.

"Why are you interested in making the change?" I asked.

"It's a long story," he replied. "But, briefly this is the situation . . ."

He went on to describe how the company, a large information processing center operating in a highly bureaucratized fashion, was experiencing difficult problems in a major segment of its operations. Eighteen months earlier, during an electrical storm that led to a loss of power in one of the company's buildings, five of the seven service staff on night duty reported strange sensations from their computer terminals and tingling in their hands. Over the following days, others began reporting similar sensations and associated problems—such as numbness, headaches, and nausea. In the following three weeks, there were almost 100 reports of continuing "electrical shocks." Union reps requested immediate action on the problem. The issue of workplace health and safety at Teleserve became a hot topic in the local media, and various health and government agencies became involved.

Reports of shocklike incidents continued intermittently and began to rise dramatically six months later, with more than 100 other reports within a space of 12 weeks. The reports had also begun to emanate from people working in other parts of the organization, culminating in a walkout lasting three days, with impacts costing the company an estimated $750,000 in lost revenue.

Graham described how the company had initiated all kinds of ergonomic and health studies. None of them came up with any evidence showing that the workplace was unsafe; the physical and medical problems experienced by staff could not be explained. There was talk within the company of the problems being "stress related." But this was hotly disputed by sections of the work force and by the union.

In the attempt to address the health and safety issues, all kinds of committees involving union and management had been established in accordance with government legislation. As a result, supervisors and middle managers were pushed to the sidelines. They lost control over what was happening in their units and were squeezed out of decision making. They were angry at being bypassed and felt that they were powerless to do the jobs for which they were responsible. As a result, they were now *demanding* action on *their* problems.

In response, Graham and a colleague had met with the managers and had facilitated a process leading to a series of short- and long-term action plans. The managers wanted to be kept better informed, and they wanted to develop new skills and competencies that would help them deal with the challenges that lay ahead. As a result of the pressure of their immediate situations, they were saying that they were not prepared to do any more work on the problems being experienced by their staff until top management made a commitment to help them with their issues.

The managers had presented their needs to senior management and received support. Graham was now approaching me to see if I could organize and present a seminar that would help them to understand and develop some new approaches to organizing their work and to acquire some of the management skills needed for survival in a turbulent world. He had been reading *Images* and was familiar with a number of successful experiments with self-organizing work teams. He wanted to help his line managers learn more about new approaches to management and empower them to go forward.

I was glued to the telephone!

The call had only taken a few minutes. But the conversation had told me so much.

My response: "That sounds very interesting. But it sounds as if you need more than a seminar!"

We shared a laugh and agreed to talk again.

AN INITIAL READING

As I drove to my meeting, my mind worked overtime, trying to gain an overall grasp on Teleserve's situation. In developing an initial reading, at least five of the metaphors discussed in *Images* seemed relevant: those of the machine, organism, brain, politics, and instrument of domination (Exhibit 5.1).*

Graham had mentioned the machinelike aspects of the organization and how the work of operational staff was closely monitored and controlled by sophisticated computer technology, though details were scanty. From an "organismic" standpoint there was clearly a mismatch between the human needs of employees and the technology used to control their work. He had also mentioned the relevance of the brain metaphor as a way of guiding the reorganization of work away from the existing bureaucratic structure, toward a system that allowed for a greater degree of self-organization.

The political issues were obvious. There were conflicts all over the place, and power relations were visibly shifting away from line management toward the work force.

Finally, there was obviously a deeper structure to the open struggle for control now shaping the workplace. The thunder and lightning storm initiating the chain of events leading to the crisis seemed to be just a trigger. Was the current breakdown a fundamental reaction against the dominating nature of the technology used to monitor and control the work force? Was the stress and alienation a direct product of the close and unremitting control? Was the situation a white-collar equivalent to the union-management revolts seen on blue-collar assembly lines? Graham had said that the line managers felt that they could no longer manage! The work force was clearly in the driving seat. Where was the current dispute going to lead in terms of the future of labor-management relations generally? I had little information on these issues, but clearly they were crucial.

---

*The analysis presented in this and the next three chapters draws on the approach developed in *Images of Organization*. While the chapters are written in a way that allows all readers to follow the basic ideas, those unfamiliar with *Images* may find it helpful to refer to the short exposition presented in Appendix A.

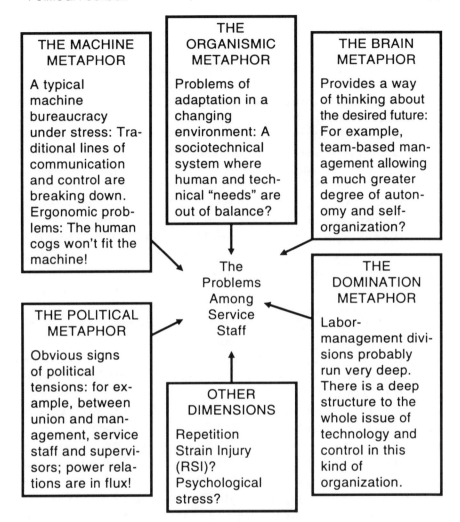

THE MACHINE METAPHOR

A typical machine bureaucracy under stress: Traditional lines of communication and control are breaking down. Ergonomic problems: The human cogs won't fit the machine!

THE ORGANISMIC METAPHOR

Problems of adaptation in a changing environment: A sociotechnical system where human and technical "needs" are out of balance?

THE BRAIN METAPHOR

Provides a way of thinking about the desired future: For example, team-based management allowing a much greater degree of autonomy and self-organization?

THE POLITICAL METAPHOR

Obvious signs of political tensions: for example, between union and management, service staff and supervisors; power relations are in flux!

The Problems Among Service Staff

OTHER DIMENSIONS

Repetition Strain Injury (RSI)? Psychological stress?

THE DOMINATION METAPHOR

Labor-management divisions probably run very deep. There is a deep structure to the whole issue of technology and control in this kind of organization.

A Key Issue: For any real empowerment of managers and their staff to occur, any seminar would have to be linked to a wider process shifting the enterprise toward more of a self-organizing model. Politically, this may not be feasible at the current time.

EXHIBIT 5.1 My First Reading of Teleserve

The physical and health problems were particularly intriguing to me. As Graham was describing the symptoms experienced by the work force—tingling, shock, numbness, headaches, nausea—and the escalating, epidemiclike nature of the problem, I had been reminded of the work and research conducted in

Australia by Fred Emery and Trevor Williams. In the mid-1980s, a similar phenomenon had emerged with Australian telephone company employees assigned to full-time computer keyboard tasks and had reached crisis proportions. The symptoms in this situation had been given a name—Repetition Strain Injury (RSI)—and had become a hot political issue nationwide. Labor unions had pressured for immediate action on the RSI problem, leading to government legislation and employment policies that discouraged full-time keyboard tasks.

The analysis of RSI offered by Emery and Williams suggested that it was systemic: an effect of the mismatch between the requirements of the new technology and the biological capacities of the human organism. Their argument was that the new technology can intensify the physical and mental effects of repetitive work, requiring a completely new level of eye-hand-brain coordination, often creating the symptoms identified as RSI. Their view was that piecemeal ergonomic adjustments, such as well-designed equipment and regular rest breaks, were only of limited value. Lasting solutions required fundamental changes in the design of the work itself: so that keyboard technology was used in a context where employees had a wide measure of control over the conduct and pacing of their work.

Against this background, Graham's instinct that Teleserve needed to move toward a system that would allow employees more autonomy and self-organization seemed sensible. A seminar on the approach to organization and management needed to support this would provide an important first step. But the context in which this occurred was all important. Was the organization open to a new approach to work design? Were the managers and other staff willing and able to make the required shifts in perspective? Could they develop the new managerial skills and competencies that would be required?

On one level, the problems being faced could be conceptualized through the well-known models of sociotechnical systems theory. Here was an organization that was quite clearly out of balance, requiring a new integration of human and technical needs. But it was also an incredibly complex political problem as well. Even if top management were prepared to consider solutions that involved a measure of technological, job, and organizational redesign, the political dynamics, especially in terms of labor-management relations, might not make this a realistic proposition.

The assignment offered by Graham seemed simple. But, if one truly wanted to do something of lasting value, it was necessary to recognize that the context was probably being shaped by powerful forces and problems, to which there may be no easy answer.

LONG-DISTANCE INFORMATION

Graham and his organization were located in a distant city, so my next contact occurred a week later through a conference call designed to broaden the information exchange. Graham involved his colleague Jenny McDonald, and I involved a colleague whom I knew could provide further input on the process of creating and managing self-organizing work teams. The inclusion of new members in the discussion created an opportunity for the story to be retold, something I always like to encourage to check my initial interpretations. So this is where we started.

Graham began the conversation, reproducing in more detail the story that he had told me earlier. He gave more data on the "shock" incidents and on the types of ergonomic and health studies that had been conducted. He said that the studies were unanimous in the view that continuing electrical shocks were not the problem. Despite the expenditure of hundreds of thousands of dollars commissioning independent expert studies, there was no evidence to suggest that the workplace was unsafe.

He described more about the problems being experienced by the line managers: how the health and safety committees were perceived as shifting power to the unions, and how terms and conditions of employment were being changed without any involvement on the part of the line managers directly responsible for controlling work performance. He described the degree of anger felt by many of these managers and mentioned how some of them had recently walked off the job.

As an example of the difficult climate faced by the line managers, he related a story where half of the operating staff on duty on a particular shift had all taken an unscheduled

"stress break" at the same time, immobilizing the unit. The
right to take "stress breaks" had just been introduced by one
of the health committees, but no one had yet told the managers!
Internal communications were in disarray, and the managers
were rightly concerned about the situation. They felt isolated
and out on a limb. The problems were further aggravated by
cuts in internal consulting services, which had closed off a
familiar path of help for managers under stress. They were now
"floundering" with reduced internal support and greater external demands.

Jenny confirmed and added to the details, and talked about
how their work with supervisors and other line managers had
allowed people to express their anger, assess basic problems, and
identify some opportunities. In the process, they had become
very impressed with the quality and potential of many of these
managers and with the action plans they had produced.

Graham and Jenny then went on to describe how top management were coming to the view that they were dealing with
some kind of "collective stress" phenomenon among service
staff and were beginning to recognize that the repetitive, highly
controlled work shouldered a lot of the blame. The internal
control systems were capable of monitoring the performance
of every member of staff on a continuous basis, producing
computerized reports on the performance of individual staff
or their aggregate work units *every 15 minutes*. Needless to say,
the effects of this surveillance created great stress. In this
context, it was easy to understand how pressures could build
up and explode. Moreover, many of the staff had pressing
concerns outside the work situation. They were mainly "work-
ing-class" women, many of whom had children in day care that
was not always satisfactory; some had marital problems; some
were single parents; many were living in situations where little
time could be spent with their family as a unit. Some women
worked the night shift to supplement income, leaving for work
as their husbands arrived home. All in all, for many, life was a
pressure pot.

In the course of providing this information, Graham mentioned the problems in Telecom Australia, where 3,800 people
had reported some kind of paralysis in their hands. He knew
of RSI and saw close parallels with his own situation. He was

leaning to the view that the nature of the work lay at the root of the problem and that the breakdown was triggered and compounded by other stress factors inside and outside the work force.

Graham and Jenny then went on to describe the specific actions taken to explore the various dimensions of the problem within the organization: ergonomic experiments changing the style of furnishings, the height of stools, the design of air-conditioning, and temperature and humidity controls. Employees had been given metal bracelets and had had metal chains attached to the bottom of their chairs to discharge any possible effects of static electricity. Even the buildings had been changed, with some employees being moved to new work locations. Experiments had also been made in terms of organizing the work force into smaller groups.

But the problems still remained. The union had resisted attempts to break up the work force. The ergonomic changes were not delivering major results. The bussing to new buildings was experienced as inconvenient and added to the overall stress. And rumors were now emerging that the problems were due to sabotage. Thirty service staff had signed a letter saying that the technicians had developed "zap devices" to deliver electric shocks! All in all, the situation was incredibly delicate and difficult.

Against this background, we went on to discuss the detailed needs of the managers. Graham and Jenny summarized the Action Plans that they had produced. These focused on getting better information systems within the organization (something that was already being worked on) and getting more knowledge of alternative systems of work organization and new management skills. As they talked, it was clear that Graham and Jenny saw the demands of the line managers as a means of opening the whole situation. If the managers could be empowered to recognize the need for change in work practices, this could then set the ball rolling for change in the organization more generally.

They then went on to describe how the idea for a management seminar represented a first step in this process and how they needed help in designing and implementing further changes that could shift the organization toward more of a self-organizing model. They recognized that this would require full partner-ship between managers, service staff, and their unions as well as respect for top management's concern that change would have to be evolutionary rather than revolutionary, probably progressing through some kind of a pilot project.

Up to this point in the conversation, which had taken the best part of an hour, Graham and Jenny had done most of the talking. The project was obviously evolving in their minds to embrace some organizational change, so we were obviously on the same wavelength.

I was still concerned about the highly politicized context in which the project was set and about the implications for a successful outcome. But there were also a number of positive signs. In their description of the situation among the managers, Graham and Jenny had talked positively of the managers' abilities and, most important, had said that they felt there was "a real will to do something." The two of them recognized that any change project would have to receive the active support and involvement of the union as a full participant in the pro-cess and spoke about how the changes would entail a culture change within the organization. They also mentioned that the natural retirement of older managers and service staff would aid this transition.

Against this background, my colleague and I entertained the possibility of getting further involved and agreed to submit a formal proposal for consideration by senior management. The conference call ended on this note, with the suggestion on my part that, if the proposed seminar for managers was to have the desired effect, it would be a good idea to think about broadening membership to include senior managers and staff representatives or at least have an equivalent initiative for these groups. In this way, they could begin to create a shared understanding of basic ideas and massage the wider culture of the organization. This would help to create the conditions needed for a successful change project. The idea was well received, subject to the line managers agreeing to "share their workshop." We agreed to talk again after our proposal had been received.

A FORMAL PROPOSAL

The conference call had confirmed my initial reading of the situation, and I felt comfortable with the overall analysis. There were gaps and unanswered questions—such as those relating to the existing "culture" of senior management and the detailed politics of the organization. I was aware that the basic problems could run very deep but felt comfortable about moving on. A project focusing on the possibilities of an organizational redesign that would modify the use of technology and allow room for more autonomy and self-organization among employees could bring relief in the short run and also open a way of tackling the deeper structural issues. *But,* there would have to be a major "buy-in" from both management and unions.

Three weeks later, a proposal was thus submitted for a two-stage approach to the problems.

The first stage comprised a seminar for people with a key stake in current problems (senior managers, line managers, service staff, and union representatives). The workshop was to be designed to explore (a) new styles of organization and management, especially those involving self-organizing work groups; (b) the values, power, and control implications of these designs; (c) the attitudes, skills, and abilities needed to manage in such situations, especially with regard to ways of empowering and motivating staff; and (d) the skills needed to manage the transition from one style of organization to the other.

The second stage offered the option of proceeding to a pilot implementation of these principles in a selected area of the organization. It was suggested that this stage should be steered by an internal "design committee," with the help of external consultants, and be evaluated independently.

Within days of submitting the proposal, Graham and Jenny were on the phone again. They liked the proposal but wanted reassurance that the workshop would allow "ample room for dialogue about the organization's current problems." They wanted to give people a chance to deal with the current reality and to understand that there was a *choice* as to how to go forward from this point. It would be ideal if the workshop could lead to a commitment to a pilot project, so that stage two would flow naturally out of stage one. They wanted further guidance as to who should be involved in the workshop, to ensure an appropriate balance and mix of different stakeholders.

The enthusiasm was evident, and momentum was building. Armed with the additional information, they planned to take the proposal to senior management as soon as possible.

THE "CONTROL CULTURE" SHOWS ITS HAND

Four weeks later, I received a call from Graham. The proposal had been presented to senior management, and the response had been positive. But there were concerns from one vice president about the pilot project, and how it would be evaluated. For the project to go ahead, it would be necessary to specify precise outcomes in advance. The criteria as to what would constitute a success needed to be clearly established. Graham and Jenny wanted to meet the team that I was putting together, to discuss the situation further.

We met in Toronto in the third week of September, in a suite at the Royal York Hotel. There were six of us. Graham and Jenny brought one of their line managers. I brought two colleagues who would be involved in the project.

The presence of the newcomers, and the fact that we had the whole day before us, created an opportunity for the basic story to be told again. It unfolded in a way that introduced further new information. We were given more data on the shock-related incidents, the latest on the medical and ergonomic reports, more information about the line manager's job and how service staff were controlled on a day-to-day basis. And we were given a clear indication of the stresses being experienced at all levels.

But the explosive news was that a year earlier the former president and several vice presidents had been fired, along with other senior managers, as a result of an unsuccessful overseas venture that had cost the company millions of dollars. Somehow or other, this had not been mentioned before! The failed venture had become a very hot political issue, because of the visibility and importance of the firm in its local community and the fact that it had received major government grants to support its activities. Under public pressure, the government of the day had become involved. There was an outcry against the misuse and waste of public funds and the fact that the top management of the corporation had allowed their attention to be diverted from the mainline business. The view in the press was that they should have been focusing on the core task of realigning the business to meet the stiff new domestic competition, rather than engaging in foreign jaunts. Government action had to be visible. Politicians exerted their influence, and heads rolled. The urgency and visibility of the action was propelled, in part, by the fact that some of the key politicians involved in the outcry were closely aligned with the labor movement. This was also a factor increasing the visibility of the current crisis around the health and safety issues, with the politicians supporting labor demands for speedy solutions to the problem.

As a result of all this, the company had become a great target for media-bashing as "the company the public loves to hate." This made it possible for almost any story of even mild incompetence or bungling within the organization to receive widespread coverage in the press, or on TV, and some employees had been getting great mileage out of this. Media attention was providing great leverage for power bases at lower levels of the organization.

My political antennae were going wild. The issues were even hotter than I first thought. Any project stood a chance of running out of control.

My concerns were further increased within minutes of this news, as we explored recent attempts at organizational change within the company. A year earlier, there had been a failed attempt at "employee participation" in decision making. A firm of consultants had been engaged to promote greater participation, as part of a corporate effectiveness program. At the second meeting, the agenda had turned to issues associated with time management and productivity. Employees and their union were completely "turned off" and had become very cynical, seeing management's interest in "participation" as a veil covering other agendas.

Here was another potential pitfall for our project. The participation experiment had been conducted in another part of the organization, but there was a real danger that our work would be tarred with the same brush.

It was against this background that the meeting then turned to the real agenda: the concerns raised by top management about the proposed project. Graham and Jenny went on to say that the crux of the issue was that the vice presidents, or at least one important vice president, were not prepared to endorse a project that looked as if it would "just help managers manage better." There *had* to be demonstrable benefits in terms of bottom line performance, such as improved customer service or reduced overhead, grievances, absenteeism, walkouts, and stress in the workplace. Graham and his colleagues had in effect been asked to do a detailed cost-benefit study and to specify *exactly* how the project would be evaluated.

As Graham talked, I realized that the control-oriented culture within the organization was now firmly enveloping our project. And it got worse. Graham was expected to show that any pilot project would guarantee current levels of effectiveness in terms of cost and service, which, on the basis of the regular monitoring of staff performance, were judged to be as high as 95% for major service operations. I could hardly believe my ears. Here was an organization in major crisis, with management problems on all fronts, with certain members of top management still believing that it was still 95% effective! I couldn't resist the temptation and asked whether the figure of 95% allowed for the loss of $750,000 every time employees chose to walk out for a few days?

My point was made. These costs were not factored in. But the problem still remained: How could Graham and his team get hard data that would convince senior management that the project would be worthwhile? They asked whether we could produce evidence from projects conducted elsewhere to demonstrate the benefits that other organizations had derived from a shift toward more self-management.

My colleagues provided lots of examples. But I was getting increasingly worried. As the conversation continued, I could feel the company's culture and values taking a firmer and firmer grip on the project. If we allowed this line of thinking to continue, Graham and Jenny's whole initiative, not just our part of the project, would be lost. Top management's concern for detailed control and evaluation—the very values underpinning the surveillance and stress in the existing situation—were now steering us in the footsteps of the earlier experiment with participation. The union would *never* join a project that was presented or justified in this way. I felt that the scope for a successful intervention was rapidly disappearing. The culture that had in part created and sustained the current problems was choking possible solutions. It was reasonable to talk about costs, benefits, success and failure, and how these could be measured, but not on the terms that Graham and his team were required to deliver.

The image of "political football" floated across my mind. We were being invited to play. And, unless I was very much mistaken, we were going to be the ball that was kicked around: between management, unions, and even the media. Graham and his colleagues were looking at their initiative as a key step on the path toward a significant redesign of work organization. I was seeing it through a more politicized lens.

I thus decided to try and turn the course of the meeting in a new direction to address the political realities.

I put the question very directly: "Is there support from the union for this approach to the project?"

The answer: "The support is questionable, but there are some hopes for collaboration."

I felt that the essential point behind my question didn't really connect, and discussion began to drift back to union attitudes on the stress studies and related matters. So I raised the issue even more directly:

"From what I've heard this morning, you are operating in a highly politicized context. The media, the politicians, the labor unions, disgruntled employees, line managers, and top managers concerned with 'bottom line' performance, all have an interest in what you're trying to do.

"Unless I'm mistaken, your project is going to end up as part of a game of political football. It's going to be kicked around!

"You have been asked to deliver a bottom line justification for the project to your vice president. But the real task should be to define a project into which all parties can 'buy in.'

"You *have* to avoid making the project a political football.

"The bottom line aspects of this project are important. But there is a more fundamental issue. It's not just a question of measurement or return on investment. It's a question about the future of the company, and whether you can get key stakeholders to join a project that will make a substantial difference to the way you organize a key element of your business.

"If you just try to justify the project in terms of efficiency and the bottom line, it's going to look like your participation project all over again."

From the silence in the room, I knew that my intervention had struck the right chord. We were now in a different meeting.

The point was taken.

The problem was not just to meet the demands of top management as laid out but to find a way of getting top management, along with other key stakeholders, to understand the importance of the project as a means of evolving to a new pattern of work relations within the company as a whole. The real objective should be to understand and address the limitations of the current approach to organization and management and the crisis this had produced.

So we began to talk about different stakeholders' perceptions of the project and the possibility of arriving at a definition that would encourage *everyone* to "carry the ball." The only way of ensuring that the project wouldn't be kicked around was to make sure that *everyone* had a realistic stake.

In effect, this meant that any viable project would require joint sponsorship and approval from both management and union. Unless I was grossly mistaken, the project could not survive within existing control systems as a variation of business as usual. New space needed to be created.

Senior management needed to see the initiative as a key opportunity for aiding transition to a new style of management. They needed to own the idea that the mode of organization that had delivered 95% efficiency in the past would not necessarily deliver this kind of success again.

Union representatives needed to understand that this was not just another participation project cloaking concerns for efficiency and control or a subversive attempt to break the power of the union.

Line managers and service staff needed to understand the project as a genuine attempt to address the very real stress and management problems with which they were concerned.

UNDERSTANDING SHIFTS
FROM

> **THE MACHINE AND BRAIN METAPHORS**
> "This project is about the redesign of work"

TO

> **AN EMPHASIS ON**
> **POLITICAL-CULTURAL-DOMINATION METAPHORS**
> This project is a politically* sensitive intervention set within a control-dominated corporate culture that can block success. To be successful, the project must receive wide support. It provides an opportunity to change the culture and style of the organization. But the first task is to *redefine the political context* of the project itself.

NOTE: The word *political* is used to convey the conflicting sets of interests surrounding the project (as discussed in Chapter 6 of *Images of Organization*) and not in the sense of being allied to a political party or ideology.

EXHIBIT 5.2 My Second Reading of Teleserve: A Key Reframing

As far as Graham and his team were concerned, my reframing worked (Exhibit 5.2). They had recognized from the start that the labor unions would have to be consulted and involved with any change initiative. But this now had a new profile and significance. They came to see that they too were holding the political football that was going to be kicked around. This was not just a project about the redesign of work or the improvement of managerial skills. It was a highly politicized project where success hinged on managing and redefining a political problem. The situation required a political strategy to produce a politically effective solution, of which the redesign of work would be just part.

As a result, the path forward became very clear. We needed
(a) to look at alternative ways of defining the core project, (b)
to focus on the issue of ownership and sponsorship on the part
of key stakeholders, and (c) to develop a concrete plan for
carrying the project forward.

THE REFRAMING CREATES NEW MOMENTUM

After a well-deserved break, the meeting resumed with new
energy. Everyone had known from the beginning that we were
dealing with a politically loaded project. But the understanding had been implicit and dominated by the idea that an
organizational redesign could lead to a solution removing key
problems. The organizational redesign had been in the foreground, with the politics lurking in the background. As a result
of my intervention, the situation was reversed. The political
problem was now clearly in the foreground. The main issues
were on the table and could be addressed directly in fresh
ways. The effect was liberating.

As we talked about the perceptions of different stakeholders, the "tug-of-war" nature of the situation with which we
were dealing became increasingly clear. There were paradoxes
all over the place.

Top management wanted a resolution to current staff problems. But they also wanted to continue to deliver on their
bottom line performance targets. Would they come to see that
the overcontrolled systems that were delivering this bottom
line performance were a part of the basic problem?

The labor union was no doubt concerned about the health
and welfare of employees, but could the conditions of collective agreements be relaxed to allow less stressful forms of work
organization to emerge? The current problems were giving the
union great leverage and power in dealings with management,
with the government, and with the media. Would they let this
power go? They had obvious and legitimate concerns about
management's overwhelming focus on issues of control and
efficiency and how new forms of organization could just evolve
into tighter managerial control over the work force. Wearing a
union hat, it was easy to see how a shift toward self-organizing

work groups could undermine the future solidarity of the work force and the long-term power of unions generally. Could a solution to these problems be found? What would prove more important: the concern to remedy the adverse health effects of the highly controlled work environment or fears about incorporation into the management process and a possible loss of power?

Turning to the line managers, could they link their immediate concerns to those of their staff and find a joint solution? Rather than seeing the problems in terms of "us" and "them," could they see that both parties were caught in a tangle because of a shared problem? If so, would they be prepared to share *"their"* workshop with other key stakeholders? They were angry about the increasing power and influence of the unions. Could they transcend this to become partners in a potential solution?

Against the background of these considerations, it became increasingly clear that the task was not to "sell" the project that we had designed in its current form but to use the project as a focus for getting a multistakeholder team together that would look at the existing proposal, change it where necessary, and carry the project forward in a mutually acceptable way. The real task was to create, at least for the moment, a sense of "safe space" free of management controls and union agreements, so that a joint attack on the problem became possible. The task, in short, was to build the commitments and energy required to explore the possibilities for genuine change.

As these issues were explored, it was clear that the meeting had made a giant leap in understanding. Everyone was contributing to the discussion on stakeholder perceptions, and, when the time came to move to the issue of *how* ownership could be created, and *who* should be involved, Graham and his team had little difficulty in taking over design of the initiative. I suggested that one way of looking at the ownership problem was to focus on *who should be involved* and *in what ways.* We developed the matrix presented in Exhibit 5.3 and set about identifying specific names and the categories of the matrix into which they would fall.

There were some people who had to be clearly visible in their general support for the project but who would not necessarily have to be involved in the details. For example, the new president

	NAMES OF KEY "STAKEHOLDERS"

TYPE OF INVOLVEMENT	1	2	3	4	5	6	7	8	9	10	11	12	13	14	***
1. Must give visible support and commitment to the initiative	*	*			*	*			*		*				
2. Must be involved in the detailed design and sponsorship of the initiative (the potential design team to be picked from this group)			*	*	*		*	*		*		*	*	*	
3. Must be involved in detailed imple-mentation (an open question at this moment)															

NOTE: The numbers shown above are used in lieu of the names of the people involved. More than 20 names were identified.

EXHIBIT 5.3 A Scheme for Designing Stakeholder Involvement

(who was joining the organization the following month), union leaders, key vice presidents, and key influence leaders from within the union, line management, and service staff had to be extremely clear and visible in terms of their commitment and support. They had to see the importance and potential of the project as a step toward creating a new restructuring of work, to take ownership, and to be committed to its success. Moreover, they had to be *seen to be* in this position. The symbolism as well as the substance of their position was of key importance.

There was another group, which included some of the above, who would have to be more actively involved in the development of the project and sign off on key strategic issues as the project evolved. They would have to be kept informed about its activities on a regular basis and have their input sought. This was the group from which the project design team would ultimately have to be chosen. It would be necessary to find the cluster of people that would provide an acceptable representation of the wider group.

Within no more than 10 minutes, the first two categories of the matrix had been filled out in a preliminary way, and the problem of identifying the representative design team began. It was recognized that the development of such a team would have to be a consultative process conducted back in the organization, but it was found useful to develop a preliminary sketch of what it might look like, just to get an idea of how everything might unfold.

With this task complete, the third problem was to develop the elements of an action plan for carrying the project from this point. *How* was a joint union-management sponsorship of the project to be achieved? This was the only way we could prevent the "football" from being kicked around. For a successful project, there had to be a way of getting key union and management people to see the potential of a new initiative and the value of getting ahold of the ball. As we raised the issue, the strategy became clear. Graham and Jenny were the ones who laid it out.

First: "Go back to the vice president" who was especially concerned about the control and evaluation of the project. Tell him about this meeting and why a relaxation of the company's usual controls and yardsticks is appropriate."

It was agreed that Graham and his team would do this and that I would be prepared to attend a meeting to clarify the issues from an independent perspective, if necessary.

Next, "Get the incoming president on board."

Graham was optimistic that the new president would welcome a fresh initiative that got a fast start on the problem and that he was the kind of person who would understand the rationale that had been developed.

Then, "Get the union leaders involved."

"No," said Graham.

He and his colleagues were leading the way.

"Get the new president and the executive VP to go to Williams [a leading local politician]. They know each other well. Let Williams prepare the ground by talking to the unions before management brings the proposal forward.

"If and when the union leaders are comfortable about being involved, a formal process can then establish the parameters of the project. We then create a design team to steer it from that point."

The basic idea was to use the existing political network to create safe space for people to explore the consequences of the commitments that would be involved. We hoped that, if we could get the executive VP and president owning and supporting the initiative, everything else would follow.

It was agreed Graham and Jenny would explain our meeting to people back home, so that everyone who needed to know what was happening would understand the realities of the situation and, we hoped, act as informal, low-profile champions and orchestrators of the new initiative. Graham and Jenny's key task was to get everyone on board. I would make visits to talk with the executive VP, president, or whomever else seemed appropriate, if necessary. But Graham and his team would be carrying the ball.

Everyone in the meeting was energized. We had a new understanding and the elements of an action plan that could evolve as events unfolded. No doubt, there would be rocks and pitfalls along the way. But we could deal with them as they arose.

It was lunchtime. After lunch, Graham and Jenny had contingency plans. Time permitting, there was an opportunity to visit a local firm using technology similar to that used by Teleserve, so that my team could see and understand the work situation more directly. This was confirmed, and the visit proved very useful in giving us a closer look at the conditions under which service staff and line managers were required to work. As we walked around, I reflected on the unusual course of this project and how I was learning about the client organization "secondhand." Geography was a real problem. The project was in effect being put together "long distance," creating all kinds of problems and information gaps that in most projects would have been rectified much earlier on. But, despite the surprises of our meeting, everything seemed to be moving along really well.

GETTING KEY STAKEHOLDERS ON BOARD

On their return home, Graham and his team took full ownership of the project, incorporating our initial proposal into a plan of their own, building around the essential idea that the aim was to launch the first steps of a change process that would attract widespread support. They knew that they had to start thinking about how to shift their control over the project to the future design team discussed at our earlier meeting. They started to call it the "Make It Happen Team" and knew that it would have to be composed of people with the potential to take the project to a successful conclusion. They began to think that the seminar that had originally been planned for the managers and service staff should now be run after the "Make It Happen Team" had been established. It would provide an ideal means of launching the project and of getting everyone on the same wavelength. They also began to evolve the detailed tactics for involving key stakeholders in a joint sponsorship of future developments.

Within a week, they had approached the organization's vice president for customer services. Graham reported that he was "excited, supportive, and accepting" of the plan. He accompanied them to a meeting with the vice president who had expressed most vocal concern about project evaluation and the "bottom line." The principle was established that, because the project was not a conventional one, the usual predetermined targets were not entirely relevant. It was also agreed that the unusual nature of the project justified an unusual style of decision making, freeing it from the regular line of command. The result was that both VPs agreed to sponsor the project to the new president and to the chairman of the board.

This meeting was held the following week. Graham and Jenny made the presentation with the VPs in support. It was very well received, and they were told that they'd "done a hell of a job!" It was decided that the president would set up a meeting with Williams, the politician, but to ask for support and advice on how the union could be encouraged to get involved rather than putting him on the spot by asking him if he would sponsor the initiative directly.

Two approaches were made to Williams, one in late October, the other in early November. They were successful in rallying his general support, leaving specific actions to his discretion. His help proved crucial in winning union support and in creating a new context in which people could see the possibility of something new unfolding.

The president had his first meeting with key union leaders, and an opportunity was created for Graham and Jenny to meet with them to discuss detailed problems at a future date. An informal meeting was held in December, and, with the support of the union's medical adviser, preliminary commitment to an initiative was achieved, provided that management also showed substantial commitment to the project in advance. In particular, the union leaders wanted management to establish parameters for the design team *before* the project started, so that the team had real autonomy and did not have to run for higher approval whenever it came up with a new idea or direction. In return, the union was prepared to specify new parameters on its side, to allow the design team to work outside the current collective agreement.

Throughout the above process, I acted as the long-distance adviser to Graham and Jenny. But no site visits were necessary. The team overcame all hurdles themselves. By adapting their strategies to meet the needs of the situation at hand, they slowly but surely created the "safe space" in which a viable new initiative could evolve. Their approach built on the reframing achieved in the Toronto meeting in September, allowing the details to be jointly determined by union and management.

By the following February, formal commitments to a joint project had been obtained. A "start-up (design) team" comprising six members was established. It comprised three union representatives and three from line management. It was mandated (a) to define parameters for the project, (b) to select a consultant to help them, and (c) to plan and implement the project generally. Graham and Jenny became their internal facilitators and consultants, playing a purely advisory role.

My direct involvement with the initiative shifted at this point. The original idea to hold a seminar had been postponed, and, through our careful orchestration of all concerned, the project now had a momentum of its own. The start-up team was in control, and a fresh start with a new consultant acceptable to both union and management seemed appropriate. They developed the selection criteria and, after a comprehensive search, found an excellent person to guide them in the detailed design and implementation of the shift toward a new style of organization and management. Work immediately got under way.

Over the following two years, the project gained slow but sure ground. Progress at first was tentative because, given the history, there was a lot of uncertainty as to whether the project was "for real" and whether it would receive support from key players at critical points. Also, everyone was a new player at this game. The organization had never done anything like this before, and the team steering the project had significant hurdles to overcome. Trust between union and management representatives was low, and their new role in working together placed their old roles and loyalties in a new and difficult perspective.

The fact that, from the start, the design team was given real "teeth" and power by both unions and management was a critical success factor. A proposal to top management resulted in the team controlling a budget of $250,000 for the start-up phase—a figure that had incredible symbolic value, because it demonstrated real management commitment and trust. The money was a significant symbol of power, because no group at this level of seniority had ever had access to such funds before. It also removed initial union concerns that the project would be dangled on purse strings controlled by management.

The process of acquiring these funds also played a key role in empowering and galvanizing the team. In addition to developing the proposal, the team had to make a formal presentation to top management and answer questions they raised. This was "a first" for everyone concerned. Some of the team had never spoken in public before, let alone defended a request for a quarter of a million dollars. They did, in Graham's view, "an outstanding job with sincerity and honesty, creating great confidence among themselves and top management. They won the support and admiration of top management, and themselves grew into people with management ability." The story of the meeting became an anchor point in the team's culture, being told and retold, serving as a "landmark event" and as a symbol of the team's ability to gain access to top management.

The success placed the design team firmly in the driving seat. They moved in a highly consultative mode, seeking input from all relevant stakeholders on the overall direction to be taken on the project as well as on specifics. They educated themselves and others as they went along, holding workshops and learning from experiences in self-organization elsewhere. They set their sights high, at one point becoming known as the "Dream Team," but delivered on their aspirations.

An experimental redesign of the work process was launched in a trial office, comprising 40 as opposed to the usual 150 staff. A letter of agreement between union and management—another "landmark event"—guaranteed the operational space needed to create possibilities for true innovation. The trial office was staffed by regular service employees who volunteered for the project and who were eventually selected by lottery because three times the required number had offered their names. The consultant and design team helped to shape the broad parameters within which the trial would work, but the detailed form "self-organized" as the 40 staff took control of development. They appointed an "office committee" of five members, elected democratically with rotating membership in lieu of a manager, and developed codes of behavior relating to decision making, budgets, resource management, communication, and staff development. They took control of performance measurement and peer evaluation. They developed means of educating themselves and of upgrading skills. Concrete innovations included the removal of hierarchy, the introduction of flexible hours of work, trading of work schedules, the removal of monitoring, and the evolution of new procedures for working with customers to ensure that service staff had optimal autonomy in meeting customer needs. The office operated on the basis of a self-organizing philosophy, stressing the importance of people being involved with multiple tasks and developing multiple skills. Clerical, managerial, and service functions were fused.

The project was evaluated by the design team at the end of an eight-month period and demonstrated a real success. The design team then formulated and presented more than 20 recommendations for further development to a committee comprising three members of top management and three union representatives, set up to make decisions on the next phase of the project. The committee agreed to nine of the recommendations, referring others to the formal bargaining table. Many of the recommendations, which incorporated the ideas described above, were controversial because they challenged the basic mode of operation and "territory" of both union and management. Basic agreements were struck, however. They were introduced and explained to staff by joint union and management teams, and the mode of operation piloted in the trial office was gradually diffused to other work units in the company.

The "political football" is still quite political, but it is now being firmly carried on all sides! A new era of collaborative relations has begun to emerge, accompanied by an improvement in many indications of success. Traditional performance measurements are showing dramatic improvement under the new work system. Customer complaints and absenteeism have fallen, and customer congratulations have soared. But, perhaps most significant, formal employee grievances are running at about 3% of their original level, and the health and safety complaints have virtually disappeared.

Needless to say, despite the success, there have been ongoing problems throughout the change. For example, many first-line managers resisted the new initiatives as they saw their jobs beginning to disappear. The trial office created a "fishbowl" effect that attracted a lot of attention and criticism at key points. Ensuring effective communications that got "the facts rather than the rumors" onto the organizational grapevine was an ever-present problem. Difficulties were sometimes encountered in finding champions for new initiatives outside the design team. The design team sometimes ran into real problems in getting the support of technical and other "experts" within the company. And many labor and management people were genuinely stretched by the new attitudes and approaches needed to make a more collaborative approach to work design a reality. Some of the problems seemed to be gender related. For the first time in the company's history, women on the design team, and in the trial office, were changing management practices originally created and controlled by the company's male-dominated management!

As Graham and Jenny reflect on the project as a whole, they emphasize with justifiable pride the success that has unfolded from the lightning storm. The project took a lot longer than they had originally expected, but the change produced is much broader and deeper. Looking back on the experience, they place main emphasis on the power that was generated by "identifying the key stakeholders and winning their support, contribution, and commitment."

As Graham observes: "The concept of stakeholder development and of building the project from the bottom up changed our whole mind-set. Winning support became the means of building momentum. We talked with people. We involved them. We got them to view the problems for themselves. We got them involved in defining the issues and developing potential solutions. They were involved in the presentations. The process was very functional in building ownership, which I now believe to be the only way to resolve human problems in the workplace. . . . The old modus operandi was to use one's power. That approach is no longer acceptable. We now begin the opposite way by building understanding and commitment. . . . This is a continuous process. Commitment has to be worked with continuously. People have to be able to express their concerns continuously. . . . Often, time isn't allowed for this to occur, and to let people grow.

"It's difficult to convince those unfamiliar with the approach that this is the best method of creating change in the long run. But, I use it in all my work, all the time, now. . . . You get all the parties participating in the joint study of a problem. You get junior and senior people on board. You get them to sell their ideas to their superiors. They then sell it to others. Everyone gets on board. There are no bystanders. The process changes relations with the people involved. There is true ownership."

THE PROJECT AS AN
EXAMPLE OF IMAGINIZATION

The Teleserve project provides a clear illustration of imaginization in practice. In relating the story, I have shown how unfolding interpretations helped to frame a new course of action. From a variety of alternative and complementary readings of what was happening within the company (Exhibits 5.1 and 5.2), a "political" explanation giving considerable weight to the dominating influence of the control-oriented corporate culture emerged. On the basis of this reading, the metaphor of political football was then used to frame an intervention capable of steering the project in a new direction, thus helping to "write" the unfolding story in a new way.

As I have tried to show, Graham and Jenny had all the skills, information, and insights needed to steer the project themselves. But, up until the Toronto meeting, they were too close to the situation to see it in a new light. Like all of us, they were caught in the day-to-day reality with which they were dealing. The key breakthrough was created by nudging them toward a slightly different view of the highly politicized context in which they were working.

The reframing helped to show them a new way forward. Rather than simply going ahead with a long-term project that was being shaped by short-term demands—especially those imposed by the vice presidents' concerns for "business as usual" on the one hand and the line managers' need for more management education on the other—they quickly saw how the initiative could be reshaped to create a project that would have significant and lasting impact on the organization. By working through a political frame, and creating a project that would gain support from key stakeholders, they had an alternative to forcing or "selling" a project shaped by parameters imposed by senior management. This was very energizing, especially when they realized that they already had most of the information and skills needed to carry the project forward themselves. As external consultants, I and my colleagues had told them little that they didn't already know. We simply made a strategic intervention that highlighted a neglected dimension of their situation and helped them to understand and handle their project with new energy and perspective.

To my mind, this is what imaginization as an approach to organizational change is all about. It's about mobilizing insights and interpretive abilities to find creative ways of reshaping situations that are stuck or unsatisfactory in some way.

SENIOR MANAGEMENT

"We don't need this problem. We have to restore normal levels of control and efficiency, based on measured results."

LINE MANAGERS

"The situation is changing on us. We're held accountable, but we don't have the power to deliver. We need to get better informed and to learn new skills for managing in a turbulent world."

THE ERGONOMISTS

"There are some routine ergonomic problems that can be improved through the physical redesign of equipment. But there is no evidence of major health and safety problems."

GRAHAM AND JENNY

"The problem rests in the stressful nature of the work itself. We need to redesign the work process. We also need to deal with the collective stress phenomenon that's emerged."

The Problems Among Service Staff

LABOR LEADERS

"This mess has got to be cleared up. The health and safety aspects are crucial. Manage- ment has to take action, but we don't trust them. We are strong and can apply a lot of pressure if necessary."

THE SERVICE STAFF

"We're working with a poor system. We don't want the strain and stress. Management has to sort the situation out. More stress breaks. Safer equipment. Find the 'techies' that are 'zapping us.' "

THE POLITICIANS

"We don't want more media coverage on this one and more charges of mismanagement that consume our time. We don't want the unions asking *us* to solve their problems."

EXHIBIT 5.4 Different Stakeholders Often Have Different Readings of the Same Situation

The Teleserve situation was stuck because, as illustrated in Exhibit 5.4, different stakeholders had different perspectives on the problems being faced and favored different courses of action. There was no easy "win-win" solution because each stakeholder group faced a major paradox in collaborating in a significant organizational change.

For top management, any change toward a more team-based, self-organizing model carried the threat of losing control. For unions, there was a risk of losing power to the team-based system and of blurring traditional demarcations between labor and management as employees assumed traditional managerial functions. And, for line managers, the change carried a recognition that they no longer had the power and role they used to have.

Given these considerations, together with the other information favoring a political reading of the overall situation, especially the mistrust between labor and management, the failed participation project, the militant line managers, and the "media-bashing," it was clear that any successful project would have to create *new space* in which a truly new initiative could emerge. It was also clear that the parameters for evaluation being imposed by top management would prevent that space from emerging and that any successful project would ultimately have to reshape relations between union and management.

Hence the image of "political football": Unless safe space was created, we were sure to be kicked around!

This was the image that floated across my mind as we grappled with the unfolding story at Teleserve. It seemed absolutely "right for the moment," because it offered an evocative means of helping Graham and Jenny recognize the harsh political realities with which they were dealing.

What could have been more evocative than the thought that "we're all going to get kicked around!"

The image resonated with the needs of the situation and created a dramatic shift in the nature and tone of the meeting at which it was introduced. It mobilized a new frame of reference for the Teleserve team and played a crucial role in allowing a successful project to emerge.

It would be a mistake, however, to see the success of the intervention as resting on the metaphor of political football per se. Rather, *it depended on the process of imaginization that led to the generation of the metaphor* and on the sustained efforts of the Teleserve team in acting on key insights. The image helped to create an imaginative breakthrough. But it was the sustained follow-through on the part of the Teleserve team that ultimately delivered the concrete results. In the Teleserve project, as in all the others reported in this book, my main concern as a change agent trying to help with a problematic situation was to arrive at a genuine understanding of the situation with which I was being confronted and to mirror it back in some way. This is basically what I did throughout the project. I listened. I learned. I used the "radar" provided by *Images of Organization* as a way of picking up key signals and organized them as "readings" that evolved throughout the project. And, when the time came to intervene, I relied on the most resonant image that came to mind. It could have been that Teleserve was engaged in a "tug-of-war" or occupying a battlefield. It happened to be political football!

POSTSCRIPT ON METHOD

So much for the Teleserve story. I have used it to illustrate how imaginization can be used as a diagnostic process through which we can "read" and help to "rewrite" what is happening in projects with which we are involved. As noted, I have tried to take you inside the process, so that we can share a firsthand experience of this aspect of imaginization in practice and will provide further examples in the chapters that follow.

Before moving ahead, however, I would like to return to a point that I made toward the end of Chapter 1, where I mentioned how the stories of imaginization related in this book are based on my experiences and are told through my eyes. I suggested that, at times, you may find yourself disagreeing with the interpretations that are made, hence the way in which a project unfolds.

Now may be such a time, for some readers.

To illustrate, consider what would have happened if the original call from Teleserve had come from the leader of the labor union, instead of from Graham. Suppose that he had invited me to help *his* team to make sense of what was happening and to develop a strategy for dealing with the problems being faced.

Or suppose that I had been approached by someone who saw the basic problems in Teleserve as a "women's issue." The service staff in the organization were almost all women; the top managers were all male. The difficult socioeconomic circumstances of many female staff were crucial factors in creating a stressful context; the systems through which they were so closely monitored and evaluated can be seen as archetypes of male-dominated management. Suppose that the mandate was to develop strategies for dealing with the basic issues from a "women's perspective."

Under either of these circumstances, the outcome of the project would probably have been completely different. I would have been introduced to the basic issues in different ways, have received different information, and, as a result of the different mandates, have produced very different readings of the basic situation. As I met different people and heard different stories, I would have probably ended up making a very different intervention.

My point is that imaginization is always perspective based and unfolds within a limited horizon shaped by the assumptions and mandates through which it is approached. As it turned out, the Teleserve project developed into one involving innovative work redesign using principles of self-organization, conducted and managed within a highly politicized context. Even though it unfolded as a joint labor-management project, it was born from a management point of view.

If from the initial telephone call it had been shaped from a "labor" or "women's" standpoint, who knows where it would have led?

Would I have ended up trying to steer a process of organizational redesign?

Would I have followed the clues about Repetition Strain Injury and advised on the formulation of general labor policy on automated workplace technology?

Would this have taken the project more toward the industrial health and safety angle?

Would I have become more concerned with understanding the struggles within Teleserve as a gender issue and in finding ways of championing women's issues in the workplace?

Who knows?

What is certain is that, whatever the mandate, I would have been able to use the process of imaginization to find a broad, creative way of dealing with the situation at hand. That's why I emphasize that imaginization rests *in the process* through which novel images, insights, and interpretations are generated rather than in the images, insights, and interpretations themselves.

That's also why I always invite readers of my "stories" to view them with a critical eye, because I recognize that, if people are approaching issues with a different perspective or horizon in mind, they will have challenging insights and interpretations of their own. And that's exactly as it should be. For, as described in Chapter 1, imaginization is about personal empowerment and can be used with many ends in mind. In sharing my stories, I am *not* trying to offer perfect, "one-and-only" interpretations or accounts that lie beyond dispute. Rather, I am trying to illustrate a general process through which everyone can develop their own ability to interpret situations in a creative and informed way. These issues are discussed further in Appendix A.

6 "We're a Blob Out of Water"

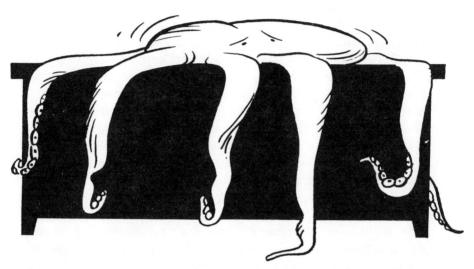

This chapter presents the story of a short intervention with a networking organization. It illustrates how rich, unconventional metaphor can capture the self-organizing qualities of an organization wishing to operate in a loosely structured style.

In Chapter 4, I showed how the unlikely image of a spider plant can be used to provide an evocative springboard for thinking about how to organize in a decentralized fashion. In this chapter, I show how staff images of octopi, amoebas, spiders, supernovas, and dandelion seeds can be used to create a shared appreciation of the ideas and principles on which an organization builds and the role they can play in helping maintain unconventional forms.

The story also highlights the difficulties that can be encountered in sustaining this kind of novelty in a politicized context where the style is poorly understood and where hostile forces wish to close it down.

*N*etwork is a dynamic youth organization established in the mid-1960s as a way of creating community among young people. Its aims: to develop and promote events, programs, and community initiatives providing opportunities for personal growth in the context of strong social values. It is run by a small team of people, committed to promoting peace and justice in the world around them. Staff are usually in their twenties and early thirties and typically spend a year or two with Network before moving on, or back, to established careers. The team leader lends continuity with a four- or five-year tenure.

Network's impacts tend to be twofold: through its community actions and programs and as a result of its influence on the personal lives of team members. Those who work on the team are usually deeply touched by the experience and often diffuse it in their new work and life situations. In its short history, Network has built an impressive record for its contribution to youth activities and is regarded in many circles as a model of how an effective youth organization should be run. Its philosophy and operating principles have been used for organizing similar groups elsewhere.

My first contact was initiated by Mike, the team leader. He asked if I could "give the Network team a couple of hours of my time" to explore some of their organizational problems. He was approaching the end of his tenure and wanted to create an opportunity for reflection on existing practice prior to the transition. I knew of Network's impressive record and welcomed the opportunity to lend a hand.

The meeting was held in Mike's home. Having come from a corporate meeting, I was struck by the relaxed informality of the team, who were winding up their weekly business as I arrived. All but one of the five team members were present and, after friendly introductions, we got down to business.

I had a simple agenda: to create an opportunity for them to tell me more about themselves and see if there was any way I could create leverage on whatever problems they were facing. So I started in a very straightforward way: "Tell me more about Network. Mike has shared some of the history. But I'd like to learn more."

They went on to describe some of their programs and activities and shared some of the processes through which they sought to "co-create community": by networking and connecting individuals and groups of young people with each other. Their purpose was to be of service to others and "to help link and catalyze communities of friends." The ultimate aim was to help young people grow and develop in ways that would allow them to realize their personal agendas and make a contribution to society along the way.

They talked of their work with schools and schoolchildren, about the "big events" and programs with which they were engaged, and about their philosophy of trying to model and "live" the social justice message in whatever they sought to do. They were practicing a form of "team leadership," based on the idea that everyone on the team could play an empowered leadership role and take ownership of the decisions and actions of the group as a whole. The salaries paid to the team by the national church organization providing Network's main funding were pooled and then reallocated according to need. Mike received a slightly higher sum, because he had a family of four children. But, it was a fraction of what he would earn in his profession as a full-time teacher. All team members were making a financial sacrifice to work with Network.

As they got into the nitty-gritty day-to-day issues and concerns, they went on to describe problems of "overcommitment," of "spreading too thinly," inadequate resources, difficulties in setting priorities between projects, in delegating work to others, and in time management—the usual organizational problems!

They were wrestling with how they could stabilize their network of activities, set realistic objectives, and get "better organized," for example, in terms of their administration and follow-through on decisions. They managed themselves through their weekly staff meeting in a consensus mode, using periods of reflection to resolve difficult issues. They believed that, given time, the right decision or way forward always became apparent. They had a strong general feeling that they were "not really organized" and that there might be a better way to bring everything under control.

They spent about 15 to 20 minutes building a detailed picture of their concerns. My initial "reading" of the situation was that the group was "culture driven" (Exhibit 6.1). They were tightly knit, bound by a shared vision and shared values,

"THE CULTURE METAPHOR"

This is an organization driven by its *culture*

—the shared vision
—common values
—a real sense of being a team
—their own distinctive mode of consensus decision making
—very democratic, very open, very equal

The bureaucratic, administrative aspects of organization have been pushed into the background; an ad hoc, self-organizing approach seems to be the rule. It operates on a loose "Model 6" style: The team is the hub of a network involving hundreds of other volunteers and collaborators over the course of a year.

No sign of *political* tensions within the team—it seems to be a truly integrated group.

EXHIBIT 6.1 A Preliminary Reading of Network

wrestling with the day-to-day administrative demands and problems that every manager knows. They wanted to get more organized. But the danger was that, in doing so, they could throw out the baby with the bath water, organizing in a way that eroded the group culture and its achievements.

To gain a deeper understanding of their issues, I decided to create another way of approaching their concerns, through the imaging methodology described in Chapter 2. Their task: to capture the essence of Network through some animal or other image that represented their experience of the organization. To create the right mood, I framed the task in a lighthearted fashion, suggesting that it offered a creative means of exploring their issues from a new angle. They were comfortable with the assignment, and so we got right into their descriptions.

The first person to speak was Louise, a woman in her late twenties. She had a metaphor on the tip of her tongue. Network was an octopus:

"[It] has many arms—it's not just two handed. Perhaps it has too many arms—bringing too many people in. . . . Most of the time it works well, but it's a blob out of water. Out of its element, it can't do much. We're great at working with people who believe in what we're doing. But we're a blob in dealing with the hierarchy that pays us. We really need to find ways of dealing with those that disagree with us. We're great at preaching to the converted!"

The second metaphor was offered by Pedro, a man in his early thirties. He described Network as an amoeba: "Small. Continually transforming. Difficult to combat. It transforms from the inside in terms of cells and fission. It subdivides. It's flexible, and it takes different shapes."

Pressed on whether he saw the image as a positive or negative one, he felt that, overall, it was very positive, because it captured how Network could do different things in different ways. But there were also negative features:

"It's difficult to control from the inside, and can be repressed by outside forces—by antibiotics!

"But it always bobs back again."

The third person, Phil, a young man in his early twenties, said:

"Network reminds me of Charlotte, the spider in the tale, *Charlotte's Web*.

"Have you read the story?"

I replied that I hadn't, so he went on to give his version along the following lines:*

Charlotte the spider was a very special spider who lived in a barnyard with a lot of animals. One of these was Wilbur the pig. Charlotte lived at the back of Wilbur's sty, and they became good friends.

One afternoon, some of the animals overheard that the farmer was going to take Wilbur to market the following day and that he would end up as bacon. Wilbur, naturally, was very upset.

---

*His account departs from this wonderful children's story by E. B. White in length and detail, but the message is fundamentally the same.

Charlotte tried to comfort him and was determined to do something to help. She had a great idea: She would build a special web that would save Wilbur. To execute her plan, she needed the help of the other animals, especially the barn rat, a rather selfish character. She persuaded it to run errands back and forth to the garbage pile in search of newsprint.

That night Charlotte went to work, and the following morning the farmer was greeted by a miracle. Spun across Wilbur's sty was a fantastic spider's web with the words "SOME PIG" right across the middle.

The farmer was awestruck and sent for all the neighbors to come and see the miracle. Obviously, there was no way that this "miracle pig" could be sent for bacon!

Wilbur was saved.

The story ends with Charlotte dying of old age, but only after laying her eggs and giving birth to hundreds of new Charlottes who spread out into the world in all directions, presumably to do something along the same lines again.

After telling the story, Phil went on to say that, for him, Charlotte symbolized the essence of Network with "its concern for caring and helping others, and its ability to act as a mobilizer and catalyst for action among young people."

Like Charlotte, Network had "a definite purpose in bringing people together, and in showing great care and concern for others. Charlotte was not glorified, and operated in a very subtle way. She was humble, subtle, and powerful . . . in no way like a peacock."

The end of the story was also significant: "All those spiders go out into the world, each having the same kind of philosophy and basic skills. The same happens when we go out . . . as people die in their immediate relationship and involvement with Network, others come to life."

This image of hundreds of new Charlottes spreading out in the world was followed by similar ones offered by Mike, the team leader. His images were of a supernova and of dandelion seeds blowing in the wind:

"Network is like a supernova—an exploding star created from lots of different elements which come together and break apart. The supernova involves death of the old star, but also gives life. In the same way dandelion seeds from dying flowers are blown by the wind in all directions, regenerating the dandelion and creating new beginnings. Network is the same. It's dynamic and going in a hundred different directions."

The atmosphere was animated. People were enjoying hearing each other's images. Pedro now had another. He wanted to add the image of a chameleon to the amoeba he had mentioned earlier:

"We change our image for different groups as we move from school to school, and talk with people with different commitments. We adapt our relationships as we go. We change color, blend, and adapt to our surroundings. . . . This is important since if we become just one color, we're dead!"

These images succeeded in creating a rich picture of Network. They unfolded with enthusiasm. It was clear that team members had a warm and positive feeling about their organization.

About three quarters of an hour had now elapsed since the start of the meeting, and the time came for me to make a contribution. I wanted to find a way of blending my understanding of the role and importance of the group's culture in shaping their way of organizing with some of the insights that had been generated through their imagery.

So, with a few preliminary remarks, I began to mirror back what they had told me: "Mike asked me to come to the meeting to see if I could help you reflect on the current state of Network.

"Earlier, you mentioned how you are facing a number of specific problems: the overcommitment, inadequate resources, problems of delegation, etcetera. But in listening to your images and stories, I gain an extremely positive view of what Network is, what it does, and how it does it.

"Your views have a lot of consistency and clarity. I have heard about Network as an organization that is continually reaching out to the community: like the spiders in *Charlotte's Web* and the dandelion seeds blowing in the wind. Through your imagery you have talked a lot about the creative and regenerative capacities of the organization and about the amoebic and chameleonlike ability to adapt and change to meet different concerns. For the most part, your images have been enthusiastic and extremely positive.

"The only real negative that I've heard is that Network is a 'blob out of water': that your 'octopus' may have too many arms, be engaged in too many activities, and may get out of control from time to time. I detected a similar, and perhaps related, concern in the way Pedro described how his flexible 'amoeba' could suffer from antibiotics administered by forces outside.

"In my experience, a lot of loosely structured networking organizations such as yours feel that they are poorly organized and are running out of control. They are often looking forward to the day when they can make their problems disappear by streamlining operations in some way. But they have to be careful that this attempt to 'get organized' doesn't kill the essence and spirit of what they are doing and achieving.

"The bureaucratic approach to organization, with its emphasis on clear rules, procedures, and systems is just one way of getting organized. There are others. For example, it is possible to organize around shared values and shared meanings, around shared understandings of what you are doing and how you are going to do it.

"It seems to me that this is what Network is doing. It's organizing itself around shared values and beliefs, through your distinctive sense of identity and culture. Network *is* organized, but in a way that promotes a lot of flexibility, autonomy, and ability to self-organize. Your images of Charlotte, the supernova, the dandelion seeds, the amoeba and chameleon all speak to this dimension of your style of operation.

"So, coming back to your immediate problems, particularly your blobbiness, and the desire to streamline and be more effective, the challenge is to find a way of organizing that doesn't undo what your current style is obviously achieving. You don't want bureaucratic rules and systems to get in the way and displace the energies and values of your members.

"So, let's go forward on the premise that you *are* organized. That you are organizing yourselves in a free-flowing manner that is appropriate to networks such as yours. The challenge, really, is to find a way of understanding and improving what you are already doing. You need to hang on to your sense of identity, expressed in all your imagery, while tackling the nitty-gritty concerns that are getting in the way, causing discomfort, or threatening your future in some way.

"So let's talk about the 'blobbiness.' Let's get back to that issue of being a blob out of water.

IMAGES OF ADAPTATION AND MALADAPTATION

IMAGES OF EXPANSIVE SELF - ORGANIZATION

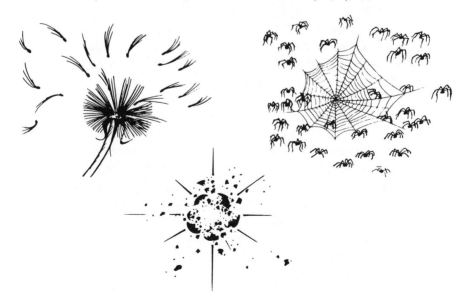

EXHIBIT 6.2   STAFF IMAGES CAN CAPTURE KEY ORGANIZATIONAL CHARACTERISTICS

"In what ways are you a blob out of water?"

The team began to talk about *when* and *where* Network was blobby, when and where it experienced the most difficulty in dealing with others. Attention immediately focused on the church hierarchy. There seemed to be a running battle with the authorities. Team members felt that "Network wasn't really understood." They felt that "their views weren't heard." Their stands on issues of social justice were "often an irritant," sometimes "an embarrassment," to the cautious bureaucrats who ultimately provided the funding and mandate for their work.

As they described the problems, they went on to say how Network had *always* been in this uneasy relationship. People had felt for a number of years that Network was walking a tightrope on the issue of how long it would be tolerated and whether it would eventually be disbanded. Despite its obvious success, Network was seen as a painful thorn in the side of the powers that be.

This information added a new dimension to the emerging picture of their problems. Clearly, the values that held them together and energized their activities were also values that threatened to close them down. It was clear that their shared values were the essential ingredient allowing the "supernova" and "dandelion seeds" to explode happily and enthusiastically in different directions within the context of their shared mission and for the "spiders" to regenerate and disseminate their basic philosophy and message into the world. Network was a "values-driven organization," where the group culture, based on a strong pattern of shared meaning, provided the glue that held it together. Their values drove them on, creating the action and excitement that they enjoyed so much. But it also led to the overcommitment, and the "there's too much going on" feeling, captured in the image of the sprawling, unmanageable octopus.

The strong political dynamic revealed in this discussion of their "blobbiness" forced me to revise my initial reading of the situation along the lines summarized in Exhibit 6.3. The "political" tensions were much deeper than I had originally thought. Indeed, the coherence inside the team could, in part, be a function of the tension outside. It was obvious that we had to find a way of continuing to energize the organization through a living of its values, but we also needed to find a way of getting a better hold on the political realities being faced.

> ## "THE POLITICAL METAPHOR DOMINATES"
> The *political* dynamics between Network and the church hierarchy seem crucial. It's here that the "blobbiness" presents the greatest problems. The strong team culture lying at the base of Network's success could be intensifying the underlying political problem.

EXHIBIT 6.3   A Second Reading of Network

To create this extra leverage, I needed to achieve a more comprehensive understanding of the political challenges. I thus invited the team to pursue the "blob out of water" image a bit further and to identify their key reference groups: the stakeholders with whom they interacted. These were listed on a flip chart, and the team was then asked to identify the relations that were crucial and peripheral as well as the degree of "blobbiness" (Exhibit 6.4). We then discussed how Network could develop a strategy for managing each set of relations. The basic idea was to build around the current strengths of the organization, particularly its ability to energize itself and those with whom it worked, while dealing with the blobbiness. The strategy was also linked back to the image of the chameleon.

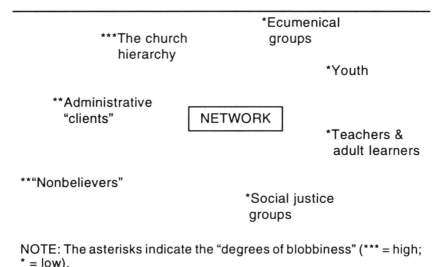

NOTE: The asterisks indicate the "degrees of blobbiness" (*** = high; * = low).

EXHIBIT 6.4   Some of Network's External Stakeholders

We wanted to enhance the organization's ability to deal with multiple constituencies in a positive way.

This was a political strategy shaped by my political reading of the basic situation. Network was a "values-driven" organization, but it needed to enhance its political skills if it was to survive in the long run. Strategies for managing relations with the church hierarchy were explored, as was the possibility of diversifying the funding base to reduce Network's dependency.

Attention was also given to streamlining the administrative base of the organization, in a way that didn't hamper its spirit and drive. Network's own administrative system was explicitly identified as one of its key stakeholders. It was represented by the people who had to be paid, or were waiting for advice or information, and others who were dependent on Network having an effective administrative capacity. Like the formal church hierarchy, it needed attention, but not in a manner that stopped other energies flowing.

In this way, the diagnosis combined the "readings" and models that I brought to the situation from the outside with the images they created on the inside. The upshot of all our discussion was that the main solutions to the problems were twofold.

First, manage relations with the church hierarchy in a much more active and positive fashion to minimize their concerns and to put Network in a better light. They had to do whatever they could to smooth relations, without violating their basic values. It was likely that better communications would help to take them a long way toward this end.

Second, manage the administrative system in a nonobtrusive way, so that the organization was efficient in basic tasks as well as being strategic, flexible, and adaptive in others. We talked about how this could be done by identifying the different kinds of decisions that had to be made and by clarifying the categories where discussion and consensus were not needed. The idea was that these could then be delegated, perhaps to a full-time administrator, leaving the team to focus their energies on key issues.

In discussing the potential streamlining, I was at pains to emphasize that their administrative problems ultimately depended on a discussion and clarification of values, and what was considered important, because routine actions and decisions are often value laden. By agreeing on the parameters relating to when detailed discussion and consensus were needed, they could free themselves from a host of issues that were brought to the whole group for a decision, instead of being made in a more timely and routine way by the person most directly involved. If people could "get on the same wavelength" as to what was likely to be important and controversial, they had a means of acting autonomously within a system that was ultimately driven by consensus. They wouldn't have to bring *all* issues to meetings for advance clearance. A routine report on decisions that had been made would suffice in many circumstances.

Many consensus-oriented organizations tie themselves in knots over this kind of administrative issue. They don't address or try to clarify the parameters for deciding *when* consensus is necessary and end up applying consensus decision making to everything—the result: administrative stalemate and ineffectiveness. The challenge, and it's often a difficult one, is to streamline those activities and decisions where core values are *not* at stake.*

In this way, I tried to nudge the team toward a more effective pattern of operation consistent with current strengths.

"Hang on to your core values. But tidy up your act, especially in terms of relations with the church hierarchy." This was the essence of the message.

The "blob out of water," the uncontrollability of the octopus, and the changing faces of the organization reflected in the chameleon and amoeba, all pointed in a common direction. In formal organization theory, we call it the problem of "differentiation and integration," a term coined by Paul Lawrence and Jay Lorsch in the late 1960s. It's the problem of having different styles of organizing to deal with different elements of one's task environment while retaining a healthy state of integration. Organizing to overcome "blobbiness" captured the same idea in a nontheoretical way.

---

*It's worth noting that the spider-plant model with its umbilical cords could have helped here. Basically, the problem was to define an umbilical cord for managing the administrative function. Unfortunately, I had not invented the metaphor at the time this project was conducted.

And so the meeting ended. It had lasted just over an hour and a half. Its main impact was to create a richer sense of self-identity:

We are Charlottes.
We are the supernova.
We are the dandelion seeds.
We are the chameleon.
We are the amoeba.
But we'd better do something about that octopus!

IMAGINIZING NEW ORGANIZING STYLES

Network provides a powerful illustration of how one can organize holographically, through a network of shared meaning that encodes the whole into all the parts, allowing staff to go out into the world like Charlotte's spiders or like dandelion seeds blowing in the wind, carrying the organizational vision and mission with them wherever they go.

Staff images captured the essence of their organizing style. They *were* like the spiders in *Charlotte's Web*. They *were* like the dandelion seeds and supernova. They *were* like an amoeba and chameleon, changing shape and color in different circumstances. They operated in a loose, expansive, and at times chaotic style, yet, throughout, they were held together in a highly coherent, organized way through their strong value base. And that's why they were so successful in discharging their primary tasks. Each of the "spiders" and "dandelion seeds" embodied the essence of the organization. They espoused and "lived" its values and could reproduce and regenerate the essence of Network wherever they went. What from the outside may have appeared a state of disorganization, randomness, and drift was in reality a powerful, flexible, yet almost invisible style of organization that allowed staff to operate autonomously yet in unison.

I can think of dozens of organizations working in difficult, changing environments that would love to be able to create the same capacities. They would love to find ways of mobilizing the same kind of teamwork and of helping staff to carry the same spirit and enterprise into far-flung corners of the environment.

But the paradox and, indeed, tragedy of Network's story is that this very successful organization has been closed down.

When I left my meeting with team members, I felt that the insights generated in our session together had really taken hold. But it was too late, because the "blobbiness" had already begun to get them. As it turned out, moves were already under way to transform Network, by reabsorbing it within a new youth initiative launched by the church hierarchy. Network was seen as powerful and effective; but it was also seen as too independent, chaotic, disorganized, and in need of control.

The story is being repeated in many other situations where flexible, "adhocratic" teams are working under the auspices of more bureaucratic partners that don't really understand or like their mode of operation. From the outside, these teams seem chaotic and in a state of drift; their principles of organization are not understood. Recall, for example, the story of Speedy in Chapter 3.

Network's experience thus offers us two important lessons.

It shows us the qualities that organizations wishing to adopt flexible, self-organizing styles need to possess as well as some of the images that can be used to understand and legitimize this approach to management.

But it also issues a stern warning with regard to the dangers that arise when new and old styles of organization clash. The problem is, I believe, archetypal and this is one of the main reasons I have chosen to include the case in this book.

In almost every large organization, there are stories of successful initiatives that have been closed down because they challenge existing power structures and cultural and institutional norms. As a result, when the choice boils down to killing a successful new initiative, or managing the discomfort, turbulence, and change created by its success, those with power often choose the former path. It's a symptom of the difficulties we face in moving from a world shaped by organization to one forged through imaginization.

Our next chapter takes another look at this problem.

7 "Futureblock"

Many organizations are caught in a syndrome of "change, change, change . . . and going nowhere!" People espouse the desire for change but all kinds of factors within the existing situation reinforce the status quo. This chapter explores some of the patterns connected with this kind of "Futureblock."

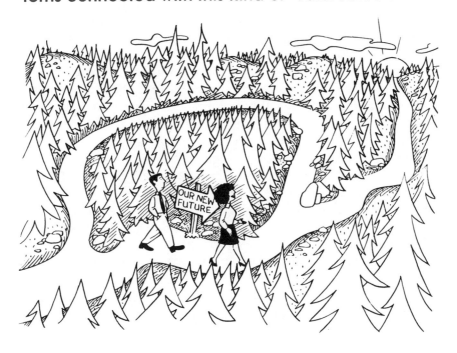

As in other chapters, I provide a comprehensive illustration of how we can invent images to "read" and understand the basic dynamics involved and to frame novel ways of managing them. The chapter features four metaphors that I have found particularly useful in helping organizations break free of immobilizing patterns. I call them "The Gulf," "Deerhunting," the "Iceberg," and "Model 3."

Peeling an onion.

Doing a jigsaw where pieces are added or reshaped as one goes along.

Both these images capture key aspects of the challenges faced by managers and consultants in reading the dynamics of complex organizations. As shown in previous chapters, one moves to deeper levels of understanding as the evidence mounts and as critical insights reshape patterns of interpretation. Throughout the process, one has to remain open to the significance of new information to grasp and understand the overall picture that's unfolding, exploring possibilities and probing in whatever way one can.

In my own professional practice, I find the conceptual framework provided in *Images of Organization* crucial for this task because the metaphors discussed there provide a powerful grasp on the overall nature of an organization. But I in no way restrict myself to these metaphors and frequently find myself inventing or searching for new ones that will provide further insights.

In this chapter, I want to focus on this aspect of imaginization in more detail and share four related metaphors that I have found particularly useful in diagnosing organizational problems. They're called "The Gulf," "Deerhunting," the "Iceberg," and "Model 3."

I will introduce the metaphors by presenting a case study capturing key challenges faced by bureaucratic organizations in times of change. The case blends information from a number of different sources, woven in a way that protects the identity of the people involved while giving an accurate view of the central issues. The pattern of "Futureblock" revealed in this case is so common that you may find yourself projecting details from your own organization onto the story. You probably "know" its characters and are able to empathize with the situation being faced. As in previous chapters, the story is told from the standpoint of an external change agent trying to read what's happening.

"WE'VE BEEN GREAT . . . AND WE'LL BE GREAT AGAIN!"

Stereotype is one of four European subsidiaries of a U.S. multinational. It produces sophisticated electrical and electronic controls used in manufacturing processes. The parent is a *Fortune* 500 company with a hefty reputation. It is wealthy and, during the last 20 years, has diversified into a number of related fields.

Stereotype represents an important part of the parent's core business. But, since the late 1970s, its foundations have become increasingly shaky. Like numerous other firms in industries as diverse as chemicals, engineering, pharmaceuticals, and telecommunications, it has built its success on a series of breakthrough products. Each decade since the 1940s has brought technical achievements that have secured financial success for the company and its salaried employees. Through the 1970s, the principle of job security was established. A strong "benefits culture" developed, with staff at middle and senior levels enjoying large company cars, cushy offices, and privileges worthy of their station. It became a rich and somewhat internally oriented company, promoting from within and commanding strong loyalty and commitment from its hardworking employees.

With the downturn in the business cycle in the early 1980s, this began to change. Stereotype rationalized its activities, closing two of its seven factories and reducing blue-collar staff by 30% and junior white-collar staff by 20%. In addition, following instructions from the United States, it put a freeze on new hires and implemented a policy designed to eliminate several layers of middle management through "natural attrition." These developments sent a chill warning throughout the organization, especially the middle ranks. But, for the most part, staff were confident that Stereotype would weather the storm.

As the 1980s progressed, this confidence was challenged on a number of fronts. The anticipated technical breakthroughs did not appear so Stereotype's products have become increasingly dated and exposed to competition from new firms and new industries. Sales on the company's most important product lines have been on a downward trend for the last eight years with Stereotype's bottom line becoming more and more negative. On paper, the firm is showing losses of more than $15 million a year, against gross sales revenue in the region of $500 million. The "real" state of affairs, however, is unknown because of a host of internal transfer payments arising from sales and other transactions between sister companies within the parent group and because of fluctuations in exchange rates. For example, Stereotype pays top dollar for products, research, and other services provided by the U.S. parent and pays a premium for components bought from sister companies in Europe. The true profitability and contribution of the company is thus extremely hazy, with Stereotype's senior management believing that the "real loss" is currently in the region of $1 to $2 million a year. The U.S. headquarters (known as "HQ") has responded by requiring Stereotype "to pay more attention to the bottom line" and by urging "tight control of variable expenses and increases in sales revenue."

There are constraints, however, on Stereotype's ability to deliver on this mandate. One of the policies of the parent company is that Stereotype use and market products researched and designed in the United States and keep local research to a minimum. But the U.S. products are not always suited to the European context. Stereotype has tried to work around the constraints by launching a number of small new business ventures showing considerable promise. But HQ will not allow further expansion, because of the firm's negative bottom line. Senior management in Stereotype thus feel caught in an extremely difficult corner, having to confine attention to core products that are increasingly unsuitable for the local market while being prevented from pursuing new initiatives that they believe will bring substantial success.

The company thus tends to be research and technology driven: building around products looking for markets. The middle and senior staff are all highly educated, strongly scientific in orientation, and technically very competent. For the most part, they believe that they work for "a great company," which, despite current problems, "will be great again."

THE DRIVE TOWARD "TEAMWORK"

Until 6 years ago, Stereotype was a model bureaucracy, set within a matrix structure internationally. Subsidiary companies were given responsibility for a geographic area but were expected to reproduce the functional structure of the U.S. parent.

Hierarchy and functional organization dominated. Stereotype was run on a tight rein by the CEO, who believed in exercising strong personal control over fragmented departments. He alone exerted overall control. Through a carefully designed system of reporting, he was able to monitor the implementation of local policies and keep close tabs on ongoing performance. In many ways, he was "HQ's ambassador": the U.S. presence in local administration. He followed central policies, making minimal amendments to suit local circumstances, and reported detailed results to HQ on a quarterly basis. He was CEO for 15 years and delivered excellent returns for the first 10. Thereafter, he faced increasingly difficult circumstances because of maturing products. Like all faithful ambassadors, he was well rewarded on his retirement seven years ago.

His successor, Gerald Wolfe, is a 55-year-old engineer. He was brought in as CEO after serving 4 years as a senior vice president (Marketing) in the United States. He recognized the severe problems created by Stereotype's aging products and championed a more entrepreneurial local approach. But his enthusiasm was restrained by his support for HQ's view that overall company success was built around being "research and technology driven."

Like many CEOs running subsidiaries of large corporations, he was split between local and central demands. He was aware that his future success in the overall company meant that he had to deliver improved financial results for Stereotype while not straying too far from HQ policy. He was committed to restoring Stereotype's financial success, but he didn't want to do it in a way that would jeopardize a continuation of his career "back home." When push came to shove, he was an HQ man!

Soon after his arrival, Wolfe began to initiate significant changes in Stereotype's bureaucratic style of management. He wanted to foster a more collaborative approach and took the opportunity created by the retirement of two of the seven existing department heads to create a top management team. He promoted two energetic men in their early forties to head the Marketing and R & D departments, joining the existing heads of the Production, Sales, Engineering, Finance, and Personnel departments. All of these were men in their early fifties, except the head of Personnel, a woman in her late forties. They were mandated to develop a "team-based approach to management," with a focus on "Stereotype 2000." Wolfe's declared aim was "to build a profitable organization for the 1990s" and "an outstanding organization for the twenty-first century."

This shift to a collaborative style was accompanied by regular Management Team meetings. He took the team on an Outward Bound course designed to foster solidarity and mutual support, and over the following year it engaged in a detailed review of Stereotype's mission, goals, objectives, and action plans. One member, the vice president for Finance, found the transition difficult and took an early retirement. The head of Personnel also experienced difficulties with what she called the "Boys' Club" atmosphere, especially on the Outward Bound trip. But she "dug in" and, along with other team members, became energized by the new approach. Joined by the new vice president (Finance), a man in his late forties, they soon became a powerful group, with meetings characterized by frank discussion over a wide range of issues.

There were lots of tensions, however. Some members felt that Wolfe, though a firm believer in the *principle* of teamwork, had difficulty in actually being a team player. He had a tendency to fall back into an authoritarian mode under stress. The difficulties around Stereotype's "bottom line" performance were a constant source of difficulty and, given the constraints imposed by HQ on new entrepreneurial initiatives, frustration was often at a high level. The constraints on internal resources, and the growing departmental demands, also injected a strong sense of internal competition between departments. This led certain Management Team members to jockey for position to show solidarity with their staff, often at the expense of overall cohesion and "team spirit."

After a year functioning in this way, the Management Team made a decision to carry the teamwork principle further into the organization. Under the banner of "Improving Quality and Adding Value"—the IQAV initiative—a series of project teams were established to attack organizationwide issues, such as quality, corporate culture, innovation, competitiveness, and organizational development. Middle managers from each department sat on these teams, and all were sent on team-building courses to improve the quality of teamwork.

Representation on one of the project teams was immediately seen as a "career plus"—"a must" for anyone seeking promotion. The Management Team selected team members and, for the most part, chose excellent people for the tasks to be performed. With rare exceptions, they were committed company men and women, loaded with professional expertise and determined to make their projects big winners for themselves and the organization.

For the first year, enthusiasm was extremely high. Project team members worked extremely hard, because the projects were taken on in addition to regular departmental duties. They produced excellent work. But, unfortunately, the results were never implemented in more than a token way. The Management Team commended their efforts but never really ran with the ideas and recommendations as the teams had hoped. Problems such as "restricted budgets," "HQ policy," "the time's not right," and "it doesn't *quite* fit the strategic plan" were used to put major recommendations on hold. Action was restricted to the more minor, immediately do-able issues.

Formally, the teams were lavished with praise and received awards for their work. But there was cynicism, and discontent soon began to grow on both sides.

The Management Team had concerns that the project groups "weren't quite clicking," because they weren't producing the results that the Management Team would have produced! But there were good reasons. The project teams weren't privy to all the information possessed by the Management Team. Certain policy issues and ideas were seen as "restricted" and, at best, were only communicated through innuendo or gentle hints.

"It all takes time."

"Given the circumstances, they're doing a great job."

"It's great training."

"We're slowly bringing along a new generation of senior managers."

Justifications such as these were used by the Management Team to rationalize the disappointing performance, coupled with the resolution that better briefings and a closer monitoring of progress would be in order. To do this, some Management Team members made a habit of dropping in on key team meetings.

For their part, project team members became more and more skeptical. The majority began to view the Management Team's response to their work as sending a double message:

"Work hard!"

"But don't come up with anything too controversial!"

The fact that minor proposals stood the best chance of implementation led to the development of team cultures preoccupied with the "do-able," pragmatic aspects of a project.

Style became as important as substance.

Project teams became as concerned with "looking good" as with developing substantial ideas and recommendations.

"What does the Management Team *really* want us to do?"

"What will they buy?"

"How can we sell it?"

These tended to be the questions on a project team's collective mind. Members of the various teams became more and more cynical, and evasive in commitment, and put less and less effort into team activities.

Project work was supplementary to a heavy load of departmental duties, all of which were monitored and assessed through the company's Management Assessment Plan (MAP). Team performance was seen as a key element in this evaluation. But most staff were not prepared to let their performance on regular departmental duties slip for the sake of project team performance. Certain team leaders who saw their projects as providing a critical opportunity for creating visibility and impact within Stereotype, and, possibly, in the parent company as well, were more committed. But they were exceptions to the rule.

After 2 years of wavering commitments, it became obvious to all concerned that the teams weren't going to deliver anything spectacular as far as the future of Stereotype was concerned. Even when project teams were given major initiatives and were explicitly invited to approach them in a creative, entrepreneurial way, the results seemed mundane. For example, one team charged with investigating broad opportunities for new products focused their recommendations on a streamlining and repackaging of the old. Another team charged with identifying key initiatives with regard to the use of information technology focused their final efforts on the identification of relevant PC training programs.

The Management Team became more and more disappointed and communicated their feelings in informal feedback sessions with each team. The aim of these meetings was to create an opportunity for frank, open exchange. But discussion on the part of project team members was guarded. They skirted the core problems. The overall conclusion reached by the Management Team was that staff needed even more formal help to improve the quality of teamwork and that, for its part, the Management Team needed to create even better briefings and controls.

And so the process continued.

Five years after the establishment of the first project team, results are still disappointing. The Management Team is still committed to its program of bringing quality and teamwork right into the organization. It has an elaborate program for developing team-based skills and has extended it to include all of Stereotype's middle managers. It has initiated a number of programs to improve "quality," with considerable success in its factory operations but with mediocre success elsewhere. It has also spent a great deal of money on programs designed to "empower staff" and "change the culture of the organization" as well as on "Stereotype 2000" workshops for staff at all levels.

The Management Team has settled into a stable membership and pattern of operation. Formally, relations are cordial. But, beneath the surface, they are strained. Everyone pays lip service to openness and teamwork. Wolfe's latent authoritarianism and rivalries within the Management Team are discussed from time to time but are never really resolved. The Management Team has gradually become more modest in its expectations of what team-work within the organization will produce. The view is that, while teamwork is essential for realizing the aims of "Stereotype 2000," "it takes time, time, time!"

Most of the organization's real work is done through its formal departments. The project teams are viewed as valuable communication and management training tools, but little more. The key to Stereotype's success is still seen as resting in "the breakthrough" that's going to come from HQ. The Management Team continues to discuss the possibility of extending their more successful entrepreneurial activities, but, ultimately, they know that they are marking time. They take comfort in the idea that "they're ready to move when the OK comes" and continue to focus on small changes that can "improve the bottom line," "add value and quality to existing operations wherever possible," "and motivate staff so that everything can switch into gear when necessary."

"READING" STEREOTYPE

Stereotype shares the fate of many bureaucratic organizations in times of change: "stuckness." The need to transform and revitalize operations is clearly recognized, but, for one reason or another, it's difficult to cut loose and do what really needs to be done. There's a lot of action: a new management structure, an emphasis on teamwork, a new vision for the year 2000, and lots of training. But the changes are hollow. They're not creating an energized organization capable of shaping a successful future. There's a sense of "marking time," with key staff "hoping things will get better" and looking elsewhere for key initiatives that will make a dramatic difference to the company. The company's main successes, such as the improved quality and the value-added orientation in production, are operational rather than strategic and alone will not guarantee Stereotype's future success.

The situation is archetypal. There are many organizations like Stereotype. Their detailed stories are different. But the themes are substantially the same. They recognize the need for change. They are initiating change upon change, upon change. But the changes don't seem to be going anywhere. They're not taking root and are not having substantial impact.

One way of capturing Stereotype's situation is presented in Exhibit 7.1. This interweaves the insights of four different metaphors drawn from the method of analysis offered in *Images of Organization*: those of an organism, culture, psychic prison, and political system.

Let's play with some of the implications of this imagery. Stereotype is an organism struggling to survive in a changing environment. The company was effective in the organizational environment up to the early 1980s, enjoying and growing fat on the substantial benefits of a research-and-technology-driven approach to product development. It produced a number of

> Stereotype is like an *organism* trying to survive in a changing environment. It was well adapted to its old environment but is struggling in the new. It has the qualities of a solid rhino. It needs to become more like an opportunity-seeking fox or lynx.

There are at least three interconnected sets of factors blocking this kind of transformation. They protect the rhinolike qualities!

Stereotype's strong corporate *culture* reinforces the status quo. Here are some manifestations:

At HQ:
—we're a research-technology-driven company
—subsidiary businesses must fit the mold of the parent
—strong control must be exercised from the center

At the local level:
—HQ will produce a breakthrough
—confidentiality is important in the Management Team—don't share restricted information with staff and project teams
—deliver on the key objectives in the Management Assessment Plan

The corporate culture is a *psychic prison,* trapping it's members into dysfunctional beliefs. For example, previous success is seen as promising future success. The idea that a breakthrough *will* happen is blocking new initiatives. The organization is now a victim of earlier success.

There are strong *political* forces reinforcing the status quo. For example:

At HQ:
—HQ wants Stereotype as a dependent company
—the politics of transfer prices and local profits
—HQ appoints loyal ambassadors as CEOs of subsidiaries

At the local level:
—the CEO is an HQ man
—the Management Team, partly because of the CEO, will not champion local initiatives forcefully at HQ
—careers are threatened by going out on a limb
—a "heads down" and "fit in" mentality dominates

EXHIBIT 7.1 An Overall Reading of Stereotype's Problems

big winners. But, in the new environment, the company is atrophying. Its niche has new competition. It is having difficulty sustaining market share, hence the resources on which its survival ultimately depends. If the process continues, Stereotype will grow leaner, become smaller, and maybe die—*unless* it can achieve a new fit with the environment. To do this, it has at least three options. It can achieve a major product breakthrough that will make new resources available. It can try to find other ways of surviving in its existing niche, for example, by becoming leaner, faster, and more opportunistic. Or it can find a new niche altogether.

Currently, Stereotype is placing emphasis on a combination of the first two strategies. But its attempt to create a more entrepreneurial, innovative organization with new products and new niches is stillborn, because of the dominant culture and defensive strategy focusing on existing core products and corporate style.

Stereotype's overall predicament from this point of view is represented in Exhibit 7.2, which profiles the company's lack of fit with the current organizational environment. Even with all the changes that have been introduced, Stereotype is still a quasi-bureaucratic organization dominated by HQ. It is unable to break into a new more flexible mode to create a new alignment with external challenges.

To understand why, we have to turn to the other metaphors identified in Exhibit 7.1.

To evolve into a new form, Stereotype has to break free of the vicious circles holding the old organization together. These are found in the cultural, political, and psychological forces that underpinned the success of the old-style organization. Over the years, the lavish benefits-oriented corporate culture has thrived on the technical achievements of HQ. The "we're great" syndrome has built a momentum that's difficult to change. Despite all the external problems, most senior and middle management, though worried about the future, are still well served by the current organization. They are thus reluctant to question and challenge the hand that feeds them.

The corporate culture thus has a prisonlike quality. It binds people into the old way of life and is supported by the overall structure of corporate politics, which reinforces central control

A PROFILE OF STEREOTYPE: 1980 AND 1990

1980   1990

THE ENVIRONMENT

Changing as a result
of aging technology
and products and
new competition

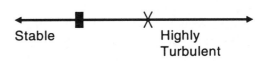

Stable   Highly
Turbulent

STRATEGY

Still primarily defensive
of the old niche; the
entrepreneurial
approach hasn't
taken root

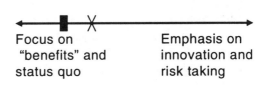

Defensive   Proactive and
entrepreneurial

STRUCTURE

Changed at the top
and in project teams,
otherwise bureaucratic

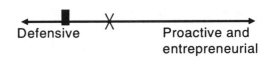

Bureaucratic   Organic
"adhocratic"
and flexible

CULTURE

Old values dominant,
despite new vision
for the year 2000

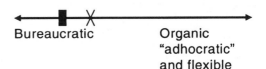

Focus on   Emphasis on
  "benefits" and   innovation and
status quo   risk taking

MANAGEMENT STYLE

Still primarily top down,
despite the teamwork

Authoritarian   Highly
collaborative

NOTE: The above profile is based on the contingency model of organi-za-tion offered in my *Images of Organization* (1986: 63) and *Creative Organi-zation Theory* (1989: 76-79). The profile is approximate and is just illustra-tive. It is an oversimplified analysis that ignores the detailed variations within Stereotype. For example, some sections of the organization are further to the left on the various dimensions than others. In some cases, this alignment is appropriate because tasks performed are more routine and less affected by external changes. A fuller analysis would give atten-tion to the need for appropriate differentiation and integration (Lawrence & Lorsch, 1967) while aligning with key external challenges. The six organi-zational models discussed later in this chapter illustrate what it takes to move toward the right of the continuum.

EXHIBIT 7.2 Stereotype Represented as an "Organism" striving to Achieve a "Good Fit" with its Environment

from HQ. Politically, one has to go out on a limb to change the course of the organization. Project teams or key individuals could do this, but, without the direct support of Gerald Wolfe and the Management Team, it's risky and unlikely to have a major impact. Hence most key players have withdrawn into a "play safe" strategy. Wolfe and his team have begun to champion significant change. But they have stopped short in really pushing their case at the HQ level—because Wolfe and others see this as a "no-go zone" as far as their future careers are concerned. This is one of the major reasons the efforts around teamwork have fizzled out. The experience of the majority of those involved has shown that, beneath the hoopla, it's business as usual. Despite all the formal teamwork, HQ and the Management Team are firmly in control.

To a degree, the focus on improving internal operations is serving as a substitute for direct action on key external challenges. In doing *something,* especially something progressive like team building, top management are unconsciously keeping their anxiety at bay. The "it takes time" phenomenon plays a similar role, as does the lack of accurate information about the "real" financial state of the company. The web of transfer prices throws a veil over the company's actual position, yet Stereotype's top management haven't really tried to pull the veil off—because this would raise questions and challenges in terms of the link between Stereotype and HQ. This is a dangerous area for any loyal ambassador who's there to keep an eye on the regional base rather than to challenge the wisdom of *being* just a regional base when other opportunities are available.

The dilemma facing Stereotype is that, to follow a more entrepreneurial route, which could lead the company to become a successful business in its own right with minimal reliance on HQ, it has to break the grip of the company's existing culture and politics. But this is like trying to pull oneself up by one's own bootstraps. The problem is symbolized most sharply in the fact that Wolfe, the champion and architect of existing changes, is also the champion and representative of HQ's control over the local situation. He is the champion of change *and* of the status quo. If he weren't this kind of loyal ambassador, he wouldn't be there as CEO in the first place!

These cultural, political, and psychological forces are three of the most powerful factors keeping organizations like Stereotype in their current modes of operation—*even when there's an explicit desire to change.* This is why so many organizational change projects run into difficulties. Consultants or managers can develop and advocate a new strategy, structure, or management style and even try to foster a new culture for their organization. But, when the time comes to work the desired changes through the existing system, everything gets "closed off" or "watered down." Results are thus often much more disappointing and modest than was hoped at the start of the change process.

The pattern of maladaptation presented in Exhibit 7.2 is very common nowadays, though the details vary. In some organizations, change is being driven by the introduction of new technology. In others, the driving forces rest in an attempt "to change the culture," "to introduce a new vision or mission," a "new organizational design," or a program to "enhance quality and service" or "empower employees." But the story is almost always the same. Changes in relation to one dimension of the organization are not accompanied by sympathetic changes elsewhere, because cultural, political, and psychological forces prevent an appropriate realignment from occurring.

PROBING BLOCKS TO CHANGE

The task of unraveling the network of factors holding an organization like Stereotype in an ineffective alignment can be daunting. For one can rarely be certain what the blocking factors actually are. Take, for example, the problems between Stereotype's Management Team and the project teams with regard to creativity and "acceptable risk taking." At first sight, these may seem to hinge on a simple problem of communication. But, pushing further, the situation becomes more complicated. For example, is the noncommunication rooted in the nature and style of the Management Team and its in-buried conflicts? Or does it stem from Wolfe's wavering loyalties between HQ and Stereotype?

This is the "peeling the onion" problem. Different readings of a situation produce very different understandings of what needs to be done. But it takes time to penetrate to the essence of what is going on. A manager or change agent can end up in a lot of blind alleys before he or she achieves the appropriate insights.

To deal with this problem, I often find it useful to test the resonance of a number of metaphors that can probe and capture key elements of "stuckness" *as I go along*. I use them as rough templates for shaping my understanding and to provide springboards for talking about key issues. They often help one to explore the complex tangle of cultural, political, psychological, and other forces reinforcing the status quo.

I call the metaphors "The Gulf," "Deerhunting," the "Iceberg," and "Model 3." All first emerged as "metaphors of the moment" in action research or consulting interventions.

"THE GULF"

"The Gulf" is a very common feature in organizations with a strong management team at the top. It arises when the top managers act in ways that, in effect, create a "no go zone" on critical issues facing the organization. Sometimes the managers are clear in stating that the issues are not open to discussion. But more often than not the process develops informally as top managers sidestep awkward issues and as middle managers "read" the grapevine and learn to see that discussion and action on these initiatives is not welcome and, if pushed, can have negative career implications. The result: Top and middle levels fail to dialogue in a meaningful way about the core challenges affecting the organization. Ongoing discussions and actions are directed elsewhere. As a result, frustration and cynicism develop on both sides, with major negative implications for the culture of the organization. Eventually, the gulf at the top also gets reproduced lower down, for example, between middle managers and operational levels, because, if people in the middle are doing a U-turn on issues in relation to those at the top, they usually have to do a U-turn below.

We see "The Gulf" operating in Stereotype in a variety of ways: for example, in the gap that has developed between HQ

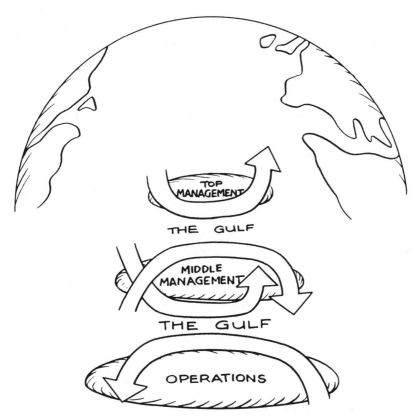

EXHIBIT 7.3 THE GULF: PRODUCED THROUGH
"U - TURNS" ON SENSITIVE ISSUES

and the Management Team, between the Management Team and
the organization's special project teams, and even between Wolfe
and the Management Team. Members of the Management Team
under Wolfe's leadership are not challenging HQ policies as they
might because to challenge HQ is a "no go," negative career
move. The middle managers are doing the same in relation to the
Management Team because they are reading the hierarchical
game. Despite the fact that Stereotype is formally committed to
progressive development and change in pursuit of "Stereotype
2000," cultural, political, and psychological forces within the
organization in effect sustain the status quo.

When encountering symptoms of "The Gulf," I often find it
extremely useful to "name it" as such and to identify it as a

pervasive phenomenon found in many organizations undergoing change. This often depersonalizes the immediate issues and makes them easier to address because people begin to see that they are produced by a much more general set of forces that transcend the immediate situation.

Silence is one of the main factors surrounding and sustaining "The Gulf" as a phenomenon. Almost everyone might have experienced its presence. People know or feel that "it's there." But no one has ever come out and said so. Yet this is precisely what's needed to make it actionable.

Take the situation of Gerald Wolfe at Stereotype. He's fighting a battle on two fronts, scoring solid marks at HQ but in effect creating an acquiescent Management Team. When members of the Management Team express their feelings to a trusted outsider about "what the team is *really* like," the bottom line is that they don't trust the team process. They feel that, if Wolfe is "pushed" to ally with one side or the other, it will be with HQ. But members of the Management Team have never openly confronted Wolfe on this issue or shared their feelings to the degree that they might have, despite all the sessions on team building. More often than not, they are resigned to dropping hints, but no more.

Yet Wolfe's dilemma is very common: It's shared by hundreds of other managers who are called "chief executives" but are in effect middle managers running "branch plants." They share the fate of being caught between the demands of their local company on the one hand and of HQ on the other. The consequences ripple throughout the organization to create "gulfs" at many levels. If one can begin by creating constructive dialogue and analysis of the gulf as a phenomenon then new insights, opportunities, and ideas for dealing with the gulf between Wolfe and his Management Team, between Wolfe and HQ, and between the Management Team and middle managers, often can emerge.

In tackling the underlying problems, however, it's vital to create a safe context and to proceed with caution. For, as has been suggested, gulfs are often underpinned by complex political and personal relationships. The political consequences of challenging established power relations are obvious. So too are the dangers of unleashing interpersonal conflicts. But, beneath all this, there may be other complex psychological factors that can make exploration of gulf-related phenomena a potential mine field.

For example, gulflike situations, though systemic, are often sustained by the personalities and psychological profiles of those involved. People in leadership positions may surround themselves with "yes-men" or "yes-women," producing distorted understandings of reality. Unfortunately, the distortions can become so idealized, and so identified with the leadership, that any challenge is interpreted as an attack on the leaders themselves. Vindictive punishment often results, as the leaders, often unconsciously, find ways of scapegoating and sacrificing their perceived critics to save their fundamental sense of themselves. The manager or consultant working on gulf issues is at as much risk as anyone else here and may end up incurring the wrath of the leadership and being shot like the proverbial messenger bringing bad news—even though he or she has been specifically asked to address the issues.

As an organizational phenomenon, "The Gulf" can be characterized by enormous inaction, stagnation, and decay, sapping the vitality of an organization. But, when tackled and addressed, it can explode like a mine field. That's why any processes dealing with gulf-related issues must be orchestrated to provide a high degree of safety for all concerned.

Hence it's often a good idea to try and create an understanding of the generic pattern, to depersonalize its nature, and to work the issues with key individuals like Wolfe and members of his Management Team on an individual basis, unraveling the connections and what's binding them into an unsatisfactory pattern. Then one can work the issues in a safer group setting. When one has the top team in a better position to move, dialogue with the rest of the organization can then often unfold in a more constructive manner.

"The Gulf," as an image that can be used to diagnose and unlock key organizational problems, shares the same "mirroring" potential that I have illustrated through metaphors presented in earlier chapters. It allows people to look at their organization in a new way. It allows them to see themselves with fresh eyes and to understand the role that they may be playing in sustaining "gulflike" situations. It is this mirroring capacity that often leads to the breakthroughs that allow new initiatives to emerge. For example, the above discussion may have performed some mirroring function in relation to yourself and the problems being encountered in *your* organization. This is how the process of imaginization works. It creates the possibility of developing shared insights and understandings to create a new context in which new actions can unfold.

"MODEL 3"

"The Gulf" is very common in what I call "Model 3" organizations. These are organizations that, like Stereotype, get stuck in their attempts to change because they are caught by the old bureaucratic forces they are trying to shake off. I have developed the "Model 3" concept as one of six templates designed to characterize organizational forms suited to different degrees of environmental change and to illustrate the difficulties that can be encountered in trying to shift from one form of organization to another.

The six templates (Exhibit 7.4) provide rough models against which people can identify the characteristics of their own organizations or organizational subunits and understand the generic nature of their particular difficulties in managing organizational change. As in the case of "The Gulf," the realization that the problems being faced are "not just ours" can have a liberating effect, depersonalizing the immediate context of the problems to create an opportunity for new dialogue, understanding, and action.

Model 3 has to be understood against the background of Models 1 and 2.

Model 1 is the classical bureaucracy, carefully blueprinted into functional departments, run from the top by the chief executive through various structures, rules, regulations, job descriptions, and controls. It is designed to work like a machine and operates very efficiently—as long as nothing changes! Bureaucracies, like machines, operate well when there are stable functions to be performed, especially when they can be broken down into a series of separate operations coordinated from the top. But, when an organization's tasks keep changing, it's a

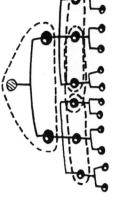

Model 3: The Bureacracy With
Project Teams and Task Forces

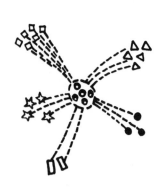

Model 6: The Loosely-Coupled
Organic Network

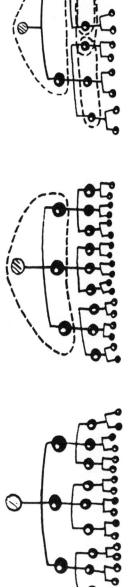

Model 2: The Bureaucracy With a
Senior "Management Team"

Model 5: The Project Organization

Model 1: The Rigid Bureaucracy

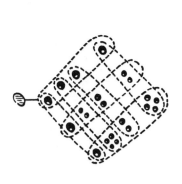

Model 4: The Matrix Organization

161

different story. The changes create a host of problems that no one is mandated to solve. The problems thus work their way up the hierarchy and eventually fall on the chief executive's desk. He or she soon gets overloaded and initiates a shift to Model 2 by appointing a top management team. Collectively, they now deal with the problems, leaving the bureaucratic machine below (i.e., the functional departments) to continue with the routine work.

Model 2 works reasonably well for dealing with moderate amounts of change. But, if the pace heats up, the top team gets overloaded, with a host of operational and strategic decisions demanding attention at team meetings. Gradually, or as a result of a specific organizational redesign, Model 2 thus gets pushed toward Model 3. Interdepartmental committees or project teams are established within the body of the organization itself. The idea is that routine work will still be conducted through departmental hierarchies, with special problems or projects being delegated to the project teams for investigation and the development of appropriate action plans.

This initiative, often heralded as a move to a "project organization," makes life bearable at the top again, because a lot of work can now be delegated. But, because the teams are set within the context of a bureaucratic structure, they often fail to take off. There are a lot of projects and a lot of meetings. But there are also a lot of spinning wheels. The team meetings, as in Stereotype, become ritualistic. Team members are usually representatives of their departments. As such, they have dual loyalties—to their departmental bosses and to their team. But, because real power over day-to-day activities and career progress rest with the departmental heads, the teams themselves do not develop any real clout. Members usually "sit in" on team meetings as departmental representatives in a "listen and tell" mode. They listen to what's being said and voice their department's point of view. If problems arise in the meeting, decisions are usually delayed until representatives have had a chance to "report back" and test departmental reactions. If the issue is truly controversial, it ends up getting passed to the top team so that departmental heads can resolve it for themselves.

Model 3 is thus an organization characterized by pseudo-teams that are only capable of dealing with relatively minor issues. In effect, Model 2 still rules.

All three of these models are evident in Stereotype, which, in effect, has shifted through Models 1, 2, and 3. It has many of the problems described above. The powerlessness and cynical culture that has developed in the project teams is generic—shared by countless other organizations caught in the same bureaucratic trap. The structure of the organization has changed, but the culture and politics are still firmly set in the old mold.

Organizations can often make successful transitions from Model 1 or 2 to Model 3. But Model 3 is only effective when the issues delegated to the teams are small in number, require consultation rather than action, and allow generous time frames for producing results. We are back to the contingency view of organization and management discussed in relation to Stereotype in connection with Exhibit 7.2, which is further elaborated in relation to the six models in Exhibit 7.5. To be effective, organizations need to structure themselves through models that are appropriate for dealing with the external challenges being faced. If the quest, as in Stereotype, is to create an organizational structure that is driven and enlivened from the middle by flexible, aggressive, innovative teams, the results of Model 3 are almost always disappointing. In my research, I encounter frustrated "Model 3" organizations time and again. Like Stereotype, they think or hope that they're unleashing the potential of a dynamic team-based approach to work, but, in effect, they are usually just involving middle managers in time-consuming processes of interdepartmental consultation. Dynamism and team-based energy in the middle is only created against the odds, by groups of managers who are so

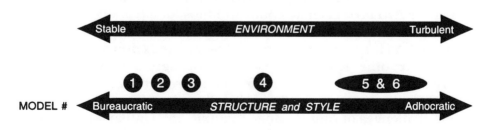

You Need a Model That Can Deal With the Challenges of *Your* Particular Environment

EXHIBIT 7.5 Different Models for Different Environments

committed to their team's overall goals that they take great personal risks to advance their cause.

To achieve the flexible, innovative, committed organization that is needed to deal with the turbulence and change found in the modern environment, organizations have to get beyond Model 3. As illustrated in Exhibit 7.5, this is where Models 4, 5, and 6 come in, especially Models 5 and 6.

Model 4, the matrix organization, is a hybrid bureaucratic form. Its special character rests in the fact that it has decided to give more or less equal priority to functional departments such as Finance, Administration, Marketing, Sales, Production, and R & D (the columns of the matrix) and to various business or product areas (the rows). Thus people working in various product or business teams within the organization have a dual focus. They must work with two perspectives in mind, combining functional skills and resources with an orientation driven by the key tasks they have been assigned. The dual orientation means that bureaucratic power typical of Models 1, 2, and 3 is diluted, because the heads of major projects, or groups of projects, can be as important and as powerful as heads of traditional functional departments. In this way, members of project teams are not necessarily pulled back into the traditional lines of responsibility. Because project heads may have a large influence on rewards and future career paths, real team commitment can develop. In successful examples of Model 4, the project teams become the driving force behind innovation, providing an ability for the organization to change and adapt along with challenges emerging from the environment.

The same is true of Model 5. This model, typical of small and medium-sized organizations that are highly innovative, is built around teams. The influence of functional departments is minimized. People are appointed to work on specific projects. One or two projects may command most of a person's energy at a particular time, but he or she may also be contributing to others. As the work on one project team winds down, commitments on other teams increase. Career progress in this type of organization rests in moving from one project to another.

This kind of organization is ideally suited for dealing with the challenges of rapid change (Exhibit 7.5). Unlike the matrix of Model 4, it does not have a heavy functional structure to carry along. Its focus is teamwork, innovation, and successful initiatives, completed in a profitable, timely fashion. Functional departments, insofar as they exist, are support departments, committed to enhancing the work of the teams who are their clients. The whole operation is controlled by the management team at the center. It focuses on strategic thrust, defining operational parameters, marshaling and channeling resources, monitoring results, and facilitating the general management of the system as a whole. The teams may be managed through "umbilical cords" characteristic of the spider-plant model discussed in Chapter 4.

The organization is much more like a fluid network of interaction than a bureaucratic structure. The teams are powerful, exciting, and dynamic entities. There is frequent cross-fertilization of ideas and a regular exchange of information, especially between team leaders and the senior management group. Much effort is devoted to creating shared appreciations and understandings of the nature of the organization and its mission, but always within a context that encourages an open, evolving, learning-oriented approach to business. The organization is constantly trying to find and create the new initiatives, ideas, systems, and processes that will contribute to its success. It is a kind of "adhocracy," finding and developing its form as it goes along.

This is the kind of organization that Stereotype, at least in part, may need to become to meet the challenge of its local environment. Unfortunately, it is stuck inappropriately in Model 3.

Model 6 provides another example of an organizational style ideal for conditions requiring flexibility, innovation, and change. In a way, it's a nonorganization in the sense that it does not exist as a physical entity. It's a subcontracting network where the team at the center steers the whole enterprise.

Take the fashion industry, where Model 6 networks flourish as ideal means of dealing with the rapid pace of change. The team at the center of the network has come together to exploit a market niche. Rather than build "an organization," it decides to subcontract almost everything: detailed design, manufacturing, marketing, distribution, communication. The "satellites" shown in Exhibit 7.4 are the subcontracting firms. They are linked to the center through specific contracts, which come and go. The membership of the network is in constant flux. The team at the center is the only point of continuity. It directs strategy, tactics, and resource flows, keeping lean, minimizing overhead, operating with maximum flexibility: no planning department, no MIS, no HRD department. Everything is contracted out, even routine finance! It often operates on "spider-plant principles," discussed in Chapter 4.

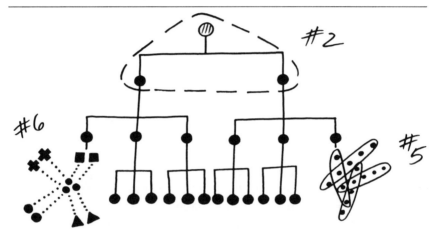

One of the key challenges in managing mixed models of this kind rests in ensuring that the dominant model doesn't impose itself too strongly on the other styles. Dominant cultures often have a cloning influence! An understanding of "umbilical cords" and boundary management play a key role in sustaining required differentiation.

EXHIBIT 7.6 The Models May Exist in Mixed Forms

These six templates, which I have presented as simplified models of a total organization, often exist in mixed forms (see Exhibit 7.6). They provide an evocative means of helping members of an organization see which model or models they are currently employing and can help them judge what's possible or ideal in terms of organizing for flexibility and innovation.

To illustrate, consider their application to Stereotype. The models provide a powerful way of helping Stereotype's Management Team understand why the project teams in its Model 3 organization are not "cutting loose" and being truly innovative. They can help them to understand "The Gulf" from a new perspective and to see that, if they truly want to create a more flexible, innovative organization, perhaps they should be thinking about Models 4, 5, and 6 rather than just pushing for more team training within a Model 3 structure. For example, they could find a way of shifting closer to Model 4 by elevating the priority of key projects and changing the composition and orientation of the Management Team to reflect this. Or they could choose to launch Model 5 or Model 6 initiatives in special areas of the organization or for special projects, as illustrated in Exhibit 7.6. In doing so, they may be able to introduce a new potential for entrepreneurship and innovation in specific pockets of the organization while still operating within the constraints set by HQ. An awareness of the six models, and an ability to see and name precisely what is wrong with the current situation, could provide a powerful lever for change.

Used and interpreted flexibly, I find that these rough-and-ready templates can have a powerful effect. They can provide the all-important "mirror" that allows people to see where their organization is and where it could be.

"DEERHUNTING"

Similar leverage can sometimes be created by evoking a "deerhunting" metaphor, developed in one of my projects by my colleague Lin Ward. Deerhunters set out for the forest, shoot a deer, and carry it back home.

Right?

Well, not exactly.

They carry the body back, but the essence of the living deer remains in the forest.

The same happens in a lot of organizational development projects (Exhibit 7.7).

Managers go hunting for the right program or concept for changing their organization. But, when applied "back home," day-to-day reality takes over, and results are often disappointing. The trophies are there, as certificates on the wall. But the essence of what the programs were trying to achieve is somehow lost.

Many organizations experience this phenomenon, with programs on "teamwork," "vision and values," "empowerment,"

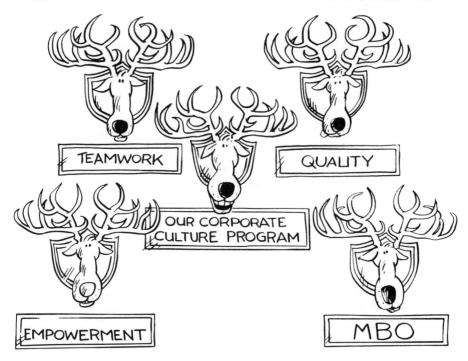

TEAMWORK

QUALITY

OUR CORPORATE CULTURE PROGRAM

EMPOWERMENT

MBO

EXHIBIT 7.7   DEERHUNTING IN ORGANIZATIONAL DEVELOPMENT

and "leadership" following each other in quick succession. Something is learned through each activity, and the organization is nudged in the right direction. But the results are often marginal, and employees often end up frustrated and cynical:

"Here we go again."

"The new flavor of the month!"

"What will the focus be next year?"

"We're engaging in change for the sake of change."

The programs eat up time, add pressure to already crowded schedules, and create a lot of disillusionment. They don't influence the organization effectively because they are introduced within the context of the old organization, the old culture, and the old system of politics, without appropriate accommodations being made. As in the case of project teams in a Model 3 organization, the changes tend to be superficial and are recognized as such by those with operational responsibilities.

To take a simple example, consider what happens when an "employee empowerment program" is introduced in a Model

1, 2, or 3 organization. The limits of "empowerment" are usually quickly felt as people run into the constraints imposed by the existing hierarchy. They quickly feel that they are "empowered in a box," and cynicism and disillusionment soon set in. Model 1, 2, and 3 organizations often plow millions of dollars into empowerment and teamwork development, because they would like to have an "empowered staff" taking more interest and initiative in their work. But they rarely "bite the bullet" and modify their basic model of organization to allow the new initiatives space to flourish. If they shifted attention and focused, for example, on creating Model 5 or Model 6 initiatives in places where teamwork and empowerment were really needed, they would have much greater impact.

The power of the deerhunting metaphor is that it can help create awareness and dialogue around the dead or dying nature of so many organizational development programs. As a result, it can create new leverage on the basic problem: that, despite massive expenditures, forces within the established organization typically work against the new initiatives, holding old styles in place. This can begin to reframe an organization's whole approach to change. It can redirect energy and focus attention on developing the living essence of programs, so that they can be kept alive in practice rather than just hang as trophies on the wall.

THE "ICEBERG"

Similar leverage can be created through the "iceberg" metaphor.

As we all know, most of an iceberg lies beneath the waterline. The same is true in our organizations. The visible characteristics are supported and sustained by all manner of hidden forces. By creating an appropriate context for inquiry, and by asking people to identify the hidden dimensions of their organizational iceberg, it's often amazing how quickly one can penetrate to key insights that would take ages to emerge through more general forms of dialogue.

Exhibits 7.8 and 7.9 provide illustrations of the use of this metaphor in relation to Stereotype and to Teleserve, discussed in Chapter 5. In each case, the large iceberg represents the

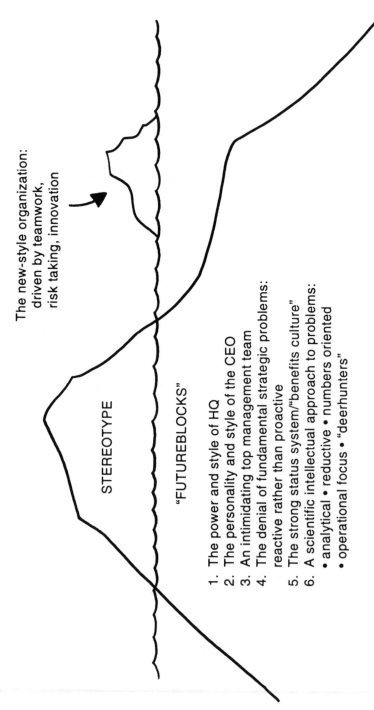

The new-style organization: driven by teamwork, risk taking, innovation

STEREOTYPE

"FUTUREBLOCKS"

1. The power and style of HQ
2. The personality and style of the CEO
3. An intimidating top management team
4. The denial of fundamental strategic problems: reactive rather than proactive
5. The strong status system/"benefits culture"
6. A scientific intellectual approach to problems:
   • analytical • reductive • numbers oriented
   • operational focus • "deerhunters"

EXHIBIT 7.8 "THE ICEBERG" AT STEREOTYPE

170

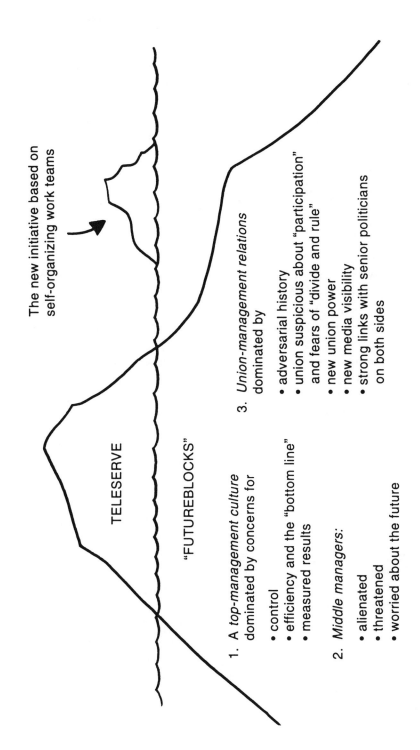

The new initiative based on self-organizing work teams

TELESERVE

"FUTUREBLOCKS"

1. A *top-management culture* dominated by concerns for
   - control
   - efficiency and the "bottom line"
   - measured results

2. *Middle managers:*
   - alienated
   - threatened
   - worried about the future

3. *Union-management relations* dominated by
   - adversarial history
   - union suspicious about "participation" and fears of "divide and rule"
   - new union power
   - new media visibility
   - strong links with senior politicians on both sides

EXHIBIT 7.9 "THE ICEBERG" AT TELESERVE

existing organization, with the constraining influences, or "Futureblocks," lying "beneath the surface." The new iceberg, which, symbolically, does not yet have anything sustaining it, represents the style to which the two organizations could move. In Stereotype (Exhibit 7.8), this could be a more innovative team-driven organization, using Model 5 and Model 6 initiatives to venture into new territory. In Teleserve (Exhibit 7.9), it was the more loosely controlled structure of self-organizing work teams. The challenge, of course, is to relax the constraints of the old iceberg and create a strong foundation for developing the new.

This method of imaging problems associated with organizational change can provide a powerful means of identifying blocks to development. Nowadays, most organizations have a good idea of the kind of organization they wish to become. The problem is getting there. The "Iceberg" provides a simple and direct means of creating dialogue about these issues. It can be used in diagnostic sessions with staff as individuals or in group settings. I find that the process can be salutary, because, as in the case of "The Gulf," most people know that the blocks are there, even though they have never thought about them in a specific manner. As people reflect on their own personal understanding of their organizational iceberg, key insights of a general or specific nature usually emerge:

"Our culture is holding us back."
"There's no real trust."
"You get your head chopped off if you say what you feel."
"The CEO doesn't always mean what he says."
"There are no real rewards for risk taking."
"The Management Team has all the power."
"Covering your ass is what counts around here."

Such responses can provide a penetrating means of unraveling the organization's detailed problems, especially when people's views can be shared and explored with those in control. A series of home truths expressed in evocative language by one's staff can often create more reflection and momentum than a dozen theories or management courses! They can provide a way of recognizing and addressing some of the hidden blocks to change and of chipping away at their restraining influence.

METAPHORS AND IMAGINIZATION

In this, as in the previous two chapters, I have tried to illustrate how metaphor can play an important role in the diagnosis of organizational problems. Using Stereotype as a backdrop, I have tried to reveal familiar patterns through which organizations block desired paths for future development. Often, the blocks involve structural, cultural, political, psychological, and other forces. A manager, change agent, consultant, or anyone who wishes to help organizations achieve new forms will usually encounter these blocks in one way or another. The challenge is to be aware of their existence, to recognize the different forms that they can take, and to find ways of dealing with them. Images of "The Gulf," "Model 3," "Deerhunting," and organizational "Icebergs" provide means through which one can begin to move toward this end.

Much of the "Futureblock" in our organizations can be captured by using one or more of these metaphors. "The Gulf" identifies a common organizational pathology in times of change. "Model 3" provides a way of explaining some of the reasons the gulf occurs and why so many people often spend so much time in unproductive team meetings. "Deerhunting" captures a syndrome in which "Model 3" organizations frequently get caught, and the "Iceberg" provides a method of identifying and dealing with the hidden blocks and problems that are creating all the above symptoms.

Hence, if these metaphors resonate with my broader reading of the problems with which I'm dealing, and no better metaphors of the moment emerge naturally, I use them as a way of creating dialogue. If they're appropriate, they create an evocative response, opening many valuable insights and paths for exploration.

In presenting and discussing the metaphors, I have characterized their role in a variety of ways: as templates, mirrors, archetypes, patterns, levers, diagnostic tools, dialogue generators, and so on. These descriptors, which of course are metaphors in their own right, capture the aims underlying their use. I employ them in an open, flexible manner to help people reframe their understandings of a situation so that they can tackle the "stuckness" problem in fresh ways. They have an important role to play in the toolbox of organization and management theory. While broad conceptual metaphors, such as those explored in *Images of Organization*, are necessary for analyzing the fundamental character of an organization, and for shaping broad strategies for management and change, evocative metaphors such as those discussed above are often needed to create detailed leverage on specific problems. The next five chapters provide further illustrations of this aspect of imaginization in practice. They provide further evidence of how simple images can capture and address fundamental issues and seed opportunities for significant change.

8 "Boiling Dry"

In previous chapters I've suggested that it's often possible to capture and address complex organizational problems through "metaphors of the moment" that emerge spontaneously during the course of discussion and inquiry.

These metaphors offer "inside theories" about what is happening and what needs to be done. They can often have a much greater impact on management and change processes than more abstract academic theories, and they should be mobilized whenever possible.

In this chapter, I provide a further illustration. It features an account of a retreat for senior management in a hospital experimenting with a holographic approach to organization. It shows how metaphors of the moment can capture key challenges and be used to help staff create a coherent story of "where they've been and where they're going." Again, the aim is to provide a detailed view of how the management of change can be driven through evocative metaphor and to provide a further illustration of some of the dilemmas faced by managers and change agents in nudging the process in an appropriate direction.

In Chapter 1, I wrote about the possibilities of creating a holographic style of organization. As you may recall, it involves trying to develop approaches to organization where the whole is built into all the parts. At first sight, the idea seems strange and paradoxical. But, as suggested, it has a lot of important implications for management.

For example, one can design an organization holographically around a basic pattern that allows "the whole" to reproduce itself. The spider-plant organization discussed in Chapter 4 provides a good example. Or one can create a holographic office or factory, building around self-organizing work groups that operate as quasi-independent "mini-organizations." The factories and offices, in effect, become groups of "mini-factories" and "mini-offices" organized around cellular principles. Or one can enhance and develop capacities in each and every employee so that they can produce and reproduce the competencies, skills, vision, values, and ethics of the organization on an ongoing basis. They become like the "dandelion seeds" and "spiders" discussed in Chapter 6, representing and reproducing "the organization" in whatever they do. This, in essence, is what many programs focusing on the development of teamwork and corporate culture are aiming for.

Many holographic approaches to organization are emerging quite naturally as enterprises try to create more room for flexibility and innovation and to promote capacities for self-organization. To do this, they are having to find ways of organizing through shared visions, values, and "culture" rather than through bureaucratic structures and rules. And they are having to find ways of developing team-based modes of operation where people have multiple, overlapping skills, so that the teams can evolve their own patterns of communication and control in addressing the tasks they've been assigned.

I take an active interest in any organization that is developing this approach to management. So it was with special interest that I received a telephone call from the head of Nursing Services in a medium-sized hospital in the United States. They were experimenting with the holographic approach among senior management. Because most hospitals are notoriously bureaucratic, I was immediately intrigued.

She went on to say that for the past year she and her senior management team had been implementing the holographic principles described in *Images of Organization* and wondered if I would be able to help them run a day-and-a-half retreat for 40 to 50 senior staff within Nursing Services. They had reached a crucial stage in development and wanted to take stock of their situation.

I expressed my interest in the project, and she went on to describe how the idea of experimenting with a self-organizing "holographic design" had been introduced a year or so earlier. It was being used as a means of creating a more innovative and responsive department, through a flattening of the structure and the empowerment of staff. She had first discussed the ideas with her three most senior colleagues, and, when an opportunity to fill a senior vacancy arose, it was decided to experiment with the new approach. Instead of filling the bu-reaucratic slot, they decided to leave the position open and to encourage new lines of responsibility and reporting. Instead of following formal lines of authority and responsibility, the top 40 or so managers were invited to strike their own patterns of connection and decision making by going to whomever they thought could help. The aim was to unite managers around the vision of creating a responsive, self-organizing department that would change its detailed form as circumstances required.

To facilitate this, managers were encouraged to see them-selves as resources to each other and to allow new patterns of organization to emerge. In organizing through core values stressing the priority of the patient, and encouraging managers to exemplify this kind of leadership orientation, it was hoped that an appropriate organizational style and structure would take form. The structure would evolve from the requirements of im-proving patient care rather than be imposed in a predetermined way. The approach was introduced gradually and quietly but also amidst some concern, stress, and uncertainty among those in managerial roles. The ideas of autonomy, empowerment, self-organization, and the holographic approach were discussed widely, and, backed by the good faith of staff, promising first steps had been made.

The role of the retreat was to consolidate and to create a launchpad for further development. My formal mandate: "to create a learning environment that would enhance the self-organizing process, in a manner promoting autonomy, collaboration, innovation, job satisfaction, and professional development, *without chaos!"*

A "READING" UNFOLDS

After a second excellent telephone briefing from the head of nursing on overall developments, and another "update" from herself and her three senior associates during an hour-long drive to the retreat center several weeks later, a consistent story began to emerge. I sensed that important strides had been made in implementing the self-organizing model, but there were real problems and concerns.

I listened carefully and detected at least five areas where problems and needs were being identified:

1. There seemed to be difficulties in integrating the "self-organizing" approach in Nursing Services with the "top-down," bureaucratic style dominating the rest of the hospital.

2. There was a need to refine and develop existing approaches to teamwork and self-organization in practice.

3. There were concerns as to when and how the "self-organizing" approach could be carried to lower levels of the organization, so that it involved nursing staff as well as the 40 or so senior managers that had provided the focus up to now.

4. There were general problems relating to the management of change, especially with regard to the quality of interdepartmental relations associated with point 1 above.

5. There was also a related problem of communicating what was happening, to others and among themselves.

I mirrored these five issues back to the top team later that evening at the final design session and suggested that I run the retreat in a way that ensured all the issues were raised and addressed in some way.

The Department of Nursing Services is in transition

FROM an "old style" MACHINE bureaucracy		TO a more HOLOGRAPHIC style

The change is set within

A *culture* that seems willing and supportive but, perhaps, somewhat confused and uncertain. There is a definite gender influence—*very* open and supportive compared with many male-dominated organizations. (All the senior managers are women.)

There are also signs of emerging *political* tensions with other departments—the hospital at large is a traditional (predominantly male) hierarchy!

EXHIBIT 8.1 A Preliminary Reading of the Department of Nursing Services

They were happy with the approach, provided that the retreat began with a strong up-front presentation from myself on ideas about holographic self-organization and new management styles, to clarify and frame key issues for later discussion. The priority for the retreat was to create a shared understanding of what was happening in the department and what may lie in store.

My reading of the overall situation at the time is summarized in Exhibit 8.1. The department was changing from a quasi-bureaucratic to a self-organizing mode. There was a definite will to see the transition work out, at least in the eyes of the top team. Indeed, they communicated an enormous energy and excitement and a feeling that they were doing something innovative and important. But the real question hinged on the extent to which this was shared in the organization at large.

I was sensing that "political" strains were emerging in relations between Nursing Services and other hospital departments as attempts were made to move toward the self-organizing model. Nursing Services, on the report of its top management, seemed unified, though I knew that the retreat might suggest otherwise. For example, it could reveal dissent among the 40 or so managers and potential resistance from specific groups of nurses or their unions. But, for the time being, I was comfortable framing my assignment in terms of the department's need to give practical help on the direction and tactics of change and to provide a helpful nudge to the "culture" of senior staff that would help to create an appropriate context for further development.

With this in mind, I thus began the retreat the following morning with a formal presentation on some recent developments in management. We discussed different styles of organization based on the "six models" presented in Chapter 7, the circumstances where they were appropriate, the styles of management required in flatter, "holographic" organizations, the nature and requirements of teamwork, and some general blocks and resistances to change. My aim was to show where the department stood in relation to what was happening on the management scene generally and to identify some of the special challenges and difficulties that usually arise in shifting from bureaucratic to self-organizing management styles. I used the iceberg model discussed in Chapter 7 to identify some hidden forces that could confront their change agenda and to ground our discussion in current reality.

The retreat was then opened to the participants. They were invited to share their experiences of the change process in the context of what had been said and to identify salient issues that they wanted to address in more detail. These included

1. finding ways of creating "buy-in" from nursing staff and other hospital departments,
2. improving communication,
3. improving the practice of self-organization,
4. sustaining momentum,

5. understanding and learning from successes, and
6. clarifying and emphasizing core values in the new team context.

The general message emerging from this discussion was very consistent with the briefings that I had received before the retreat. They were flattening the hierarchy, striking new patterns of communication based on "need" rather than on traditional lines of authority; people were being empowered to take on new responsibilities and decision making; and "team cultures" seemed to be emerging. The self-organizing approach was definitely taking root. The department was energized and open. The "culture" in the room seemed incredibly supportive. This wasn't your typical male-dominated organization! Or was it the values of the nursing profession coming through?

In any event, I felt that the mood was open and, at least from my point of view, very motivating. The department was in the middle of an exciting phase of organizational development and progressing well. I thus felt very comfortable in helping the group organize the above topics under two general "umbrella issues" to provide a focus for the afternoon discussion groups. These were

(a) the values of the department and the challenges of self-organization in practice and

(b) the problems of integrating the new management style with the rest of the organization.

The group discussions were lively, and reporting back to groups raised a host of issues and ideas in relation to these topics. The remainder of the afternoon was then devoted to exploring their implications.

By the end of the day, a lot of clarification about the challenges and difficulties in moving to a holographic/self-organizing approach had been achieved, but a host of other questions had also been raised. For example, the problems of creating "buy-in" and commitment from others, of developing required skills, of building on successes, and of sustaining momentum while recognizing the limits of the self-organizing approach were still big concerns.

These issues were listed on flip charts, and it was resolved to examine them in more depth during the course of the following day.

Reflecting on the day's proceedings that evening, I was struck by a number of thoughts. There seemed to be an extremely strong commitment to the new style and direction, combined with concerns and uncertainty. I was impressed by the proactive and committed attitude among the nursing managers. The top team had done an excellent job in bringing them this far.

On the other hand, my radar was picking up a number of warning signs. The people at the retreat seemed highly competent; many seemed "naturals" in moving toward the more flexible, self-organizing style of management. But, at times, there seemed so much commitment to the *concept* of self-organization, and to the *concept* of holographic management, that there was a real danger that the theory could get in the way. For example, I was struck by the frequency with which the problem of communicating the way they were now organized had been discussed. The problem had been raised during the car ride to the retreat and had also cropped up in group discussions and in reportbacks. In particular, I recalled one humorous story relating to the difficulties staff experienced in telling people outside the department, especially potential recruits, how the department worked. Staff seemed to have no way of telling them what it was like in practice. The meaning of *holographic organization* and *self-organization*, used as buzzwords inside, was not shared by the outsider. So, recourse had to be made to saying that the department was "*not* like a traditional department," that managerial roles "were *not* traditional management-supervisory roles," and so on. Obviously, the communication was judged unsatisfactory on both sides of the information exchange. The story, told by one of the senior managers, had attracted hoots of laughter, acknowledging that the problem was widely shared.

The problem seemed crucial to many of the issues raised during the afternoon. I thus decided that it would be helpful to start the second day of the retreat by getting all of the managers imaging the *past, present,* and *future* of the department. I wanted them to leave the detailed concepts of holographic management and self-organization behind for a moment, to see if they could approach the issue in a new way. The problem of "telling our story" seemed a paramount one. They were having difficulties explaining their position to new recruits, to senior medical staff, and to bureaucrats in other departments. People could not understand their style. At best, it seemed as if they were strange; at worst, chaotic. If my hunch was correct, a part of the problem was that they were unclear about their story themselves. If we could create a focus on this, it would be possible to create a strong sense of shared understanding internally and find a way of communicating key aspects of their message externally. In the process, we would have a powerful means of getting to the heart of many of the issues they had raised the previous day.

"TELLING OUR STORY"

I thus started the second day of the retreat by inviting people to break into smaller groups and introduced an exercise using the imaging methodology discussed in Chapters 2 and 6. Each person was invited to think of an animal or other image that captured the Department of Nursing Services *"as it was* before the changes 2 years ago, as it is *now,* and as it will be *5 years in the future."* Each group was then asked to discuss their images, and how they saw the department changing over time, and to report their insights back to the total group.

Exhibit 8.2 summarizes the results. The reports were humorous and animated. They captured some of the fundamental characteristics of the department and people's aspirations for the future organization. As you can see, the images were incredibly varied but captured the confusing and uncertain stage of development in which the department now found itself.

Note the pattern as well as the progressive nature of the change. Note how the dependence of the adolescent gives way to a state of interdependence; how the strictness of Queen Elizabeth I, the order and discipline of the old woman in the shoe, and of a formal classroom give way to fluid images of sea gulls in flight, owners of a building in an earthquake zone, and a jamboree. Note how the passivity of the Olympic spectator gives way to control of the race; how the fledgling bird grows into an adult with distinctive competence; how the linearity of train and snake become more complex systems with an unfolding, self-organizing character; how the traditional Norman Rockwell becomes a self-organizing Etch-a-Sketch.

IMAGES OF NURSING SERVICES

Two Years Ago	Now	In Five Years' Time
1. Dependence: an adolescent thinking about "breaking curfew"	Independence: We have broken curfew and are now dealing with the consequences	Interdependence with the rest of the organization
2. A part of the court of the queen of England	The old woman who lived in the shoe	Sea gulls in flight
3. The old woman who lived in the shoe	A school of whales in a sea of sharks	Owners of the top floors of a building in an earthquake (in control but in a situation that is uncontrollable!)
4. A schoolroom with students and teachers	A camping trip (with fewer rules)	A jamboree
5. Spectators at the Olympics	In the race	Holding the stopwatch
6. A bird coming out of a shell	The bird trying to fly	An owl? or eagle? or crow? or vulture?
7. A train in motion, speeding, undirectional	Grand Central Station: organized chaos	A transportation system
8. A snake with its head leading and tail following	A pot of boiling water	A galaxy: ordered but undiscovered
9. Norman Rockwell	A fuzzy French impressionist	Etch-a-Sketch

EXHIBIT 8.2 Metaphors of Past, Present, and Future

Clearly, there were many avenues that could have been followed in developing the implications of this imagery. My approach as facilitator was to encourage a rich pattern of storytelling, knowing that the process would help to energize and frame the context for future action. There was so much consistency in the various images. Everyone could relate to what was being said, and the humor allowed difficult issues to be expressed in a constructive way. When the process had run its course, I then made what I hoped would prove to be a few well-chosen remarks.

I noted the theme of transition. The images only covered a span of seven years but contained *major* shifts. They reflected the journey on which the department was engaged, with all its uncertainties. There was a pattern in the transition from the rule-based, unidirectional messages contained in the images of two years ago compared with the new capacities and fluidity of five years hence. The *now* was characterized by confusion, difficulty, and, in some cases, danger.

I knew that my intervention was critical in shaping what was to follow. There was no overwhelming convergence on any one image of the future that could provide an integrating frame of shared meaning. In telling their transition stories, people seemed comfortable with the idea that the current confusions and uncertainties would eventually give way to a feeling of competence. They seemed comfortable with the journey away from the old bureaucratic model to a more fluid situation. The main concern rested in shifting from the confusing *now* to the desired state of increased competence. The problem was *"getting there"*! I thus decided to select one of the metaphors of the present situation as a way of focusing attention and energy.

I selected the pot of boiling water and invited reflection on this image.

"What happens to boiling water?"

"It evaporates."

"It boils dry."

My point: "Is that what will happen in relation to the current initiative toward self-organization?"

There was a lot of action in the department.

There was a lot of excitement.

But was it going anywhere?

I selected the boiling water metaphor as a way of focusing on this key problem. In any change process, one often reaches a point of high energy and excitement where commitments are flowing and promise is high. But all too often this energy dissipates, because, unless there is follow-through and sustained progress, crises of confidence and wavering support often arise. As a result, many people fall back into the old style. In my reading of the situation, this was the main danger facing Nursing Services. They had achieved much, and the energy and understanding for achieving further change was there. But it could easily dissipate.

The image of boiling water captured the energy and strength in the present situation but also the pitfalls. I was thus determined to work it for all it was worth, with a view to avoiding the state of "boiling dry." I sensed that, if I could use the metaphor to focus on this danger, and get everyone to focus on what needed to be done to avoid boiling dry, I could help the department become aware of the specific strategies and tactics that could be used to manage the difficult path ahead. The process would also help to fill out the details of their emerging story.

The focus on "boiling dry" allowed us to embrace the issues that had been left hanging overnight. The problems of creating "buy-in," of developing required skills, of building on successes, and of communicating with others were precisely those that needed attention. The metaphor helped to create a sense of realism: that all this stuff could go nowhere unless the ongoing transition was appropriately managed.

To address the details, groups were formed around these issues, and the discussion and the subsequent reporting back raised a lot of concerns and provided many ideas through which further progress could be made. The retreat was now *really* addressing the details of its emerging story, not just the broad imagery. It was addressing some of the core issues about self-organization in practice and building a real head of steam.

But was it going too fast? I felt that I was dealing with a really empowered group of people. There was no way that they were going to let the pot boil dry! There was a lot of talk about how achievements could be sustained and how they could begin to take their story and new management practice into the rest of the organization. There was talk about how the problems and lack of understanding on the part of doctors, bureaucrats, and senior administrators could be managed.

But, I could see that the department head and one of her senior associates were getting visibly worried. I sensed that they were concerned that the process was going too fast and could fly out of control: into the chaos that I'd been mandated to avoid! The senior managers were in danger of running ahead of where the head of nursing and her associates wanted them to be.

They were empowered all right.

But were they *too* empowered?

At the coffee break, these concerns were communicated to me by the head of nursing and the senior associate sitting next to her. She reminded me, with a touch of humor, that the main aim of the retreat was to "empower *ourselves* as a group of 40-odd managers, not to carry the changes into the hospital at large." I was also reminded that I was dealing with a group of more than 40 ex-nurses. There was a fear that the retreat could lead to the view that "we have to overthrow the paternalistic system in which we work."

I listened, saw the potential dangers, and decided to check the situation. I talked to several key people to sense the mood among participants and to judge whether they too felt that everything was going to swing out of control. Fortunately, I found the situation to be much more stable than the top managers feared. There was a genuine energy and excitement, but not radical furor. People seemed to truly believe that it was possible to carry their approach to self-organization forward in a significant way, and they wanted to do everything possible to create "the story" that was within their grasp.

I, too, felt very comfortable with the situation. I had experienced the same phenomenon in different forms before. Often, in sessions like the one I was running, people *do* get excited by the possibilities. They *do* feel empowered. They *do* want to reach as far as they can. And, as a result, the sponsors *do* get anxious, because they are the ones that ultimately have to manage the consequences back in the regular work setting. This is what I saw in the top team. There was a genuine and understandable fear that their good work would be set back in some way. They were outside their comfort zone.

I thus returned to the head of nursing and asked for her trust in steering the process to a satisfactory conclusion. Rather than trying to close the situation down by imposing a "cooling off" agenda, as had been more or less suggested to me, I asked her and her senior associate if they would be prepared to share their concerns with everyone present, trusting me to facilitate the ensuing debate. They agreed.

In starting the next session, I thus approached the issue very directly and posed the question of whether the process was running too fast and whether it should be slowed down. I then turned the stage over to the head of nursing to express her views. She did a beautiful job, noting with considerable humor the paradox she now faced. The retreat had been intended to empower everyone. She was the one who had wanted to get everyone going. Now, she wanted to slow things down.

Her colleague also made a statement, focusing on the need for realism. She mentioned that the paternalistic system within which nurses worked had been around a long time and wasn't going to disappear overnight! In essence, she was worried that staff, in their enthusiasm to create change in the hospital as a whole, could antagonize the powers that be.

The two statements, and audience response, created an excellent environment for further progress. The enthusiasm of staff was undiminished, yet there was now a fuller appreciation of some of the dangers and concerns.

To build on this, I knew that I had to make another critical intervention. A little while earlier, one of the managers had evoked the story of the Wizard of Oz and the Yellow Brick Road and had drawn parallels with the current state of the department. She had suggested that they were on the Yellow Brick Road, with all its uncertainties and confusion. I thus decided to use the metaphor in a way that linked to my earlier insight that one of the critical requirements facing the department was to learn how to communicate the story of what it was trying to do. The earlier imaging exercise hadn't really helped here. It had opened a way of identifying key concerns and for mobilizing energy and shared understanding. But there was no overall frame that communicated the central message.

The image of the Yellow Brick Road seemed to fill this gap.

The Yellow Brick Road, with all its challenges, was the existing reality and also pointed to the desired future. Could we use the metaphor to get a better understanding of the emerging story? I suggested that one way of doing this rested in tackling some of the choices that lay ahead. Building on earlier discussions and concerns, I framed these in terms of four options, using their words as far as possible:

1. Stop or contain the self-organizing process within current limits.

2. Allow the process to "trickle" or "spill over" into other areas of the department, and the hospital at large, but in a controlled way.

3. Allow uncontrolled "spillover," leaving the process to evolve at will.

4. Try to produce radical reforms in the wider "paternalistic" system.

I invited the retreat to form into groups around these issues and to tell the story of the Yellow Brick Road from the point of view of their favored scenario. What would they wish to see unfold?

No one wanted to stop or contain the process.

A large number of managers wanted to work on the "controlled spillover" scenario and divided into two groups to do so.

About a third of the total group opted to examine the "uncontrolled" scenario.

A small group opted to examine the possibility of "radical change."

The groups quickly got down to work and produced excellent results. There was a high degree of convergence between the views of the three groups examining the process of controlled and uncontrolled spillover. The two groups examining the controlled strategy saw great potential in building around naturally occurring opportunities for spreading the self-organizing approach: for example, through role modeling, championing, and a sharing of core values. They saw great opportunity in using this kind of initiative for overcoming the systemwide recruitment problem in relation to staff nurses, who were leaving the profession in droves as a result of the lack of autonomy within more traditional bureaucratized systems.

They wanted to build around successes and to handle relations with other departments with care and skill, educating them without trumpet blowing or fanfare.

The group examining the uncontrolled spillover scenario built around similar ideas but argued that the whole story should encourage staff empowerment on a broader scale. They wanted to continue what they were doing, building on the successes, but being much more forceful in promoting and seeking new empowerment opportunities.

The "radical" group didn't produce the expected scenario for overthrowing paternalism. Rather, they focused on developing a new approach to organization, building around the patient and patient care. They saw opportunities for resolving many of the current crises in the health service by adopting a customer service orientation, with the nursing profession as primary care giver and focal point of the whole system. They wanted the nursing profession to see "service to the patient" as a way of transforming the organization of medical services and of existing power relations—but in an evolutionary rather than a revolutionary way. They invoked a variation of "Model 6," discussed in my earlier presentation to the group and in Chapter 7 of this book, as a means of organizing the network of required services on a subcontracting basis. It was a story with which almost everyone present could empathize because it built on so many of the core values of the nursing profession.

The four stories were thus highly complementary. The first three offered a clear vision of how the self-organizing process could evolve in a fairly orderly way and also addressed practical tactics. The fourth story placed everything in a more heroic, transformational context, building on the vital role of the nursing profession in future health care systems. Together, they created an exciting and empowering vision of what the future could hold.

The storytelling exercise thus helped to bind members of the retreat together. The challenge was clear: to continue their journey along the Yellow Brick Road, building on the ideas offered in the four presentations. Rather than worry unduly about the theory and concepts of self-organization, they needed to continue developing and communicating their story, so that they could empower themselves, sustain a sense of shared understanding and shared experience, and, in the process, help others to understand and join their quest. The concept of holographic self-organization had served its purpose. It had created a broad frame of reference through which they could develop an alternative to the bureaucratic mode. They understood the basic principles. Now, they needed to let the practice continue to unfold. During the course of the retreat, we had discussed numerous ideas and tactics through which this could occur. The challenge was to incorporate these ideas into the unfolding story, trying to shift toward a more patient-oriented approach, building on successes and small steps in a comfortable, incremental way. They needed to think about their "iceberg" and tackle the blocks and barriers being faced. If everyone at the retreat could go forward and play her part in creating the shift toward the new model, it would surely emerge in practice.

The storytelling made the task of closing the retreat a relatively easy one, because it was clear that the required vision, ideas, creativity, and general ability to make the transition a success were already present in the room. The group *was* an empowered group. It consisted of extremely able women with the ability and experience to carry the initiative toward self-organization a lot further. All they had to do was follow the path of what they were already doing.

And so the story ends, as far as my direct involvement in the project was concerned. The retreat was a step along the Yellow Brick Road—a high-energy session that would require further energy and action to deliver concrete results in practice. In leaving, I was confident that those present had a solid understanding of what was required and that their process would succeed.

In the two years since the retreat, much progress has been made in helping the core group of senior managers improve their self-organizing approach and its influence on the delivery of patient care. New initiatives have sprung up and been developed as a result of people seeing and working on good opportunities rather than by driving the process in a directive, centralized manner. Managers within the leadership group have carried the self-organizing approach back into their spheres of responsibility, allowing the various groups of nurses and other professionals involved to develop their own specific modes of operation. As a result, processes of self-organization are developing on a broad front, but at a differential rate, as people find ways of integrating the self-organizing philosophy with the various tasks that have to be performed and the various subcultures found within the department.

The new style of management has been allowed to evolve and find its own form. Throughout the process, every effort has been made to communicate with the rest of the organization, "telling the story" in a positive, low-profile way. As a result, members of the department are now helping to introduce similar organizational changes elsewhere.

As the head of nursing puts it: "Our old parochial view of nursing is disappearing; the boundaries between departments are beginning to break down. We are inviting and allowing more people into our circle, and doing more to empower others. We are much freer in letting responsibilities go to other departments if necessary and in working collaboratively. We don't feel that we have to be in charge. As people have become comfortable and more confident, they've become more open. . . . We have moved beyond our early insecurity and right into the promotion of autonomy. The main problem is that some of our staff are getting so proud of the creativity, and of our vision, that they sometimes neglect the day-to-day details. It's so much more exciting to get involved in the romance of empowerment and autonomy!

"As I look back on our process, I think this is the major thing that I'd now emphasize. As well as avoiding the chaos, you've got to be sure that people don't forget the details. But people have definitely become more empowered and more open. . . . I have a passionate belief in the ability and potential of the people that I work with. If you can provide them with the knowledge base to have successful autonomy, the right things usually happen."

SOME CLOSING REFLECTIONS

In this and previous chapters, I have invited you to join me on a journey of imaginization that has taken many twists and turns. We have talked about spider plants and dandelion seeds, political football, strategic termites, octopi, gulfs, icebergs, and now boiling water and yellow brick roads. This seems very far from the serious endeavor known as organization and management theory.

Yet, I believe that it illustrates the essence of what the theory and practice of organization and management are all about. For the most part, organization theory has built on *theorists' metaphors*. They often create important insights but run the risk of remaining abstract and distant from the situations in which they are applied. Also, the tendency is to switch power and dialogue to the terrain of the external theorist-interventionist and away from that of the people living the day-to-day reality.

In many respects, this is what was happening in Nursing Services. The idea of creating a holographic approach to organization had created an important breakthrough for the department. But, at the time of my intervention, it had begun to get in the way, because it was making discourse in the department too theoretical. They were trying to mold themselves in accordance with the theory and principles of holographic design rather than enhancing and developing the potentials for self-organization they already possessed. Hence the whole thrust of my intervention was to avoid getting entangled in a discussion of theory and technique and to find ways of empowering them to continue what they were already doing.

This insight accounted for my decision to move into the storytelling mode, building around images of past, present, and future. It also explained why I chose the metaphor of "boiling water" from all the others generated through their imaging session (Exhibit 8.2) to symbolize what I saw as the dominant problem: that of "boiling dry"! And, later, when the issues associated with this problem had been explored, it explained why I hooked onto the Yellow Brick Road, another evocative metaphor that was theirs rather than mine, to carry the storytelling forward.

In this way, my intervention was shaped by my ongoing reading of the situation (Exhibit 8.1) and an attempt to find the most appropriate way forward, unfolding the retreat in a manner that would meet the needs of those involved. In line with the reading in Exhibit 8.1, my dominant interpretation throughout was that, above all else, I needed to find a way of empowering the department to create a sense of shared understanding about the implications of self-organization in practice (the cultural dimension of the change) and for managing political realities within the wider organization. The idea of getting them to "tell their story" seemed to provide an excellent means of doing this, because I was picking up so many signs that they were experiencing difficulties in communicating what the new style of organization involved. I knew that, if they couldn't tell others what they were doing, they really didn't have an adequate shared understanding among themselves. Hence the storytelling metaphor became the primary one through which I framed the rest of the retreat. It seemed ideal for creating the kind of experience that would help to develop the shared meanings on which a strong and robust culture depends.

The images of "boiling water" and the Yellow Brick Road were convenient focusing devices that could help to achieve these aims in practice. I thus selected them in turn as a means of making our way forward. Obviously, at the time, I had no means of envisaging the detailed outcome. But I knew that the image of boiling dry could tap into the core problems of sustaining the change process, a central aim of the retreat. I realized that the Yellow Brick Road was perfect for capturing the uncertainty and confusion of a journey that had a happy ending.

The metaphors seemed perfect for the task at hand, so I used them, and went with the flow.

As it turned out, even the crisis about whether everything was going to fly out of control also proved ideal, because it created a perfect opportunity to clarify the issue. If I had backed off and slowed the process down, I suspect that the decision would have squashed a lot of the empowerment that was beginning to emerge. By confronting the crisis, and building it into the process, I was able to dramatize the choices facing the department and to help build clarity and commitment to a way forward.

The Nursing Services story, like those in earlier chapters, symbolizes the free-flowing yet grounded interpretive style that lies at the core of imaginization in practice. It illustrates imaginization as an attitude of mind that can help us to find creative images and ideas that will resonate with the needs of the situation being faced and hence help us go forward in new ways.

The following chapters provide further illustrations of how the approach can be applied in practice.

9 Imaginizing Teamwork

The above cartoon begins to say it all.

What's teamwork?

In this chapter, my aim is to throw light on some taken-for-granted images that shape how we think about teamwork and to offer some fresh ideas for developing teamwork in practice.

TEAM METAPHORS

"Come on, Jack. You're not being a team player."

It's one of the ultimate corporate insults.

The accusation has great normative power, because team-work has become a sacred aspect of management. It conveys the idea that Jack, like every reasonable person, *should* be "pulling his weight" or devoting himself to the cause.

Yet what does teamwork mean?

In what ways is Jack out of line?

The word *team* was originally used to describe a "family or brood" or a set of draft animals like oxen, horses, or dogs harnessed to pull and work together.

Is that what we have in mind?

Are we asking Jack to act like one of the family?

To pull like an ox or draft horse?

Or, as is more common nowadays under the influence of sports culture, are we asking him to play some kind of game?

If so, what's the game?

American football?

Soccer?

Basketball?

Baseball?

Hockey?

Rowing?

Volleyball?

Rock climbing?

Tug-of-war?

As Robert Keidel shows us in his book *Corporate Players,* each image carries very different implications for the role of team members, for the role of "coach" or manager, and for how the detailed "game" unfolds. Compare, for example, the regimentation of American football with the free-flowing self-organization of basketball, hockey, or soccer. Compare the uniform pulling together of rowing with the diversity and role differentiation of baseball.

There's a world of difference between these games and the kind of teamwork implied.

American football and rowing are attractive metaphors for managerial "coaches" who want to remain firmly in control. In these sports, the coach is in command, defining the basic strategies, calling detailed plays, communicating to the "team" through a "second in command"—the quarterback or coxswain. Football and rowing provide perfect models of teamwork for authoritarian leaders and, in an organizational context, provide a new way of reproducing bureaucratic forms of organization. If the enterprise in question has clear, stable goals, and a compliant work force, then it often provides an effective recipe for management.

But, if you're calling for "football" or "rowing," don't expect the fluid self-organizing performance of a soccer, basketball, or volleyball team.

These other sports share important qualities with football, in the sense that they require close, coordinated efforts to achieve a common goal and depend for their success upon a

highly motivated group of people who understand the basic
strategy. The group must also be able to trust each other to play
to their best as they take on the competition. But, look at the
differences. Look at the rigidity and narrow task specialization
of football and the broader, multifunctioned roles of players in
the other games. Look at how much more power is delegated
to the players in soccer, basketball, or volleyball. The manager
or "coach" of teams in these sports is fully involved in selecting
players, developing strengths, working on broad strategies,
and motivating people to produce peak performances. But,
when it comes to playing the game, the players are given much
more responsibility and control over decision making. The
room for spontaneous, creative, intuitive judgment, within the
natural flow of play, is much greater.

As a Welshman who was brought up with the fluidity of rugby
and soccer, I find it interesting to observe how American football

has mechanized and bureaucratized the original game. The challenge of moving or carrying a ball 100 yards in a continuous flow has been split into the task of moving a ball ten yards ten times. The field of play is clearly marked to show one- and ten-yard objectives, and results are always *precisely* measured. The moving of the ball is broken into discrete plays, each of which is carefully planned and executed. It's as if Frederick Taylor, creator of work study and "scientific management," had been given the assignment of reorganizing the game! No wonder then that the image of a football coach provides such a popular metaphor among bureaucratic managers. In effect, it allows them to imaginize a style of teamwork consistent with the hierarchical mode of operation that makes them feel at home.

So, if we are to use sports metaphors for thinking about teamwork, let's be sure about their appropriateness for the

game being played. In any organization of any complexity, there may be a need for different kinds of teamwork. Some areas may need to have the direction and synchronicity of a rowing crew; others may need to be guided by the strong hand of a football coach. Others, as in baseball, may need to cultivate cooperation between a group of solid players who rely for their ultimate success on the unpredictable efforts of a few true stars. Others may need the self-organizing qualities of volleyball, soccer, or basketball. Others may need to develop the organizational equivalent of rock climbing, creating a sense of interdependence and mutual trust that will allow people to take great personal risks. And so on!

Each of these images of teamwork implies a very different strategy for creating effective teamwork in practice. So, as suggested in Exhibit 9.1, it's often a good idea to think quite

---

Here's a simple exercise for thinking about teamwork:

What team-building metaphors are appropriate in *your* organization and *where?*

Appropriate metaphors

Organizational unit	
Type and quality of existing teamwork	
The teamwork we should be aiming for	

EXHIBIT 9.1 Teamwork Can Take Many Forms

systematically about the kind of teamwork that's required and about the team metaphors through which it is best shaped.

That's one of the central messages of this chapter, and it helps to explain why so many attempts at creating teamwork have run into trouble. The harsh reality in many organizations is that, while teamwork is a high priority and has often been the focus of massive expenditures, results are mediocre. Indeed, in many organizations, the concept of *teamwork* has become discredited; it exists as an empty buzzword.

Yet, to find the reasons, one only has to look at the incongruities that are usually reflected in the results of an exercise like that in Exhibit 9.1 and identify where the ruling team metaphor breaks down.

I don't think we need to say any more about the oxen. For who, after all, wants to be driven in this way?

But, when it comes to the failure of sports metaphors, the situation is a little more interesting. One important factor, as I've mentioned above and illustrated through some of the cartoons, is that people are not always playing the right game or even the same game. Another rests in the fact that managers can easily get carried away with the kind of experience that they've had of teamwork in sports settings. It's great to be on a team that's playing well. And knowledge of great games, great teams, and great coaches can provide wonderful role models and points of reference for shaping activities in one's organization.

But it's easy to forget that there's an enormous distance between "the big game" on the television, or on the sports field, and the humdrum existence in the factory or office in which the team metaphor is to be applied.

The situation here can be completely different:

No big game atmosphere

Sometimes, no obvious competition in sight

Diffuse, ambiguous goals

Political conflicts

Divergent interests

And, in an era of staff layoffs, no guarantee that you will be a member of the club, let alone be playing on the team!

No wonder, therefore, that team members often don't want to play!

When you can offer the promise of a wonderful experience or objective, when you have a cause that is able to galvanize people's effort around something worthwhile, when you are able to communicate that a job is worthy of best efforts all around—these are the circumstances in which teamwork comes alive in organizational settings. We see it at its best in the efforts to save a life in an emergency ward; in responses to a disaster situation; in "beating the competition," when beating the competition is seen as being important and worthy!

When there are clear parallels with teamwork in sports settings, teamwork in organizations can flourish. The metaphor works! But, in other situations, it can often stultify. The call for teamwork becomes no more than rhetoric, producing cynicism, superficial compliance, and, eventually, stalemate. Even teams that are successful in the short run often encounter this experience over the longer term. They run out of steam as the practical weaknesses and contradictions of the underlying team metaphor become evident.

BUILDING TEAMWORK IN DIFFICULT SITUATIONS

The reality facing many managers is that simple calls for teamwork are likely to fall on deaf ears.

We've gotten beyond the stage where a "Let's Go . . . Ra Ra" approach will suffice.

Most employees are far too sophisticated to take such calls seriously, especially if they are working in difficult, fragmented, and politicized contexts or where diversity and creative dissent are essential to the work being done. Simple sports metaphors or packaged approaches to teamwork don't resonate. They tend to be too superficial. And they tend to stress and encourage more uniformity and coherence than the nature or demands of many situations allow.

In these circumstances, it is often much more productive to turn our capacities for imaginization in a new direction. Instead of just calling for teamwork, or extolling the virtues of great causes, great games, or great players, it may be much more effective to initiate processes that create new patterns of shared understanding that address the barriers and blocks to teamwork in practice and find realistic ways of mobilizing and coordinating efforts.

To illustrate, I will draw on the work of Michael Walton, a British management consultant who uses a highly visual method of imaginization to explore organizational problems and to find ways of building team cultures in difficult settings. One of his approaches involves creating a context where individuals and groups can develop independent and shared images of their situation and explore common and divergent understandings in novel ways.

For example, in the course of a typical "team-building" process, he asks those involved to take a few moments to describe their *current situation* in terms of whatever images come to mind. They are free to capture and express their views through images, feelings, words, drawings, colors, or whatever medium seems most appropriate. Each person spends a few minutes on the assignment as an individual and then shares what has been produced in a small group of up to four or five people. The group is then required to create a composite image in the form of a picture or drawing that can be presented to the total gathering.

As each group presents its composite image, an opportunity is created for everyone present to ask for further descriptions and clarifications—but without judgments. This helps to create a shared sense of what everyone thinks about the current state of affairs. Even when the total gathering is no more than six or seven people, it's a good idea to break the group into smaller subgroups, because the resonance or differences between the various images produced can provide an important boost to overall insight and understanding.

Once the groups have completed this task, the whole process is repeated with an eye on the *future.*

What would they *like* future relations in their department, team, or work unit to look like? They are given a few minutes to collect and express their own thoughts and feelings before returning to their small groups to share and discuss their views and produce a group image that is then shared and discussed in the total gathering.

Once all groups have had an opportunity to share their views, Michael then explores the similarities and differences, asking further questions, juxtaposing the images presented, and probing for further clarification. The process helps to highlight genuine differences and concerns and to explore the scope for a shared view of the future to emerge.

The following illustration of the method in practice involves the Personnel Department of a large energy company.

Football, Skiers, Rockets, and Racing Cars

The situation is a common one.

The Personnel Department, which was responsible for the whole spectrum of human resource management functions, had been charged with helping the company adjust to major new changes in management practice. Its task was to develop a corporate culture that encouraged managers to help, encourage, support, motivate, and coach their staff rather than just to engage in "top-down" evaluations focusing on "bottom line performance."

But Personnel was in a state of major disarray itself. The department was internally fragmented and overloaded with work. There had been an influx of new staff, and there was a wide variety of skill levels. Internal cohesion was at an all-time low.

To remedy the situation, Michael was invited to help. Fourteen senior managers attended a two-and-a-half-day meeting to set the stage for a formal review of the department's role and responsibilities and to explore links with the rest of the organization. The imaging process described above was used to tap into the existing culture of the group and to get a preliminary definition of where they were and where they wanted to be. After a brief introduction from Michael, two groups of seven managers were set to work imaging current and future realities.

One of the groups represented the current reality within Personnel as the dismembered football player illustrated in Exhibit 9.2. As can be seen, each part of the body is solid and well proportioned but disjointed. The strong, capable image stands on a firm base of professional personnel management, but, as the group reported, it couldn't get its act together because the legs are not connected with the trunk, and the trunk is not connected with the head, the directing force. There was a real sense of surprise and shock when the image was disclosed. It immediately seemed to make sense, but there was embarrassment about being so split into separate parts. At the same time, there was deep recognition of the inherent strength of the image and an immediate sense of just how able, powerful,

EXHIBIT 9.2   THE DISMEMBERED FOOTBALL PLAYER

NOTE: The illustrations presented in this and the next three exhibits
were originally drawn on large sheets of flip chart paper with colored
pens. They have been reproduced to scale.

and influential the department *could* be if it could find a way
of working together.

The group went on to describe the effect of the current
organizational changes in terms of the motifs surrounding the

football player. The new management style was presented as a dark rain cloud accompanied by the cryptic comment: "Washes whiter than white." The slogan played on the laundry detergent commercials that promise perfect results. Cynicism was rife. The group felt that management were making great promises but, in a way, whitewashing the reality. It took more than words on paper, or a directive from above, to create a new culture. They felt that top management would have to show their continuing commitment to the desired change, through deeds as well as words. There would have to be new recognition of the importance of collaboration and rewards for working in a different way.

Further aspects of this cynicism are captured in the side comments around the football player: about "scrap management" and "crap management" and the accompanying fighting motifs of "Pow," "Zap," and "Take That." These slogans were used to convey the macho bottom line culture that dominated the current organization with its win-lose undertone. A clash with the more collaborative culture that management was now calling for seemed inevitable. The organization was very macho, a point captured in the very idea of representing the department as a football player. It was unlikely that the strengths of the current style of organization would be thrown away lightly, so the Personnel group felt quite intimidated by its task.

Further concerns and cynicism were symbolized through the famous image of the three monkeys—one closing its eyes to what was happening, the other refusing to hear what was happening, and the third shouting, "Do it my way!"

The image of current reality produced by the second group featured the chaotic ski school illustrated in Exhibit 9.3. Skiers on all three runs, colored green, blue, and black to characterize three levels of increasing difficulty, are in various states of disarray. Those on the beginner's green run are confused and calling for help. Those on the blue run are crashing and buried in snow. Those on the experienced black run are having a better time, negotiating their obstacle course, enjoying the risk, and moving toward the finish. Meanwhile, the instructors are shown removed from the immediate problems and concerns, enjoying the bar and chalet. The recent movement of staff in and out of

EXHIBIT 9.3 THE CHAOTIC SKI SCHOOL

the department was represented by two buses, one bringing people in from other locations in the company, the other taking them to company headquarters. Meanwhile, the sun shines in the top left-hand corner, and a helicopter is hovering overhead, ready to remove casualties when necessary.

Michael Walton reports that the overall mood of this group's presentation was one of anger and great annoyance with senior management. There was a feeling that those at the top perceived them as novices and that inadequate support was being given to them in undertaking what was an extremely difficult task. This is reflected throughout their image of the ski slopes and in the separation of interests between the instructors in the bar and the people on the ski hills. The mood was one of great worry, concern, and conflict. Even though top managers regarded Personnel Department staff as novices or, at best, as intermediates, they *still* expected them to deliver the new culture in a "hard-bitten" and "hostile" environment.

Here was the contradiction between the macho and supportive cultures highlighted by the first group, but in a new form. It was believed that top management, critical and judgmental in the manner encouraged by the old culture, could not be counted on for support in developing the new. They were "boozing it up in the bar," waiting for people to either crash or make it down the hills by themselves. Given these circumstances, the group felt that it was vital for the Personnel Department to become as professional and mutually supportive as it could in approaching the current challenge.

The images created by both groups thus had a great deal of consistency, speaking to the stress, division, contradiction, and frustration inherent in the current state of affairs as well as to the challenges that lay ahead. There was an emotional atmosphere, with the main messages ringing clear and true. With appropriate integration and development of their fragmented skills and abilities, and support from top management, staff believed that they *could* make a major contribution. But the route was uncertain and paved with problems. The imagery helped to express many of the hidden feelings and insecurities that were lurking in the group.

With these feelings fully vented, and the issues placed clearly on the table, attention was then directed to the future. Following individual reflection and group desired discussion, the two groups produced the imagery presented in Exhibits 9.4 and 9.5.

The dismembered-footballer group developed the theme "Personnel Strikes Back" (Exhibit 9.4). Their image, rich in bright, fluorescent color, created an overall shining effect, with a rocket ship being launched toward the organizational problems, represented by a planet in space, but supported by mission control (top management) back on the ground. Flowers bloom in red and yellow. The person riding the rocket ship (symbolizing the staff of the department) and the senior manager, in mission control, are smiling and positive, approaching the organizational

EXHIBIT 9.4   "PERSONNEL STRIKES BACK"

problems directly, together, and with confidence. But the image also recognizes some of the difficulties. Parts of head office are still lost in space, symbolized by the person riding the set of golf clubs. The mood of the group was, however, optimistic and communicated its hope for an integrated and well-focused department.

The image of the desired future situation produced by the second group (Exhibit 9.5) was also very positive. It showed the company winning the "Energy Grand Prix" as a powerful,

EXHIBIT 9.5 "ENERGY GRAND PRIX"

smart, effective, well-tuned racing car about to take the check-
ered flag. Personnel is depicted as the racing support team in
the pits, providing the "Superlube" and the "Can Do" attitude
required to make the car run well. The staff are smiling. The
spectators are supportive, enjoying the achievements of the
number-one car as it speeds ahead of its rivals, the firm's main
competitors. The competitors' cars are smaller, less glamorous,
and less colorful, and one is skidding off the track.

In this way, both images emphasized a sense of integration,
momentum, direction, and collaboration—qualities that were

conspicuously absent in both groups' descriptions of their current reality. The images were still very macho and closely linked with the current culture but were much more colorful, positive, and optimistic in basic orientation.

The team-building session had a major catalytic effect on those present. It surfaced key problems and provided vivid illustrations of what people wanted to achieve. In just a few hours, Michael was able to take a group that was cynical and divided and help them talk frankly and freely about the difficulties in their situation. As Michael puts it, "It was as if a curtain had been drawn back as they confronted what they were dealing with. They were fragmented, drifting, and faced with an extremely difficult task. The imaging process allowed them to develop a deeper shared understanding of what lay ahead. . . . The humor lightened the atmosphere, and helped to release a positive energy that began to create a feeling that 'we're a team; we can work together to overcome our difficulties!' It was as if a magnet had been introduced into the situation, and all the iron filings that were lying in different directions came together."

The process helped to draw the head of the department closer to his staff and allowed them to work on the challenges being faced. They now had common reference points that they didn't have before and began to become much more collaborative and cohesive. The positive energy also spread beyond those involved in the exercise. As new staff picked up on the energy, a new team culture began to emerge. The whole experience became a major staging point in the development of the department.

DEVELOPING TEAMWORK FROM WITHIN

Most of the images selected by members of the Personnel Department in the above example have close connections with sports. But look at the interpretations. They are so unique. Football and skiing are very familiar images. But who'd have thought of a dismembered football player or a chaotic ski school? Yet, it's this possibility of creating highly personal and unique understandings of situations, and the problems being faced, that makes this kind of imaging process so much more powerful than trying to "drop" teamwork from above.

If teamwork is forced on a situation through the exhortations of an eager manager, or just developed through packaged "skills programs" that don't tackle underlying realities, the kinds of problems, distrust, and potential dissent observed in Michael Walton's case study are usually pushed underground. They deenergize, foster politicking and cynicism, and often erupt in negative, unhelpful ways. Walton's intervention helped the Personnel Department group avoid this and go forward during the rest of their retreat to produce a concrete action agenda, which was then followed up on and had a strong impact on practice.

The message implicit in this case, and developed throughout this chapter, is that our capacities for imaginization can play an important role in developing teamwork in difficult settings. Of course, there's no guarantee that the process will provide a magic wand and that entrenched difficulties will just disappear. Life's just not that simple. Despite a successful imaging process, the staff involved in Personnel still faced major challenges in gaining support from an apathetic and remote senior management group. But, as a result of probing the core issues, and of developing their own personal understanding and action agendas, they were able to go forward and, over time, gradually push the departmental culture in an appropriate direction.

This is the basic promise of the approach. It provides a means of breaking the usual patterns of discourse in an organization and of helping new insights, new dialogue, and new action opportunities emerge.

In many organizations, teamwork has become trapped by formal team building, because, in more ways than one, it has become just a game! In such circumstances, it is much more powerful to develop processes of imaginization that will help people build from their own feelings and experiences, so that they can create a truly shared understanding of problems and challenges rather than operating within frameworks imposed by others.

The next chapter provides further illustrations of how this can be done.

10 Picture Power

Imaginization is about the creation of "new space": new space in which new thinking, new insights, and new dialogue can develop and from which new initiatives can emerge. This is one of the key themes that unites all the chapters in this book. Whether talking about issues of management style, organizational design, the management and facilitation of change, or the development of teamwork, emphasis has been placed on finding imaginative ways of helping people break into the space that they need to act differently.

In the previous chapter, I began to show how this can be achieved by encouraging people to create pictures of their present and future realities. The current chapter continues this theme, providing a further example of how this kind of "picture power" can create opportunities for reshaping the culture and general development of an organization.

Suppose that I were to draw a picture and ask you to use it as a way of thinking about your organization.

You might think it a strange assignment. But, with a little thought, I'm sure that you'd come up with some interesting insights.

For example, here's a summarized response from a group of senior human resource managers who invited me to help them create some new theory for understanding their organization.

I drew a carton of yogurt and asked them for their response. This is how it went:

The Group: Our organization as yogurt? . . .

It's a culture.

It reproduces itself.

It's like yeast.

It takes time to mature.

It's sour.

It's boring.

You have to sweeten it up.

Comes in many flavors.

Very primitive.

But very middle class!

Full of bacteria.

You add some of the old culture to a new batch and before long it's all the same.

GM: What, among all these ideas, is most important for understanding your organization?

The Group: We have a tendency to make everything the same.

> We bring in newcomers, and before you know it
> they're like the old. . . . It's amazing how quickly they
> adapt to the way things are.

GM: How does this process of assimilation occur?

The group went on to discuss the detailed ways in which the corporate culture reproduced itself on a daily basis. They drew parallels between the bacterial functions in yogurt and how corporate "bacteria" work to convert staff into corporate clones. They began to see how the bacterial imagery was identifying a problem. But they also saw how it could be turned into an opportunity.

"How do we create opportunities for new 'strains' [of bacteria] to establish themselves?"

"How do we develop different subcultures?"

The discussion took on a very positive tone and created a platform for identifying specific strategies and tactics through which human resource management could have a positive and diverse impact on an organizations's culture.

So, a seemingly strange image, just like that of the spider plant in Chapter 4, produced a flow of creative discussion that helped people see and talk about their organization in new ways. It created new space in which new ideas could emerge.

My aim in this exercise, which also introduced pictures of an umbrella, an iceberg, a pot of glue, and a fish in a bowl of water, was to help the group become their own theorists. They'd asked me to work with them because they felt that I had a lot to tell them about "new theory" and the ideas that would be in vogue in the years ahead. We addressed this agenda, but the most important message that I was able to give them through the exercise was that *they*, their experience and imaginations, were their own most important resource.

Too many managers are looking outside themselves for answers to their problems. They are looking for the latest theory and at what successful organizations are doing. They are trying to spot the latest trends. In reality, they would be better off engaging in some critical thinking for themselves, recognizing that they and their colleagues already have a vast treasure of insight and experience, which they could and should be using. The challenge is to tap this insight and understanding in a constructive way.

In previous chapters, I have presented many means through which this can be done. All, in one way or another, have created visual images that allow people to see themselves or their organizations anew. That's the message that underlies the spider plant, the strategic termite, the political football, the "blob out of water," the yogurt, the iceberg, and all the other specific images that have been discussed. They create a distance and detachment from existing concepts and existing thinking, distance and detachment that allow fresh perspectives to emerge.

The visual element in all this is of key importance: because it helps to create a new *picture* of the situation with which one is dealing.

If I ask you to "see your organization as yogurt," you are obliged to get into a completely different frame of reference from that which governs your normal thinking. And that's what seeds the creative possibilities.

In the rest of this chapter, I want to illustrate this aspect of imaginization in more detail by showing how the method of getting people to develop their own pictures of their situation can unleash enormous potential for fresh understanding and change. I began to introduce the approach in discussing the development of teamwork in Chapter 9. Now, I want to feature a case based on the work of my colleague Joe Arbuckle, a management consultant who uses a similar method to help organizations create new futures.

CREATING A "NEW STORY"

One of Joe's methods focuses on the idea of helping people create a "new story" for their organization. Every organization is located in a past and present: its "old story." This often acts as a prison, locking the future into the past. Joe addresses the problem by creating opportunities for people to express their images, thoughts, and feelings about their old story to see whether a change is in order. He then uses further imaging exercises to help people identify the new story that they would like to create and to develop the personal and organizational competencies that will be required to make it a reality.

The approach can be used with top managers interested in reimaging and reshaping their organization, with groups of middle managers concerned to revitalize the work of their unit or department, and with "diagonal slices" designed to provide a representative view of the total organization. It can be used by a manager who wishes to create new relations with his or her staff. Here's an example drawn from Joe's work with a retailing firm with annual sales of more than $1.5 billion The firm employed 4,000 people, managed 400 retail stores, and was trying to create a major transformation in its approach to business.

The organization, which we'll call *Transform,* was in an important stage of transition. After many years of profitable operation as a distribution network organized as an extension of its warehouses, the company was interested in becoming more "market driven" and "customer sensitive." At the initiative of its new president, Joe was invited to help develop and disseminate a new sense of vision throughout the company. The president wanted his staff to grasp new possibilities for the future and to create a radically new form of organization for managing day-to-day practice.

As part of the process, two three-day workshops were conducted in a retreat setting. Each involved the president and a different group of 35 people drawn from top to bottom of the organization. The mandate was to help create a "market-driven organization." Joe organized the workshops around an Old Story-New Story format. The first day was spent imaging "the Old Story" in terms of existing concepts of the business, the existing features of the organization, and the general feelings and experiences of staff. The second day was devoted to creating a vision of "the New Story," again by focusing on the business, the organization, and its people. Day three, chaired by the president, focused on "Inventing the Future": on finding ways of making the "New Story" a reality. In the following pages, I want to capture the composite nature and mood of the two events and illustrate some of the key ideas that emerged.

After appropriate introductions, and an exploration of the workshop aims, the process began with an exercise designed to help participants get outside their usual frame of reference for viewing the business. Each member of the retreat was asked to describe the difference between going into one of their retail stores and going into a store of their major competitor. The exercise was explicitly designed to highlight the differences between being "supplier and warehouse driven" on the one hand (their existing situation) and being "market driven" on the other (the position of the competitor). Participants were asked to generate images for capturing the two experiences and to use colored pens to depict customers, and customers' feelings, in the two stores. The images were then shared in small groups, and the drawings that best represented the views of each group were then presented to the total gathering.

The response was vivid and direct. In both workshops, customers were viewed as having extremely negative "in-store" experiences.

For example, group images depicted customers as being exposed to robotic, "Yes sir. No sir," "Yes sir. No sir," "Yes sir. No sir," dialogue.

There were pictures of long lines of customers.

A sales representative was shown performing a "hold up" on the customer, waving a gun and saying, "What do you want?"

There were lots of frowns and stop signs.

The stores were drawn in black and white. They were featureless.

In the competitor stores, on the other hand, the images were more highly colored: smiles, close interaction between sales assistants and customers—an altogether more integrated and harmonious experience.

The message was clear: Customers don't have a good experience in our stores. The competitor has the edge.

After this simple, yet very powerful exercise, there could be little doubt about the need for change and about the new customer and marketing orientation that provided the frame for the retreat. Relations with key suppliers had dominated the organization's past. Relations with the customer needed to become more prominent in the future.

The understanding was there for everyone to see. The resonance between the images generated by the groups in each retreat created a shared appreciation of problems and challenges on which each workshop could build.

From there, the participants proceeded to take a closer look at their current organization and the role of staff within the organization. For each part of the exercise, people were invited to develop and draw their own images, share them in a small group, and then present the images that had most meaning for the group back to the total gathering. The process resulted in dozens of creative images, most of which were drawn in evocative color. For example, *images of the current organization* included the following:

- A green tortoise carrying some of the company's products on its back (symbolizing slow movement)

- An old-style gramophone (symbolizing the organization's old style form and message)

- A rudderless boat facing contradictory directions (symbolizing drift)

- A fire-fighting brigade with hoses that weren't reaching the fire (symbolizing a basic incompetence)

- An octopus juggling a set of tools (symbolizing multiple and conflicting work demands)

- A headless horseman (symbolizing how the current emphasis on low-cost productivity eliminated the use of people's brains)

- A pyramid with people at the top and bottom, with headless chickens in the middle (symbolizing the confusion and lack of direction in the core of the enterprise)

PRODUCTION 2500

The images of the current organization in both workshops had this overwhelmingly negative tone.

So did people's images of the *roles of staff within the current organization*.

To launch this second phase of the exercise, Joe seeded the creative process by inviting everyone to draw a character that they would like to bring to an "Organizational Theme Party": the character that they felt the organization invited them to be while at work! The assignment was to draw a picture of their character's costume and to depict whether the costume helped or hindered the organization's overall performance.

Here are some of the guests that turned up:

- A blind person wearing three different hats with a ball and chain around his feet, being pulled in different directions

- An all-purpose sports person, with a football helmet, a basketball, a hockey stick, a skate on one foot, and a studded soccer boot on the other

- A serpent

- A piece in a jigsaw puzzle

- A person that was bound and gagged, with a light bulb symbolizing his bright ideas

- A fireman, orchestra conductor, and football referee, all in one person

- A knight of the round table defending the faith

- A person that was half saint and half devil (symbolizing "how to get on around here")

The images in general communicated the sense of stress, frustration, and multiple demands that people experienced at work. As in the case of the images of the current organization, there was a deep sense of discontent.

With this exercise complete, Joe then invited each team to create a mural describing the current reality of the organization, based on all that they'd seen and heard during the day. They were invited to look over all the drawings produced in the workshops, which were now posted around the room, to discuss the implications in their small groups, and then to represent their group's overall view of the current state of the business, the organization, and its people. These "Old Story Murals," twelve feet by three feet in size, were then presented to the total gathering at the end of the day.

The murals were all brightly colored imaginative renderings that tapped heartfelt feelings about current problems. For example, the mural *A Journey into Spring* represented the organization as a horse-drawn cart on a railway track about to go through a tunnel. At the other side of the tunnel, the track forked, one fork leading toward a dangerous set of rocks, the other, into a beautiful spring scene.

Repainting the Volkswagen symbolized the company as a series of old-style Volkswagen "beetles," repainted in several different colors over the period from the 1920s to the 1990s, with the background scene capturing key aspects of the organization: a tug-of-war team battling between productivity and service, bleak warehouses, controlling suppliers, stop signs, frowns, walls blocking new ideas, traffic lights constantly on orange.

Another mural captured the organization as a "juggling octopus," at first happy, then confused, and finally completely overwhelmed. Another depicted the history of a caveman wearing different fashions—superficially different but a caveman throughout!

Sailboats represented the organization as a boat caught in a storm, with its competitors racing ahead. The sails were tattered, and the boat was surrounded by mines—the competitive threats from the environment. The wind was blowing and the crew was bailing out. Overhead was a large productivity blimp, about to blow up because its fuse was running out. But in the sky beyond was an optimistic rainbow, symbolizing a possible future for the organization.

The Olympics featured an organizational Olympics with events that captured key aspects of the current enterprise: a "Paper Pole Vault," featuring a person trying to vault a mountain of paper; a "Tug-of-War"; the "Running into a Brick Wall event"; the "Scowling event"; the "Fire-Fighting event"; the "David and Goliath event"; the "Lost Soul event"; and the "Square-Peg-in-the-Round-Hole event." The humor penetrated to the heart of many aspects of the organization's malaise.

Ready to Burst, shown in Exhibit 10.1, is reproduced here to illustrate the richness of the images that were produced. As in the case of the murals described above, color, humor, and insight were intertwined to create a powerful view of the organization's old story.

EXHIBIT 10.1 "READY TO BURST"

NOTE: Both exhibits in this chapter have been redrawn to scale from murals 12 × 3 feet in size.

As can be seen, the mural starts at the left-hand side with a serpent blowing bubbles. The serpent had emerged at the theme party earlier in the day, symbolizing the "official questioner of reality" in the story of Adam and Eve. But, in the mural, staff placed the serpent in a new role. Instead of questioning reality and trying to play a liberating role, the serpent was blowing self-sealing bubbles, within which the organization was now caught.

The first bubble represents the organization as a box containing robotized people: featureless, boxed, lacking initiative and creativity. The second bubble contains an octopus with three different hats: a fireman's hat, a cowboy hat, and a hard hat, representing the different roles and demands placed on the octopus (the people in the organization). The octopus was colored red to symbolize its anger and frustration. It was angry and frustrated because the tools it needed to do its work lay outside the bubble! It was doing its best to break the bubble— the needle held by one of its tentacles being pushed hard against the inside wall. But the bubble won't burst.

Another serpent is watching what the octopus is doing. But it's wearing earmuffs! The official questioner of reality does not want to hear what's being said! The serpent has become a part of the problem. The role it could play in helping to burst the bubble from the outside is not operational.

The third bubble contains a jester with a serpent's tongue. The jester, of course, tries to convey fundamental truths in a humorous way, as is happening through the images represented in all the murals. But, even though he is trying to speak to the serpent, he is not being heard. He too has a needle and is trying to burst the bubble. But it just won't burst.

Bubble four contains a hatching egg, with a hand beginning to reach out. But the bubble is still sealed. New life in the egg is thus in danger of suffocation. It needs air to breathe. The bubble *must* be burst if there is to be new life and a future (for the organization). There is now a needle outside the bubble. Pressure is being exerted, but we are left anticipating the result.

The richness and continuity reflected in this mural are typical of the others that were presented. Each group took the task of producing a mural to heart and produced fundamental and challenging insights about their organization, presented with a humor that, in the style of the jester, made fundamental truths more palatable and manageable. Joe Arbuckle's role in all this was to facilitate their storytelling and then to draw out and integrate its common themes. In bypassing the organization's usual modes of dialogue, the visual imaging and storytelling created an opportunity for fresh insight and momentum to emerge. The process allowed people to tap into what they really thought and felt, and it allowed them to dig into depths of creativity that they were rarely able to express at work. Collectively, the process helped to create a shared understanding of common problems that could act as a powerful platform for change.

The focus of the second day of each workshop was "Creating a New Story." Joe took them through a new imaging process focusing on the business, the organization, and its people, this time with the future in mind. The day was framed by the president's aim of creating a more market-driven organization, the importance of which was now owned and thoroughly understood as a result of the previous day. Again, the imaging process produced a colorful and inventive response from staff.

The images of the *new business* were captured in pictures that replaced the stern, plain, staid images of the present with colorful, dynamic, fun, exciting retail stores that could be "experienced." They had more in common with a Disney theme park than the warehousing mentality driving the old organization.

The *new organization* was captured through images of hearts, brains, bridges, and spacecraft, for example:

- A large red heart connected with a large gray brain to show how successful innovation needed to have an emotional and integrated base as well as a conceptual one

- A bridge connecting innovative ideas with corporate goals, supported by pillars of resolve, determination, and teamwork

- A customer pulling all the different pieces of the organization together

- A spacecraft fueled by training, motivation, and a new culture: to replace the repainted Volkswagen that had been passed down over the years

Images of *the people* required in the new organization reflected similar themes:

Variations on the Wizard of Oz theme featured people that were whole and connected.

Multicolored Lego people were used to symbolize how staff should be different yet able to put themselves together in various combinations to create a variety of shapes. The differentiated yet interchangeable parts of the Lego set sent a powerful message about the power of diversity and the possibilities for new forms of organization and self-organization!

- Astronauts
- Windsurfers
- Mountain climbers
- Explorers of the unknown

- A party invitation inviting guests (staff members) to "Break Conformity," "Unleash Potential," and "Just Do It!!!!"

With all these images producing a rich and creative environment, the groups were then set to work creating a *New Story Mural*: one they believed could realize the potential of the enterprise in practice. The mandate was to review all that had gone before and produce a pictorial story that integrated the best images and ideas for shaping the future enterprise.

The murals again presented an impressive and colorful set of insights, for example:

- Space voyages decorated with symbols of the new retailing philosophy

- "The Store Is Our Stage": a new vision of the business as a form of theater with management as a performing art

- An innovative organization dominated by heart and brain, decorated with visual representations of progressive new forms of management

- A mural featuring sequences of a horse jumping a series of fences: As the fences got bigger, so did the horse! The mural was designed to communicate the idea of an organization that can grow with its challenges. In the background of the mural, there was a well-equipped barn, symbolizing the organization's capacity to produce great horses!

The images were all much more optimistic and empowering than those featured in the old story. Exhibit 10.2 illustrates how the suffocating and frustrated story captured in the "Ready (But Unable) to Burst" theme in Exhibit 10.1 became an optimistic and aggressive "Catch This!" challenge to the firm's competition. All the murals reflected this kind of general transformation and expressed the potential of the organization to move into an optimistic new future.

As can be seen, the *"Catch This!"* mural begins in the bottom left-hand corner where Exhibit 10.1 ended.

It features the bubble, the hatching egg, and the old serpent.

EXHIBIT 10.2 "CATCH THIS!"

But the serpent now has a needle. The earmuffs are gone, and it's breaking the bubble!

Inside, the egg has hatched. There is new life spreading upward. Pieces of Lego in orange, red, and blue sit side by side, symbolizing the diverse and flexible image of staff that had emerged in earlier discussion.

Above them, a butterfly is leaving its cocoon, symbolizing the transformation required in the existing organization.

Higher still floats a hot-air balloon. The Lego people are now connected in a new form, sitting in the basket. Above them, as a large motif on the balloon itself, we find an image of the customer-centered organization. The customer is drawing different parts of the organizational world together, building on an image that the group had discussed earlier in the day.

The balloon is linked to its basket through different colored ropes, all of which are equally important, representing the essential contributions of executive staff, head office, full- and part-time staff, clerical workers, and field management.

At the very top of the balloon is a purple Lego person symbolizing the creativity of people. This is linked through a flash of insight to an image of the new-style customer-oriented retail store, an image used to capture the vision of the new market-driven approach to business.

In the top right-hand corner of the mural is a baseball glove. Hence the message: "Catch This!" The whole story represented in the mural is being thrown as a major challenge to the competition that, until now, had left the existing organization way behind.

The invitation of all the new story murals was to develop a future that represented a dramatic rift with the past. The imaging process created enormous leverage for change, allowing staff to see and express existing reality in a fresh way and to come up with their own ideas for shaping a path to the future. Joe integrated the various insights emerging from the workshops, spelling out and consolidating the connections between the various murals, thus creating a valuable foundation on which the change process could build.

By the end of the second day, the mood in both workshops was extremely positive. Everyone seemed very pleased with themselves, and for good reason. In just two days, they had tapped an enormous amount of creativity, showing that, though people had joined the workshop in a rather tired, disillusioned, and frustrated state of mind, the opportunities were enormous. They had every reason to be very impressed with themselves. They were store clerks, accountants, middle managers, and vice presidents, not artists and storytellers. But they had brought out the artistry and storytelling from within themselves to forge an emerging vision of the way forward. Moreover, this was no abstract vision "out there" in a consulting report or strategic planning brief. It was a vision that used many different modes of expression to tell the same story. It was a vision that was a product of personal experience, personal feelings, personal reflection, and genuine dialogue. It was a vision over which they had direct ownership and of which they felt part. The vision was really an extension of themselves. In breaking free of the old-style images, they had created a valuable opportunity for remaking themselves and their organization.

Against this backdrop, the third day presented Joe with a relatively easy task.

The success of what had gone before created a new energy in which to explore the action agenda needed to realize the new story in practice. Continuing the theme of the previous two days, the president was placed in charge of a process designed to explore concrete ideas on how to "invent the future" by transforming current reality. Instead of focusing on fixing the old, attention was placed on creating the new. The mandate: to find the big ideas that could help to transform the business, its organization, and its people and to develop the implications of the ideas that seemed to offer most promise. The day created a vibrant exchange on specific policy initiatives, creating a detailed action base on which the change initiative could build.

As a result of the retreat, the president launched a major change initiative using the images and ideas emerging from workshop seminars as design principles for shaping the new organization. The transition from the repainted Volkswagen beetle to the futuristic starship was selected as a central guiding theme for throwing a "Catch This" challenge to the competition. Decisions were made to redesign retail stores to create a "high-tech," "high-touch" customer experience. The metaphor of store manager as "drama director" was selected as a means of making this a reality, with the president urging the company to rethink and refocus its activities to support the "on-stage performance" of the managers and their staff. To achieve this, decisions were made to restyle central organizational activities so that support to the stores, rather than control from head office, became the overarching theme. The roles of existing vice presidents and their staff were changed, so that they could become "resource partners" in the emerging network of stores rather than old-style line managers. Because the abilities of staff were crucial for making this new story come true, a search was initiated for a new vice president of human resources. This was accompanied by a clear commitment that the new-style employee would be valued as a creative partner in developing the new customer-centered approach to business. The images of employees as self-organizing "Lego people," windsurfers who can quickly adapt to a changing environment, and innovators who fuse the caring of "heart" and the creativity of "brain" were selected as central ways of expressing the challenge.

In this way, the emerging strategy sought to break the self-sealing bubbles that were holding the organization into its old alignment, to provide the vital "jab" needed to provide life-enhancing air!

VISUAL IMAGING CAN PRODUCE POWERFUL RESULTS

Joe Arbuckle's intervention provides a wonderful illustration of "picture power" in practice. It shows how people can be encouraged to tap their creative insights. It also shows how these can then be molded into a strategy for change. We have here an illustration of the enormous creative power that rests within each and every organization. In looking at the images and murals that were produced, and in reflecting on the themes and messages they communicated, it's easy to forget that they were generated by a normal, everyday group of people, in a normal, everyday organization. There were no Picassos and no great philosophers or well-known storytellers among their number. They were regular people using basic insights and imagery to communicate what they felt were fundamental truths about the state of their organization and its possibilities.

The case thus speaks to the power and possibilities of imagin- ization in practice. It illustrates how modes of visual imaging can break the constraints of an organization's conventional discourse and create the new space or new ground on which new developments can be built.

Rudderless boats
Headless horsemen
Firemen with defective hoses
Self-sealing bubbles
Repainted Volkswagens
Starships
Lego people
"Catch This" challenges

These and the other images illustrated in this case speak far louder than any words, concepts, and theories about the orga- nization could ever do. They are unique, personal, and powerful. That's why this kind of process can provide such an effective means of mobilizing organizational change.

11 Living the Message

New images, new insights, and new understandings provide a springboard for successful imaginization. But new actions make it a reality.

The current chapter places special emphasis on the "action side" of imaginization, showing how images and metaphors can be used to create experiences where key messages are "lived," not just spoken. In times when people are often cynical and tired of rhetoric, this can have great impact. The chapter gives special attention to actions that can send "holographic messages" conveying the essence of change initiatives and illustrates how the "lived metaphor" theme can be used in managerial practice and for shaping organizational development and training experiences.

MANAGING THROUGH "LIVED METAPHOR"

Brilliant ideas and great insights often go nowhere. Most of us have had the experience of making a breakthrough in our understanding of a situation only to find that it eventually withers away. As we encounter the idea months or years later, we are left wondering, "Whatever happened there? A great idea. Why didn't it take off?"

The reasons explaining the failure of promising initiatives are often complex. Sometimes they contradict the existing culture of an organization and mobilize political opposition. Sometimes they touch "psychic nerves" or get lost in the heat of fighting other battles. At other times, they just atrophy as a result of dwindling commitment or lack of understanding. As a result, we have a variation on the "Futureblock" syndrome, with change processes that go nowhere.

There's an old golfing adage that says, "Drive for show. Putt for dough."

It carries a very important message for the way we approach the process of imaginization and, indeed, all organizational change initiatives. In golf, "the drive" is the most powerful shot in the whole game. It can be magnificent. But it counts for little if there is poor follow-through in terms of other strokes on the fairway and the green. The metaphor speaks to the fate of so many change projects. Imaging and visioning style can be expansive and exciting. People can get thoroughly involved and even get carried away with their creativity and the possibilities this opens. But, unless this is brought back into the realm of action, and means are found to ground the insights in practice, the process counts for nothing. Indeed, the outcome can be worse. For the absence of successful follow-through on a project often makes it extremely difficult to launch another.

If we review the insights presented in previous chapters, it's the action side that presents the biggest challenges:

"How do I *implement* the spider-plant model in managing the groups for which I am responsible?

"How can we *get* the right people to carry the ball?"

"How can we *overcome* our blobbiness?"

"How can we *prevent* boiling dry?"

"How do I begin to *practice* being a strategic termite?"

The insights create an enormous drive forward, but there is still the challenge of putting the ball in the hole!

In my practice of imaginization, I find it crucial to find ways of going beyond the imaging process. That's why I've become so interested in patterns of "Futureblock" and in developing exercises and tools based on images of "The Gulf," the "Iceberg," and "Deerhunting." They help to identify and probe potential barriers to change and in discovering ways in which they can be overcome.

At its simplest, the message being presented is this: "Ensure that good insights receive good follow-through."

But there's more that can be done here. For example, it's often possible to take a holographic approach to the problem and find "key actions" or "key communications" through which one can *live* the message one is trying to convey.

For example, in developing a "spider-plant" approach to organization where the aim is to empower decentralized units to become more autonomous and self-organizing, a critical point is always reached when the time for defining an appropriate "umbilical cord" arrives. The traditional bureaucratic way of doing this would be to define the cord from the center, leaving the decentralized unit to operate within the parameters thus imposed. A more self-organizing approach calls for what I described in Chapter 4 as "cord dialogue": a process that allows the cord to be defined through mutual agreement. The definition of the cord can thus be used as a "key action" that either empowers or destroys the whole initiative. According to the way it is approached, it can be used *to live* the spirit of the new organization or to reinforce the spirit of the old.

This kind of "key action" or "key communication" has a holographic quality, because the event, simple as it is, embodies the character and spirit of the whole initiative. The whole is in the part!

We see the same phenomenon in the Teleserve case discussed in Chapter 5. The critical point in this intervention hinged on the readiness of management and union to create "space" for the new design initiative—space that lay outside the constraints normally imposed by budgetary procedures, signing authority, management controls, and collective agreements. Management engaged in a "key communication" in granting "new space" for the project, to which the union then responded with additional "new space" of their own. The communication embodied the essence of the whole initiative; it *lived* the new direction by symbolizing that the project was *not* just another case of business as usual.

In the Nursing Services case (Chapter 8), one of the key actions involved in sustaining their self-organizing initiative rested in using the image of "telling our story" as a concrete strategy for improving communication within the department and the rest of the hospital. It provided an easy, nonthreatening means of creating shared understanding of a new approach to organization that *theoretically* would have seemed very abstract and confusing.

In Network's experience (Chapter 6), the challenge was to find ways of overcoming the "blobbiness" in encounters with its hierarchical parent. Unfortunately, the intervention came too late to find a key communication that could reverse the decision to close Network down.

The message that I'm communicating through these examples is that in all change initiatives critical points often arise where the whole project is on the line. If we can recognize this, and be aware of the importance of finding holographic actions that reinforce the spirit of what one is ultimately trying to achieve, the chances of success can be much improved.

This idea has great relevance for how we guide processes of imaginization into an action stage. It also has implications for how managers and organizational development professionals can find ways of designing action-based programs that *live* the message they seek to convey.

Here are some more examples.

ACTIONS AS LIVING METAPHORS

The Fax

The president of a large manufacturing company is intent on reimaging managerial styles throughout the whole company. Traditionally, it has been a "top-down," highly controlled organization. He wants it to become more "bottom up," with managers playing support roles to their staff. A management development process for senior managers is put in place, including a seminar on the new styles in practice. On the morning of the seminar, the president faxes his job description to participants, with a request for suggestions on how it should be changed so that he can better serve their needs. He will attend the last hour of the seminar to hear their initial ideas.

The fax is a "lived message." It is a metaphor of what needs to happen in this company. The president wants to change the managerial and organizational style. What could be more appropriate than starting with himself? What could be more appropriate than opening himself to the ideas of his senior staff? What could be more important than doing this in "real time," immediately after the managers have participated in a seminar on the topic?

In effect, the fax says, "You are not just being invited to apply the ideas in the seminar to yourselves. Apply them *to me!*"

As a metaphor, the fax communicated a sense that change was urgent and "for real." The president modeled what the senior executives would need to do. The total communication created a powerful motivational context in which effective change could unfold.

The Move

A regional sales manager in a large computer company has been extolling the virtues of teamwork among his sales staff. The company is trying to develop "partnership" relations with key clients. Results are modest. The teamwork is just not taking off in the manner that was hoped. The sales manager suspects that staff are locked into old patterns. Hence he decides to do something about it.

His office is located on a different floor than the sales team. As he sits behind his desk, he can sense the remoteness. So he experiments for three weeks with not having an office. When he is comfortable with the new style, he joins the sales team. His new desk sits in the same area as theirs.

"The move" had enormous symbolic power. It communicated that the changes toward the team approach were genuine, and not just a passing fad, and that old structures and practices would have to change. Like the fax, it was a living metaphor loaded with meaning about the future direction of the sales effort. It succeeded in improving the quality of communications and teamwork and initiated a significant restructuring of the organization as other managers followed suit.

Graffiti Boards

A foreign subsidiary of a large U.S. conglomerate has just experienced a major change in top management. Its long-serving and highly respected chief executive has retired and been replaced by a senior executive from the U.S. parent. In addition, there are three new vice presidents, one of whom is a relatively unknown quantity, again brought in from the United States.

The company is very concerned about creating a smooth transition to the new management team, but the grapevine among the heads of the various businesses down below is working overtime.

"Who are these guys?"

"What direction are they going to bring?"

There are questions, concerns, and a lot of issues bubbling away.

The company is committed to a philosophy of open dialogue, so that irks and frustrations can be brought right into the open.

So the answer is simple.

Flip charts are placed before each of the business heads, and they are asked to record any questions, concerns, comments, suggestions, or ideas that they wish to communicate to the newcomers. These temporary "graffiti boards" are then physically carried into the offices of the new executives, so that they can see and "hear" what is being said.

The graffiti board comments are extremely frank.

The issues are in the open.

Everyone knows where they stand.

The newcomers have an opportunity to reflect on the significance and implications of what is being said and to prepare an appropriate response.

But, most important of all, this formalization of the grape-vine sends a strong message to the organization: We have new people at the top, but we are still an organization characterized by frank, open communication and will continue to be so!

The "graffiti boards" communicated key information to the new executives. But they were also "living metaphors" that affirmed the open and direct nature of communication within the organization. The charts themselves, and their physical movement from office to office, spoke as loudly as the words written on their pages.

In all these examples, we find action-based metaphors that have a holographic quality. Each makes a "key communication" capturing the essence of where the current situation is and where it needs to go. They capture and address the "whole" dilemma facing the people involved through actions that have enormous symbolic value. The *lived dimension* of the communication goes well beyond what words can say:

"Here is *my* job description: *Change it.*"

"Here's my desk: I'm *with you*."

"Here's a flip chart: *Write* what you've got to say."

Think about the power of the *actions* here as opposed to the more usual forms of verbal communication about, for example, "the need for a new approach to management"; "the need to intensify our commitment to teamwork"; "the importance of frank, open communication."

Managers often place too much emphasis on words. They can often be far more effective by adopting the approach of the managers described above: by finding ways of *doing things* that will symbolize the key messages that they want to get across, rather than just *saying* what needs to be done.

This challenge defines an important frontier for the development of imaginization through *action-based metaphors* that both symbolize and "live" desired changes. It seems somewhat contradictory to talk about actions as metaphors, because we tend to equate metaphor with the realm of thought and imagination. But there's absolutely no reason preventing the symbolism embedded in significant actions from being mobilized in exactly the same ways that we mobilize images to create new insights. Skilled politicians have long been masters of this craft, using significant *acts* to create new realms of meaning.

The same can be true in management generally, especially with regard to the management of change. The injunction is to search for significant actions that serve as holographic metaphors for communicating the essence of what needs to be done.

"LIVING THE MESSAGE" IN TRAINING AND ORGANIZATIONAL DEVELOPMENT

In applying the above ideas in my own work on the management of change, I have been particularly intrigued by the possibility of using metaphors for shaping the structure of learning events. Hence, when asked to design a novel intervention or learning experience that will communicate key information or messages to those involved, I frequently find myself searching for a resonant image or metaphor that will provide a design principle for shaping how we approach the task. The aim is to get beyond *telling* people what you think they may need to know by creating an experience that allows them to *live* the reality of what needs to be done.

Here are a range of illustrations.

Dealing With Earthquake Zones

The CEO of a manufacturing organization wishes to "open" and "acclimatize" staff to the challenges of the firm's changing environment. His first thoughts are that they need a series of talks or seminars.

Adopting the "lived message" approach, we build on a different principle. Staff are invited to a session designed to explore "earthquake zones." After a short overview of how social, economic, technological, and political trends are reshaping the world economy, they are invited to identify the "earthquakes" that could transform their organization or even put it out of business: just as automatic teller machines and home banking are reshaping financial services and fax and courier services are reshaping the postal system.

The "earthquake exercise" produces a vivid and penetrating analysis of key challenges. Staff confront the turbulence of the world around them, exploring how new technology and "Just in Time" management is likely to reshape the workplace; how information networks facilitate the emergence of new organization structures and managerial styles; how occupational health and safety legislation demands a new philosophy of workplace management; how problems of literacy and cultural diversity demand new forms of communications; how new economic trends are influencing the marketplace. They examine the problems and opportunities associated with these "earthquakelike" changes and identify strategies and ideas for shaping a corporate response.

In engaging in this process for themselves, rather than just reading the latest consultant's report or attending a series of seminars or briefing sessions on the various topics, staff internalize the challenges. They understand and "own" the significance of upcoming changes, because *they* are the ones who have identified the "earthquakes" and unfolded their consequences.

It's often amazing to see how this kind of process can mobilize key insights from "regular" employees drawn from the middle or lower levels of an organization, even though they have never engaged in any form of environmental analysis or strategic planning exercise. If the "earthquake exercise" is appropriately framed, so that participants are given an indication of some of the changes unfolding in the world at large, they usually have great competence in seeing the relevance for their organization and in anticipating likely consequences. By "living" through the earthquakes metaphorically, they put themselves and their organization in a much better position to deal with them.

Blocking Change

A group of middle managers in a telecommunications company have come together to develop an action plan to implement a new phase of their organizational development strategy. They have a history and reputation for being expert planners but also for getting blocked when it comes to implementation. Their plans are such great accomplishments that they often become ends in themselves!

To aid their process, it is decided to perform the "iceberg analysis" discussed in Chapter 7. They are asked to identify the kind of organization and managerial competencies they wish to develop as well as the forces beneath the surface of the existing organization that could prevent them from getting there.

They are then presented with the challenge of developing a detailed plan for *blocking* key changes. In essence, each person is asked to reflect on a key aspect of the desired change and to identify the six most effective ways of ensuring that there will be an *unsuccessful* outcome. The ideas and results of the exercise are then used as a basis for discussion with colleagues in the wider group.

Paradoxically, by focusing on what they can do to ensure failure, the group is often able to discover what needs to be done to ensure success. The approach obliges the group to confront and metaphorically "live" the reality of how they are experts at blocking change! The exercise confronts the fact that their expertise at planning, even action planning, lies at the foundation of their problems and, in so doing, creates an opportunity for them to move forward on their current project in a different way.

Corporate Theater

A European multinational comprising six businesses in the consumer products field is interested in helping senior HRD consultants from across the company improve their internal consulting skills. They want to create a "live" experience, using one of the companies as a site for applying the methodology to be used.

The first morning of the three-day workshop is spent exploring the approach. All 25 consultants have done some preparation in advance, so the session focuses on practical details.

In the afternoon, the president of the company whose operations will provide the focus of study attends the workshop. He provides a briefing on recent history and identifies some of his current problems, challenges, and concerns. He will return on the final day of the workshop, along with his senior management team, to hear the results of the consultants' analysis.

The following day, the 25 consultants arrive on site. Senior staff have made themselves available. The consultants are free to roam wherever they will and talk to managers and staff in all sections.

Later that day, they reassemble to "process" and discuss what they've learned. There have been surprises. The company, as the president explained, has major strengths and achievements. But there also seem to be major problems about which internal discourse was constrained.

As the consultants develop their conclusions, it becomes increasingly clear that their report on the final day will be difficult. The president had opened his operation because he was understandably proud of its achievements. As one of the HRD consultants put it, he felt as if he had "been invited to someone's house for dinner and was now faced with saying that he didn't like the wallpaper."

As the consultants wrestled with the situation, it was obvious that they had a major dilemma on their hands. A creative approach was needed. If the president were coming on his own, the task would be simple. But he was bringing his whole team!

A decision was thus made to "live the message" metaphorically. Rather than present a formal report, it was decided that six of the consultants would role-play a top management meeting of a key competitor and, in the process, communicate the key problems that had been found. The agenda for the meeting: to decide whether the competitor would try to purchase the company just studied.

The following morning, the president and his team arrived as scheduled. They were given a brief presentation on the work performed, and the meeting then moved into the role-play.

The effect was dramatic. The president and his team were taken right into the heart of the competitor firm, eavesdropping on what they had to say about the company. The message hit right home. It was obvious from the reactions that what "the competitor" was saying was ringing true. The president and his team were smiling at the humor injected by the consultants, looking around and nodding at each other, and taking a lot of notes. In a sense, this was no role-play. It was *exactly* what the competitor might be doing and saying at that very moment.

The "competitor" could say everything that "polite insiders" felt constrained to say. The president could "hear" messages delivered by the competitor, despite the fact that they were unpalatable, especially when expressed by his own staff. Discussion following the role-play was animated and focused. The president and his team were delighted with the results. The experience succeeded in opening a new area of discourse and development for the top management team.

Bringing a Network to Life

Link is a not-for-profit service network linking hundreds of handicapped people and their families. It has reached a crisis in its development. After 10 years playing an advocacy role for its constituents, networking with schools, boards of education, business, government, and a variety of social service organizations, its core of volunteer staff are feeling "burned out." They are tired and worried about whether Link has a future. Despite its obvious contributions to the community, and its support to members as "the door that never closes," important questions are being asked. Over the years, Link has managed to create and "spin off" several sister organizations serving special needs. Therefore: "Does Link need to continue to exist?" "Has it served its purpose?" "Can the sister organizations go it alone?"

A year earlier, a strategic review of the organization had been conducted by a team of consultants who did a thorough analysis of the nature and requirements of the organization, but in a way that drained its energy. At a retreat convened to discuss the findings, the idea of terminating Link gained ground to such an extent that people began to feel it was already dead. The meeting, later described as "the death meeting," overpowered participants, pushing them into a deep negativity.

But a hard core refused to let it die. They felt that Link was playing a crucial role in holding the sister organizations together and in allowing them to speak with a common vision and voice. Without that focus, they felt the "spin-offs" could begin to lose ground. They stumbled on in a disempowered state, recognizing the strong potential for development if the current malaise could be broken. They sought new board members to inject new energy and looked forward to the network's tenth anniversary as a breakthrough point.

They wanted an energizing, upbeat "birthday party" to spark and reaffirm the power of Link's contribution.

Invitations were mailed, and just over 20 people arrived for the celebration, a good turnout given the current malaise.

Everyone sat in a circle, and after a short introduction several rolls of party streamers were placed at the center of the group. One of the pivotal members of the network was then invited to unwind one of the rolls and ask others in the room with whom she had had significant contact in recent weeks to hold onto the streamer. Other people were then asked to do the same, using different colored streamers. Within minutes, the circle was crisscrossed with lines of colored paper, with the different colors highlighting diverse patterns of interaction.

The effect was quite astounding. Within ten fun-filled minutes, the *reality* of the network had been physically re-created before everyone's eyes. It was there for everyone to see.

"What's this about the network being dead?"

There were hundreds of interconnections.

Whatever the talk of death, the reality was life.

To show its depth and vitality, those present were then invited to share their stories and feelings about the people at the other end of their streamers.

People held those streamers for more than two hours as stories and tears flowed. Everyone spoke. They discovered the reality of their immediate history. They celebrated each other. They celebrated Link. And, as they listened, they gleaned new insight and new inspiration and made new connections.

The sheer strength, power, dedication, and potential of the people sitting around the circle were there for everyone to feel and see. Link was alive before their eyes. It was no abstract concept. It was no hollow organizational form. This was no institutionalized system of obligations and responsibilities. It was a real community with a shared vision, a shared energy, a shared understanding, and a shared burden.

There were no conclusions, no action plans, no resolutions—just a knowledge of the living reality of the network in practice.

After lunch, and a large birthday cake, attention moved on to the Annual General Meeting—one of the shortest, most positive, and upbeat Link had ever had!

The birthday was a watershed. It created new commitments and new energy, allowing Link to move into one of the most active and productive periods in its history.

All the above interventions around earthquakes, the blocking of change, the competitor role-play, and the party streamers provide examples of how action can be shaped and directed through "living metaphors." In each case, an attempt was made to structure the intervention around a metaphorical experience that would communicate central messages and insights. The aim was to help people "live the message" rather than just hear or see the message in a more abstract form.

"We're in an earthquake zone."

"We block change—so let's find how to do it *really* well!"

"Our competitors can see that we've got real problems."

"Our network is alive and well."

The four interventions built around these key messages, using evocative, dramatic, and highly visual metaphors to create an effect. Along with "the fax," "the move," and "the graffiti boards" discussed in the first half of this chapter, they illustrate how the process of imaginization can provide a creative toolbox for shaping detailed interventions of almost unlimited form. Whether one is a manager wishing to make a key communication to one's colleagues or staff or an HRD practitioner seeking to develop creative, impactful learning processes, the message is to use resonant metaphors for shaping key learning experiences where actions speak louder than words.

12 Rethinking Products and Services

Previous chapters have shown how we can use the process of imaginization to reshape the nature and style of organization and management. Now, I want to take the process a step further and illustrate how it can be used to rethink an organization's basic products and services.

Most of the chapter builds around an exercise. It invites you to use the metaphor of an Einsteinian world to think about how products and services can be reconfigured by focusing on relations between mass, space, and time.

Many products and services become "prisoners" of their underlying concept. They are usually generated by bright ideas. But those ideas often become constraints, creating patterns of thought that are rarely challenged. As a result, the products and services became vulnerable to new competition and are often caught off guard by developments outside the confining frame of reference.

Here are some well known examples:

Watches to swatches

Zips to Velcro

Cash registers to information systems

The watch industry was transformed in the 1970s by a reframing that switched the focus of attention from time-telling to fashion. Many traditional products were leapfrogged by new products based on digital and quartz technology that had more in common with disposable fashion goods than the solid timepieces of old.

Zippers, buttons, and laces have experienced a similar challenge from Velcro-style products. The reframing underlying the new development was stimulated by the metaphor of the hooked spines of the common burr. We all know how difficult it is to remove burrs from one's clothing after a walk in long grass. Velcro was born of the idea: "Why not make fasteners work that way too?"

Firms producing mechanical cash registers received a rude awakening from competitors that computerized the basic product. You only have to walk into your local corner store to see the extent of the transformation. Cash registers now form part of integrated information systems that compute and report tax, control inventory, and help in the analysis of sales. The development has turned the traditional "cash register" business upside down.

All these examples illustrate the power of reframing that lies at the core of imaginization. Just as images like the spider plant, political football, iceberg, and evaporating water can be used to create a fresh vision of a situation, and a new way forward, the new images underlying the above inventions opened paths to new development.

Donald Schön of MIT has given close attention to the study of innovation and was one of the first to recognize the role of metaphor in the reframing process. One of his famous examples focuses on the problems experienced by a group of product development researchers concerned with improving the performance of a paintbrush made of synthetic bristles. They tried a number of improvements, none of which really worked. Then, someone observed, "You know, a paintbrush is a kind of pump!" The insight led them to focus on exactly how paint flows between the bristles as they press against a surface and how the channels were defined through the bending of the brush. By designing the new brush to enhance a smooth pumping action, they improved performance considerably.

Paintbrush as pump

Watch as "fashion"

Fasteners as "sticky burrs"

Cash register as "information system"

The process is the same. By using metaphor to create new resonant frames of reference, it's possible to unleash many possibilities for innovation.

For example, a small California-based aeronautics company is developing a flying car. If successful, it will be able to fly out of the family garage, rise vertically, and then move at speeds of more than 600 kilometers per hour. The vision of its inventor, Paul Moller, is that this new kind of air traffic will be controlled by satellite, with the pilot entering the destination and relaxing for the rest of the trip as computers take over.

Moller's "skycar" is inspired by the image of a hummingbird beating its small wings at enormous speed. These birds can hover in one spot like an insect, fly backward, and move at high speeds. The key problem in using the image has been to find a way of developing a light, efficient structure that can produce the energy needed to keep the car aloft. By using composite materials that are as light as magnesium, and as strong as steel, it looks as though Moller's project will succeed, at least in prototype.

Just as the image of the common burr helped the inventor of Velcro find a way of replacing laces, zippers, and buttons, hummingbirds may guide Moller to create a new form of high-speed transportation.

In the rest of this chapter, I want to explore the implications of this kind of imaginization to illustrate how managers may be able to rethink their basic products and services on an ongoing basis. Rather than provide a broad range of illustrations, I will explore the implications of a single metaphor that has relevance for almost *every* product and service one can imagine.

The focus is inspired by Stanley Davis's book *Future Perfect*, in which he offers the challenge of thinking about the implications of a world in transition from the world of Newton to that of Einstein. Most of our organizations are based on the equivalent of Newtonian principles. What if they were to become more "Einsteinian"? Can they be reshaped by rethinking relations between mass, space, and time?

In his book, Davis gives a stimulating account of how organizations can use this reframing to overhaul almost every aspect of their activities, showing how many developments in the organizational world are in fact moving us closer to an Einsteinian point of view. As suggested in Chapter 1, organizations and their structures are physically dissolving and diffusing across space and time as they decentralize, globalize, and move toward flexible networking forms. Organizations used to be *things* defined by a specific location. Now they can be everywhere. Some are nowhere, using a "Model 6" style to subcontract virtually every activity in a way that renders an integrated organization unnecessary.

New technology is facilitating this development, creating a world where an emphasis on mass and tangibility is giving way to a focus on information and diffuse interconnection. Increasingly, we live in an information economy where meaning and value can be created in diverse ways. Information is interesting from an Einsteinian point of view because it doesn't really have mass. It is diffuse, abstract, and highly relativistic. It has no absolute value, only a value in context. The most valuable information today, for example, about an impending collapse of the stock market, will be useless tomorrow after the market has collapsed. As Gregory Bateson observed many years ago, information is a difference that makes a difference! What could be more symbolic of the amorphous nature of an Einsteinian world! Information, perhaps the key resource for adding value in modern times, is just a difference that makes a difference!

If you wish to open your organization to an Einsteinian revolution, Davis's advice is to rethink the role of time, space, and mass in almost everything you do. To illustrate, let's focus on how this image can be used to rethink products and services. Here's a checklist to get you going:

Rethinking Time

How does time affect your products and services?
How can you reshape the different aspects and implications of time?

For example,
    manufacturing time?
    service time?
    development time?
    consumption time?
    idle time?
    speed?
    other?

    _____
    _____
    _____

Rethinking Space

How can you reshape the spatial dimension of your products and services?

For example,
    size?
    shape?
    dimensions?
    location?
    other?

    _____
    _____
    _____

Rethinking Mass

How can you reconfigure the concentration, contact, and "feel" of your products and services?

For example,
  density?
  tangibility?
  feel?
  visibility?
  other?

  _____

  _____

  _____

As Davis suggests, many organizations and industries have made major breakthroughs by focusing on the ideas contained in the above list.
  Here are some examples.

RETHINKING TIME

- Note the revolution being created in manufacturing by taking time out of the production process, through, for example, Just in Time management and a general reorganization of work. It now takes hours instead of days to produce a car; weeks or even days instead of months to publish a book. We are moving toward instantaneous manufacturing systems that link producer and customer through the shortest route.

- Note the tendency toward the instantaneous in the service sector: microwaves, fast food, Polaroids, one-hour film developing, one-hour eyeglasses, shoe repair while you wait, guaranteed 30-minute pizza delivery, instant reservations on airlines, direct debiting in banks, partial automatic refunds on insurance claims.

- Note how idle time can be reduced through time sharing, for example, of vacation homes, rent-alls, computers, and through "Model 6" subcontracting.

- Note how competitive advantage in many high-tech sectors is developing around the speed of developing new products and bringing them to market.

- Note the "24-hour service" philosophy that's developing in sectors as diverse as television, banking, and retailing.

Just *one* breakthrough on the dimension of time could make a major difference to any organization! Sometimes the relevance of the idea may pop effortlessly into mind. At other times, one may really have to work for it.

To illustrate, let's take an extended example of a possible thought process.

Gasoline: How can you take the time out of this product?

We can push at reducing manufacturing and service time by streamlining the logistics of production and delivery to gasoline stations, with many potential cost savings. We can consider streamlining self-service systems, perhaps through more robotic pumps activated by your credit card. Perhaps the robot will even wash your car while you wait inside!

But let's push the time-saving dimension even further.

How can we save the customer even more time?

Perhaps by eliminating the journey to the gasoline station.

How can this be done?

A valet gasoline service: "Let us collect and clean your car while you work?"

Relocate gasoline stations at supermarkets, convenience stores, or other places drivers spend other time?

Or, perhaps, find a way of delivering gasoline at work or home?

The ideal solution would be for the customer to get his or her car "filled up" with *no* time or effort and at no extra expense.

Valet gasoline may be an answer. But it may be expensive with that extra service, unless there's an economy of scale. Perhaps it's possible to develop a contract serving all the cars in the office parking lot!

Or, perhaps, another look at the "service at home" idea may provide a better answer.

What if the customer is able to fill up before leaving home?

Our first reaction, it's impractical because of the storage problem!

But not if it's *natural* gas, especially if the gas is already being piped right into the home for other purposes!

But that's outside the gasoline industry.

Precisely!

There may be a long-term competitive advantage in service delivery to natural gas companies rather than to gasoline companies. Perhaps they should be expanding their horizons to embrace the automobile customer.

But, if we're talking about natural gas as an alternative fuel, what about solar energy?

You can "fill up" on solar energy at least 12 hours a day while parking or driving, so long as the car is in the open air.

Perhaps the long-term future lies here: with cars that don't need gas at all.

And, as an aside, what do you know! Solar energy has no mass and doesn't take space, though solar batteries and chargers do! Perhaps our gasoline company should be thinking about a realignment with auto producers to make this future come true!

The example is intended to be no more than illustrative of how a reframing of "gasoline" in terms of "time" may lead to any number of insights that have a potential to reshape and redirect product and service development. One key workable insight could have a dramatic influence.

RETHINKING SPACE

It's possible to create similar breakthroughs by rethinking spatial dimensions. For example:

- Note how design, a key influence on *shape*, is becoming a key feature of all goods and services. Increasingly, consumers demand elegance and relevance. They want products that are finely tuned to perform required tasks and services that are tailor-made to fit individual requirements. The age of giving the customer what the *producer* wants to give is rapidly disappearing. Customization is the rage: in insurance and financial services, pizza, cosmetics, and a host of other product and service sectors.

- Note how products are shrinking. Whether we are talking about computers, radios, chemicals, clocks, furnaces, or calculators, you can get more bang for the gram than you could just 10 years ago. Checkbooks and wads of cash are giving way to slim credit cards. Packaging is becoming more compact.

- In the service sector, the physical and psychological space allocated to the customer is expanding: more room, more comfort, more ways of making an impact on customer perceptions, more catering to customer needs.

- Note how products are becoming multidimensional: stereo TVs; holographic advertisements; multiple-use video display terminals; multiple-head screwdrivers; "smart cards" that can access your bank account, pay your bills, provide insurance coverage, buy travelers checks, obtain discounts on purchases, and even pay for subway rides. The trend is toward products and services that do many things simultaneously and cover a range of potential contingencies.

- Note how products and services are becoming more portable: cellular phones, pensions, pizza, temporary buildings, banking services, Walkmans. Important competitive advantages can be found by enhancing the mobility of products and services, locally and globally. Even factories are being taken to their customers. For example, with developments in Just in Time manufacturing, it is not uncommon for suppliers to locate their manufacturing units on their customer's premises.

To take an extended example of how the implications of some of these spatial characteristics may unfold in a single context, let's take the case of business school education.

How can one reframe the spatial dimensions?

Let's start with the idea of location and then work into issues of shape, size, and dimension.

A business school is usually a place. But it doesn't have to be. We can decentralize and break the concept of place altogether by taking instruction to the students.

Traveling professors?

"In-house" company MBA programs?

Mobile classrooms in high-tech buses that meet in different parts of a city according to the clustering of students?

Rent space in a convenient downtown parking lot and you will be right on hand to suit the convenience of executive MBAs. You could even run lunchtime classes! You'd also be in the right place to run special seminars and programs for alumni!

You could develop videotapes and audiotapes that allow students to take home all the noninteractive elements of an instructional program, for example, exercises developing knowledge of basic tools and techniques.

One can "clone" outstanding professors, getting key elements of their contributions on videotape so that they are accessible to everyone.

One can build on the same idea, reaching worldwide for one's professorial staff. Target world-class professors and practitioners. Get them "on tape" and into the core of your program. Bring them alive instead of just getting students to read their ideas. Live conference calls can add another dimension.

A spatial rethinking of business education creates great opportunities for distance learning networks. They could use their mastery of technology to create the finest business programs in the world. Using a "Model 6" distribution system, or some variation on the franchising model, they could perform a vital role in making many of the above developments happen and in providing support services to local institutions delivering their programs.

One can use the same principles to build national educational programs, as some distance learning networks have already begun to do. One can use new technology such as teleconferencing and videoconferencing, fax, and air transportation to link students and professors in a variety of regional centers. This kind of distributed delivery system offers a great opportunity for prestigious business schools who wish to reach outward and make their programs nonresidential.

The possible variations are boundless.

Once one tries to break down the concept that "the business school is a place," many new options emerge.

The above discussion has focused on the idea of physical space. But it's also possible to explore the idea of reshaping intellectual space. Who dominates the curriculum: the professors? the students? the needs of business? the needs of wider society? In many business schools, intellectual space is defined academically; it is shaped by academic instructors with academic preoccupations in mind. In some schools, it is a business-dominated space, with practice and technique being all important, excluding everything else. Clearly, the whole concept of intellectual space can be examined, challenged, and reshaped in a variety of ways. It can be used to redefine the territory of business education to meet the interests of various stakeholders as well as the needs of society at large.

This discussion of location and space has already brought us to issues of shape, size, design, and the multiple dimensions of business education. Reshape content. Reshape style. Reshape delivery mechanisms. Reshape the temporal dimensions by shrinking, expanding, chunking, or modularizing programs. Concentrate on customization, perhaps by allowing students to shape their own personal program as far as possible, selecting content and preferred methods of learning.

Issues such as these force a basic rethinking of what constitutes a business education program. They show how a systematic attack on the concept of space may lead to many potential lines of development. As we look to the future, it is clear that the bulk of business education will *not* be offered on the pattern established over the last few decades. The new technological age is creating new capacities that promise to transform the whole educational process. The Einsteinian metaphor provides an excellent means of grasping some of the opportunities in a very direct and comprehensive way.

RETHINKING MASS

Here are some ways in which products and services are being physically transformed:

• Mass is giving way to information. Products are becoming smaller and more intelligent, rich in complexity, design knowledge, and information: Pocket-sized computers, activated by electronic pens, can recognize handwriting. Soon they'll be recognizing voice. Photocopiers can diagnose their own problems and, if necessary, use a modem to call a repair person. Seeds that are genetically engineered have the ability to resist insects and diseases. They are being loaded with new information, reducing the mass of the chemical and other mixtures that used to be sprayed on the growing plant. Genetic engineering, an information-based industry, is replacing the traditional mass-based chemical industry in agriculture!

In all these examples, it's the intelligence rather than the size of the products that counts.

- Many products are becoming more concentrated, more dense. In chemicals, we have the emergence of "gram chemistry," where thimblefuls can replace bucketfuls in terms of potency. Bank cards perform many functions. And think of steel, ceramics, windshield wipers. There's more power and ability for the same weight and volume.

- The tangibility of products is changing and becoming more ephemeral: "no film" cameras; the "experience," "ambience," and "delicacy" of a good restaurant; the secure "feel" of a bank or insurance company; the "sensation" of the new vacation spot or nightclub. Many firms are selling the intangible. People are buying things for qualities that hang in midair. They are being sold on perceptions. Firms that are rethinking tangibility by emphasizing desired qualities and reducing undesirable ones are gaining important competitive advantage.

- Along similar lines, visibility and invisibility are becoming important. In some industries and services, it's important to seem bigger, more powerful, larger than life. Auto firms work hard to create the image of "spacious" subcompact cars! Media and sports stars are promoted as giant superheroes. Advertising and design combine to highlight desirable features of a product or service, downplaying others. Visibility is an asset in some circumstances. At other times, it's a hindrance. Invisible, unobtrusive support, for media star, student, manager, or surgeon, can be extremely valuable.

So there are many ways in which we can begin to rethink mass! As an extended example, let's look at the relationship between mass and book publishing.

"Have you heard *a good book lately?"*

This slogan advertising audiotapes captures a key challenge.

Books can be dematerialized: in the form of audiotapes, computer discs, and TV images and through remote-access electronic storage.

People do not need books in the way they used to. Reference books, manuals, textbooks, directories, recipe books, and the like often occupy valuable space and are rarely read in total. If the reader can access the information he or she needs electronically, without much fuss, it's easy to envisage books being replaced by computers or modems linked to information systems. As is well known, the publishing business is becoming part of the information technology business and has to embrace the world of electronics and audiovisual media, not just that of paper and print. If "readers" of the future want to know about a topic, they will probably access an information network that will give the facts they need, and more—at your fingertips: five sample recipes for Quiche Lorraine, instructions for producing a small business balance sheet, a short sci-fi story by Isaac Asimov, printed on command!

Of interest, these new possibilities also help to identify niches where the product will still be wanted in a traditional form. Attention is directed to books that are likely to read in detail and where feel, relationship, or tangible contact with the book is important: novels that are read in bed; ornamental books for coffee tables, display cases, and waiting rooms; gift books that have personal significance.

A focus on visibility, feel, texture, contact, and personal identification with the reader may lend insight here. How can one enhance touch and feel and, perhaps, smell? How can one develop books as physical artifacts that have intimate appeal because of the nature and quality of their physical properties?

As in earlier examples, the above discussion is no more than illustrative, showing how it may be possible to open a line of thinking that can generate a key breakthrough or significant new idea. Note how many of the new opportunities in all three of our extended examples lie outside the bounds of the traditional industry or service in question. The Einsteinian metaphor helps to create a focus on emerging developments and provides a challenging means of opening traditional mind-sets to the needs and opportunities of change. Like all metaphors, it can help an organization think creatively about the new frontiers of its business as well as identify specific opportunities and ideas for product and service development. The trick is to find an insight that provides the germ of an idea that one can really build on.

Smelly books?

It seems an unlikely line of development.

But who knows?

13 If You Only Have a Hammer . . .

Imaginization provides an approach to organization and management that can contribute to processes of individual, organizational, and social change. As shown in previous chapters, it helps us to

—understand and approach situations with
 fresh perspective,
—find new ways of organizing,
—create new patterns of shared understanding,
—enhance personal empowerment, and
—develop capacities for continuous self-organization.

This chapter, along with the theoretical appendixes that follow, seeks to place the approach in broad perspective and to encourage its use in developing more creative approaches to management.

In discussing the role of language and communication in human and insect societies, Lewis Thomas tells an intriguing story about the wasp called *Sphex*. At egg-laying time, she flies looking for caterpillars. When she finds one, she swoops down, paralyses it, and carries it off to the entrance of the burrow to her nest. The caterpillar is placed right at the "front door," and the wasp goes inside to check that everything is still in order. She then returns to pull the caterpillar in. If, however, the caterpillar is moved just a short distance while she is inside, we begin to see the limits of her well-managed behavior. She will search for the caterpillar, deposit it at the front door, and engage in the nest-checking procedure all over again. If the caterpillar is removed a second time, the dragging back and checking procedure will be repeated in exactly the same way. If you wish, by moving the caterpillar every time the wasp enters the nest, you can lock the creature into an endless cycle of mindless behavior.

Thomas uses this story as a way of reflecting on some of the characteristics of human intelligence and the role that language plays in helping us to explore and understand our world. The wasp gets locked into unproductive patterns of activity because it cannot imagine any other way of doing things. We humans, on the other hand, have an ability to be much more flexible. When confronted with new, ambiguous, or paradoxical situations, we have the capacity to intensify our search for meaning. As a result of language, which gives us a capacity to play with nuance, we can reflect on the contexts in which we find ourselves. We can make sense of problematic situations and create opportunities to act in new ways. As Thomas puts it, one of the great things about human language is that it prevents us from sticking to the matter at hand.

I have chosen to use this image of the wasp as a way of introducing the conclusion to this book, because I feel that it captures so many of the problems and challenges facing the world of organization and management today. As humans, we have amazing capacities for creative thought and behavior. We have an ability to use these capacities to do wondrous things. But, all too often, we get stuck. We get stuck in taken-for-granted ways of thinking and stuck in actions that are inappropriate for dealing with the problems and situations at hand. We become like the wasp. Or, to change the metaphor, our ways of thinking become hammers, and every problem becomes a nail.

The concept of imaginization is offered as a way of dealing with this dilemma. As has been shown in all the preceding chapters, it encourages us to look at ourselves and our situations with fresh eyes and to mobilize and use our capacities for imaginative, innovative thought and action. It encourages us to recognize that we can become skilled "readers" or "interpreters" of the situations in which we find ourselves and produce novel understandings that will allow fresh actions to emerge.

Throughout the book, I have demonstrated this in practice, showing how the approach can help us to develop new ways of thinking about management styles, organizational design, approaches to planning and change, and basic products and services. I have shown how it can be mobilized through the use of images that can help to frame and reframe situations in new ways. I have shown how it can emerge through creative "metaphors of the moment" that pop into consciousness as a means of understanding and dealing with problematic situations. I have shown how it can be developed in a more systematic manner through imaging processes that invite people to generate creative metaphors for describing the problems and challenges being faced or by drawing pictures that communicate their point of view. I have shown how this process can be tactile, intuitive, and governed by insights and gut feelings and how the process can be captured and carried into the realm of action through "lived metaphors" where the medium becomes the message. And, in demonstrating all this, I have tried to emphasize how this capacity for imaginization is an innate skill that we all possess to various degrees.

One of my primary aims in writing this book has been to show how we can place these capacities for imaginative, innovative thought at the center of managerial activity to unleash that burst of creativity so badly needed on the management scene. As I go about my work in the field of organizational change, I never cease to be amazed at the creative possibilities that are waiting to be tapped and the developments that can unfold. They lie waiting in the individual and collective minds of those who work in organizations on a daily basis. But they have usually been pushed into the background and been replaced by more narrow technical concerns, which are characteristic of the machine age in which so much of our thinking about organization has been developed. As I have emphasized, we are now living in a new age, in an age where the stability of the world of Newton is giving way to the flux and relativity of Einstein. The challenge in this world is to develop capacities for self-organization rather than to "get organized," to develop organizing styles that can flow with change. The process of imaginization provides an ideal means of approaching this task.

In presenting the approach in practice, I have focused on the role of the manager and change agent and placed a lot of emphasis on telling stories of change projects with which I have been involved. I have tried to take you right inside the process so that you can see what it involves in practice. I have also tried to emphasize that the perspective can serve many different purposes and that the stories and cases presented are just illustrations of *how* the perspective can be used.

In the most basic sense, they offer an invitation—an invitation to make the process of imaginization *your own*. Whether you are a chief executive or factory worker, a manager or trade unionist, a youth club leader or computer designer, this invitation is the same. It is to take the stories and ideas offered in this book as a resource for developing your own style of imaginization, mobilizing your own creative intelligence to shape and reshape situations that are of concern to you. You may want to take away specific ideas like those generated by the spider-plant or the "termite" approach to strategy. You may be inspired to rethink your management style by "looking in the mirror" through metaphors generated by your staff. Or you may wish to develop your company's products and services by rethinking relations between mass, space, and time or through any other creative images that come to mind. If so, all is well and good. But, in taking away specific insights such as these, it is important to recognize that it is the idea that we all have the capacity to imaginize on an ongoing basis that's most fundamental. The invitation, as I say, is to make the process of imaginization *your own*.

In a way, the approach that I have described provides us with a creative toolbox for approaching managerial and other situations that can be replenished and refurbished on an ongoing basis. It's the generative toolbox provided by our individual and collective intelligence, a "toolbox" that can be used to grasp key insights about the problems and challenges that we face and to create the shared meanings that are so essential for organized initiatives to emerge. It's a toolbox that encourages us to use a hammer when a hammer is needed or else to develop another, more appropriate tool.

The invitation of imaginization is to become what Donald Schön calls a "reflective practitioner": someone who is aware of how images and assumptions shape how we "see" and act in the world around us and who is able to mobilize this to act in more informed and productive ways. The invitation is to become more effective "readers" and interpreters of situations so that we can become more effective "authors" of these situations.

In describing the approach in practice, I have tried to present as realistic an account as possible, highlighting both strengths and limitations. As I have stressed above, imaginization offers some ideas and techniques that can help us find more creative ways of managing and shaping situations. But it cannot be reduced to a simple recipe, and it certainly doesn't provide a magic wand. Creative insights and breakthrough ideas often run into problems if they encounter hostile power structures or are interpreted within the context of old values and old "cultures" that limit their impact to a variation on the status quo. The most creative and powerful imaging session goes nowhere if there isn't "follow-through" or if it fails to command the degree of shared understanding necessary to ground the ideas in practice.

These are the harsh realities facing any person interested in generating some kind of change. And they are not easily removed. As I have tried to show, especially in Chapters 6 and 7, it is important that they be recognized and that the idealism that we can achieve creative breakthroughs always be tempered by the realism that breakthroughs often have to be grounded in corporate cultures and politicized contexts that can make change a difficult and uphill task. Success has to be earned, often against the odds. It would be nice to have that "magic wand" or the "elixir" that will guarantee Hollywood endings every time. But, as every realistic change agent knows, Hollywood endings belong to the silver screen and to popular books on management that gloss and oversimplify the way in which success actually unfolds.

Imaginization is about empowerment and the art of the possible. But it's also about realism and the need to deal with nitty-gritty barriers to change. To be successful, we need to hold both these perspectives in mind.

In selecting a focus for the book, I have chosen to deal with the problem of managing in a changing world and of developing managerial styles and organizational designs that can self-organize and flow with change. This, in many respects, defines the frontier of management at the current time. Developments in information technology and the restructuring of our global economy are creating unprecedented challenges with which old mind-sets are unable to deal. We need new ways of thinking and new ways of acting. We need new modes of shared understanding, based on new images of what we need to do. As I have tried to show, I believe that the concept and practice of imaginization provides a powerful means for achieving this end.

But, as I write, I am aware of the broader challenges that we ultimately have to face. As management writers are urging, modern economies need to develop fast, flexible, adaptive organizations that possess all the qualities that I mentioned in the opening pages of this book. They need organizations that are able to "self-organize," "thrive on chaos," become more creative, "foster entrepreneurship," "stress quality," and so on. These are basic requirements for survival in a world of rapid change. But, when all is said and done, where does this lead? As the new global alignments and realignments emerge, and unfold in whatever way they will, we are still left with some basic questions about the kind of society this new flux is creating and about broader relations between the corporate world and planet Earth.

The dilemmas are clearly revealed in the challenges facing corporate leaders today. Because of the changes occurring in the global economy, they are having to downsize and streamline; they are relocating to Third World countries to take advantage of lower wage rates and looser environmental and labor legislation. In the process, they are contributing to the decline of traditional urban centers, adding to levels of unemployment, creating dichotomized societies, and perpetuating the degradation of the environment. As some freely admit, they are building a world that they would not necessarily wish on their children. Yet they continue to do so because they feel that they have no choice. They have to downsize, relocate, and follow the logic of the system, because it appears that is the only way that their organizations can survive.

My point is that the whole global economy seems to be locked into a logic of action that has a momentum of its own. But if we delve beneath the surface, we find that it is being imaginized and shaped by implicit and unquestioned images, exactly as the world of bureaucratic organizations was shaped by mechanical principles. To illustrate, take, for example, the influence granted to the metaphor of global competitiveness. Corporations and nation states seem to be gripped by an image of the world as an elaborate competitive game where there are winners and losers, and where the ultimate aim is to be on the winning side, or at least to end up with a reasonable scorecard. Competitive win-lose relations tend to dominate. Teams merge and take new forms to tackle new competition. The teams once played on national playing fields. Now they play internationally. Governments try to act as referees and rule makers, and to shape and reshape the game. They get very concerned when one team or group of teams seems to be getting too strong or seems to be taking unfair advantage. They try to create level playing fields. And so on.

My discussion is intended to be no more than illustrative. I have focused on a metaphor that seems to capture the spirit of the age. We are "playing a game" that demands fast, flexible, adaptive, self-organizing organizations. But are we giving sufficient attention to the rules of the game? Is the game the one that we ought to be playing? Is it the best way of shaping the kind of world that we want to see?

Global competitiveness, as a metaphor, highlights the importance of competitive cut and thrust, but glosses and downplays the importance of values associated with tradition, community, neighborhood, quality of life, balanced economies, social sensitivities, ecological issues, and so on. Like all metaphors, it skews understanding, because in creating one set of insights it obliterates others. The metaphor is, in many respects, being elevated to the status of a ruling ideology, and like all ideology, tends to create a form of tunnel vision. As a society we have a choice of allowing the metaphor to create a rather one-sided transformation of the social, economic, and ecological landscape, as the mechanistic metaphor did in the wake of the Industrial Revolution, or to imaginize in a more balanced way.

This seems to be the ultimate challenge lying before us. It's a challenge of imaginizing on a global level. Of course, this will not come easily. But, as globalization progresses, it's interesting to note that we are already having to question many basic assumptions. For example, we are beginning to talk about the image of a "borderless world," in which once-sacred nation-states are having to question the significance of their identities. The rise of global corporations and of organizations that can have a simultaneous presence more or less everywhere is also demanding that we rethink traditional relations between nations, governments, and business. Nations can no longer control their economies as they did in the industrial age, because the new forms of organization are shifting the power base. And, with the continued degradation of the environment, global warming, and the depletion of the ozone layer, planet Earth is also having its say.

All these conditions are creating a new context in which new forms of imaginization may be able to flourish. In particular, the rebellion of nature seems to be giving a new twist to the possibilities and to the urgency of the situation, because, as Thomas Berry and other ecologically minded philosophers are showing, evolution, as far as humans are concerned, now rests with the "mindsphere," with how we think! The stark reality is that we have to think differently. As I have shown in this book, we have to reimage the basic ideas and relations that shape our organizations. But, more fundamentally, we have to reimage and reshape relations globally and between ourselves. The challenge is to find new images and visions that can help us to deal with the new realities. This, I believe, is the real frontier with which our individual and collective imaginizations will ultimately have to deal.

APPENDIX A The Theory Behind the Practice

In the foregoing chapters, I have presented a view of imaginization with practice in mind. Now, it's time to address the theoretical base.

In the following pages, I provide a reflective essay on the key ideas shaping the approach. It includes a discussion of the role played by images and metaphors in the social construction of reality and provides a more detailed discussion of the principles of imaginization as a mode of personal empowerment and an approach to change.

SOME PHILOSOPHICAL BACKGROUND

As the twentieth century has progressed, increasing attention has been devoted to understanding how language, images,
and ideas shape social reality and our understanding of the
world at large. Interest in this notion can be traced back to
ancient Greece, but it's only in the last 80 or 90 years that the
view has achieved real prominence.

It is difficult to put a finger on the turning point. The whole
ferment in science and philosophy toward the end of the nineteenth century played a major part. Growing interest in electricity, electromagnetism, and the discovery of the subatomic
world in science was paralleled in the humanities by the discovery of the unconscious and a growing interest in phenomenology. The everyday world, while concrete, real, and or-
dered on the surface, seemed to be underpinned by more
complex structures and forces beyond the reach of traditional
explanations.

Reality was not what it seemed to be!

The new insights were also mirrored in the world of art as
strictly representational forms gave way to impressionism,
cubism, and searches for the hidden structure of things. The
work of Picasso stands as the most obvious example.

The ferment and change underpinning these developments
shook the roots of knowledge and spun off in many directions.
For example, in science, the stable worldview of Newton gave
way to the relativity of Einstein, with the relativity of the
physical universe becoming mirrored in a relativity of knowledge as scientists like Werner Heisenberg (1958) and Neils
Bohr (1958a, 1958b) showed how even the most scientifically
controlled experiments are shaped by the assumptions and
views of the scientists involved. If one studied light as a particle, it revealed itself as a particle. If one studied light as a wave,
it revealed itself as a wave. As Thomas Kuhn (1970) later
formulated the idea, it seemed that the mind-set or "paradigm"
of the scientist played a powerful role in shaping the nature of
scientific knowledge. In the nineteenth century, science was
seen as providing a foundation for generating objective knowledge. But, as the twentieth has progressed, it has become clear
that science, despite all the claims for objectivity, is just produc-

ing a form of socially constructed knowledge and that scientific "truths" are only "true" under accompanying sets of assumptions.

Similar ideas have emerged in the humanities. Take, for example, the relationship between language and reality. The early view, expressed in Wittgenstein's (1922) "picture theory" of language, was that reality *gives us* language: that our words, images, and ideas are reflections of the world "out there." The newer view reverses this, suggesting that words, images, and ideas are not neutral reflections of reality. They are the means through which we *make* our reality. This perspective, found in the work of the later Wittgenstein (1958) and philosophers like Derrida (1978), Gadamer (1975, 1976), and Rorty (1979, 1985), emphasizes that there are no sharp distinctions between subjective and objective worlds and that language and reality are part of an integrated life-world in and through which humans and their realities are coproduced. For example, in his later work, Wittgenstein emphasized how language and action are interwoven, creating a kind of "language game" through which people engage, understand, and experience their reality, shaping their world through the constructs, actions, and processes embedded in the game itself. In his view, we live our language as part of a broader activity or "form of life." Or, as Heidegger has put it, it seems that "language speaks us as much as we speak language."

The focus on language as a means of revealing how humans construct and *make* reality has proved very insightful, because, as philosophers like Jacques Derrida have shown, its use illustrates the complex yet fragile and tentative webs of meaning on which so much social practice is based.

Take, for example, the process through which we use language to construct meaning. Words, at face value, are clear and precise. They depict an image, idea, and agreed meaning. But is the process this simple? As Derrida (1978) and his interpreters have shown (e.g., Cooper 1989), language in the form of written and social text is never self-evident. Meanings and actions are always mediated by external contexts and points of reference. *Black* only acquires significance in relation to the concept and meaning of *white*, just as *day* takes form in relation to *night*. To grasp and understand even the simplest meanings, it seems that we have to draw on all kinds of implicit knowledge and engage in complex acts of social construction and interpretation that are tentative, paradoxical, and always in danger of breaking down. The worlds in which we live, it seems, are truly extensions of ourselves and the forms of life through which we experience and engage them.

All these ideas have been enormously influential, laying the basis for a general social-constructionist view that, whatever the characteristics of the "objective" world, they are *always* known and experienced subjectively. Humans play an active role in *constructing, making,* and *enacting* their realities (Berger and Luckmann 1966; Gadamer 1975, 1976; Gergen 1982, 1985; Weick 1979). But this view itself raises fascinating paradoxes, for, while humans can in principle be seen as active agents in perceiving, constructing, and acting on their worlds, they do so in circumstances that are not of their own choosing. For example, as philosophers like Michel Foucault (1973, 1980) have shown, there are all kinds of power relations embedded in the language, routines, and discourses that shape everyday life. People's views of reality are influenced by conscious and unconscious social constructions associated with language, history, class, culture, and gender experience. Often, these exert a decisive impact, locking people into a feeling that they are hemmed in by deterministic forces over which they have no control. As a result, despite our ability to enact or make our world, existing social constructions of reality often become difficult to break, with people becoming no more than passive "voices," reflecting and "speaking" their social contexts.

These paradoxes have brought the social-constructionist movement to an interesting point in its development, which can fork in at least two ways. One path leads to the view that, whether they know it or not, humans have the potential to make and transform themselves and their world through individual and collective enactments that can "real-ize" new images, ideas, and worldviews. The other leads to the conclusion that, while this may be true in principle, the deep structure of power relations lends the world a resilient logic of its own. While the former encourages people to see and grasp the liberating potential of new individual and collective enactments, the latter tends to dwell on the idea that, to change the social constructions that shape our world, one has to begin by addressing underlying power relations.

IMAGINIZATION AND THE
SOCIAL CONSTRUCTION OF REALITY

Imaginization, as an approach to understanding social reality and as an approach to change, belongs to the social-constructionist school of thought and follows the former path. It is underpinned by the idea that human awareness and knowledge have an unfolding transformative potential and that the images and ideas people hold of themselves and their world have a fundamental impact on how their realities unfold. Like those writers who emphasize how the social construction of reality is embedded in deeper power relations, I too believe that we act on a stage shaped by deeply ingrained assumptions and discourses, where certain groups and individuals have much greater power than others to shape the infrastructure of what we do. Knowledge of these deeper power relations can be instructive. But the image that we live in a world shaped by forces over which we have little control is generally overwhelming. It tends to create complacency and feelings of futility.

Hence, in my work, I try to strike an intermediate and positive stance. Along with educators like Paolo Freire (1970), who emphasize the liberating potential of human consciousness, I believe that people *do* make and shape their world and have the ability to do so anew. As the "power theorists" suggest, people often get trapped by the cultural beliefs and social practices through which they make their reality "real." They frequently lose sight of the ideas, attitudes, assumptions, and other social constructions that are ultimately shaping the structure and experience of their daily realities. But, despite this, they always have the potential to break into new modes of consciousness and understanding. This, I believe, can be a fundamental source of individual and social change and is the premise on which my approach to imaginization builds. I believe that change, though often difficult, begins with individuals; that, if people want to change their world, they have to start with themselves; and that individual change becomes social change when a critical mass of people begin to push in the same direction.

The basic perspective is captured in the so-called "hundredth monkey syndrome," related by Lyall Watson (1979). As the story goes, when sweet potatoes were introduced as a new food for monkeys living on an island off Japan, they got a poor reception. The potatoes were dropped in the sand and, while tasty inside, were unpleasant to eat. Then, one day, one of the monkeys was observed washing the potatoes before eating them. Gradually, the process caught on. Each day, increasing numbers began to wash their potatoes. Then, when a critical point was reached (the symbolic hundredth monkey), *all* the monkeys, including those on neighboring islands, engaged in the potato-washing procedure. Social change in human societies often has the same quality. When resonant ideas or new practices "catch on," whole fields of action can be transformed.

Imaginization, as an approach to change, seeks to mobilize the potential for understanding and transformation that rests within each and every one of us. It seeks to challenge taken-for-granted ways of thinking and, in the process, open and broaden our ability to act in new ways. While stressing the art of the possible, and of finding means of helping people to discover and shape themselves and their realities in new ways, it is sensitive to the realities of power. But it does not allow those "realities" to create a sense of immobility. Hence, throughout this book, I have tried to show how it's possible to increase individual and collective consciousness of how our realities are constructed and how we can tap our individual and collective imaginations as a source of change. While I have focused on applying the basic ideas to the field of organization and management, which is my sphere of professional interest, I believe that the basic philosophy can be applied to most aspects of daily life.

THE IMPORTANCE OF IMAGES AND METAPHORS

In terms of specific background, my interest in this social-constructionist approach to change originated in a study conducted with Gibson Burrell on how different worldviews shape how we understand organization and management (Burrell and Morgan 1979). One of the main insights emerging from this work was that social scientists, like people in everyday life, tend to get trapped by their perspectives and assumptions. As a result, they construct, understand, and interpret the social world in partial ways, creating interesting sets of insights but obliterating others as ways of seeing become ways of not seeing. It was the old story of whether light is a "wave" or a "particle." Pursuing the insights, I became interested in exploring how different theoretical perspectives could be used to broaden fields of study and to help people generate deeper understandings of the issues addressed.

This eventually led to further investigation of how social scientists working in the field of organization and management construct their theories and perspectives (Morgan 1980, 1983a) and to the role played by images and metaphors in shaping domains of study and in the social construction of reality. As I explored, I came to realize, along with other theorists, that metaphor is not just a literary or linguistic device for embellishing or decorating discourse. It's a primal means through which we forge our relationships with the world (see, for example, Brown 1977; Lakoff and Johnson 1980; Morgan 1980, 1983a, 1983b; Ortony 1979; Schön 1963, 1979; White 1978). Metaphor has a formative impact on language, on the construction and embellishment of meaning, and on the development of theory and knowledge of all kinds.

To illustrate, consider a young child who catches his first sight of the moon and says "balloon" or who, on seeing a tiger at the zoo, says "meow." The child is engaging in metaphor whereby familiar elements of experience (the balloon and cat) are used to understand the unfamiliar (the moon and tiger). This process, it seems, lies at the root of how meaning is forged: from the development of language to how we think and develop formal knowledge.

Language develops as concepts associated with one domain of meaning are extended metaphorically to another. To illustrate, consider the history of the word *organization*. It stems from the ancient Greek word *organon,* meaning a tool or instrument: "something with which one works." Gradually, the use of *organon* was extended metaphorically to describe musical instruments, surgical instruments, and body organs of animals and plants—hence the English words *organ, organize,* and *organization.* *To organize* came to mean putting connected "organs" into a systematic form, and the word *organization,* a collection of organs used to perform other ends. The idea of describing a group of people as "an organization" became popular in the wake of the Industrial Revolution and acquired mechanical overtones. Organizations, like machines, came to be viewed as instruments that could be rationally designed and managed, so that their human and technical "organs" behaved in a rational, predictable way.

The same process can be observed in the development of everyday knowledge and in scientific theory. Knowledge emerges and develops as a domain of extended metaphor. For Newton, the world was seen as a kind of celestial machine. Einstein's breakthrough on relativity came through imagining what it would be like to "ride on a light wave." The images thus created allowed reality to be seen in new ways and to be studied in detail through more reductive (metonymical) processes whereby the implications of the guiding image are elaborated in detail (Morgan 1983a, 1983b; White 1978).

Unfortunately, the key role played by metaphor in helping us to understand our world has become obscured. As the word *reality* signifies, people have come to believe that they are living in a domain of meaning that seems much more real and concrete than it actually is. The same is true in science. Scientific knowledge is often seen as searching for, and offering, "the Truth." If we take a close look at the process, however, we find that science is just offering an interesting and useful metaphorical perspective, an interesting and useful way of seeing and thinking about the world! This may allow one to act on the world and to produce predictable results, as in scientific experiments, but the broad context of interpretation and meaning is ultimately grounded in the linguistic and other socially constructed frameworks within which the experiments and knowledge are set.

This is a controversial and unpopular view in the scientific community because it undermines the idea that science *should* involve the generation of some kind of literal truth (e.g., Pinder and Bourgeois 1982; Tsoukas 1991). Indeed, metaphorical knowledge is often distinguished from "literal knowledge." Metaphor is seen as belonging to the realm of creative imagination. The "literal" is seen as something that is real and true, as something that has an unambiguous empirical correspondence. Yet, if we examine the very concept of *literal*, we find that it is itself a metaphor. The word plays on the image of a letter or letters and is connected with the notions of literate and literature. The connection would no doubt be much clearer if the word were spelled *letteral*! By *evoking* the idea of a "literal truth," scientists are in effect *creating* the idea that there is a nonmetaphorical realm of knowledge. But it's no more than a metaphorical idea, one through which we try to create the notion that our understanding of reality is a little more "real" than it actually may be.

All this may seem to be playing with words. But, at a deeper level, it concerns basic issues relating to the nature of knowledge. In the early eighteenth century, the Irish philosopher George Berkeley (1910a, 1910b) noted that objectivity belongs as much to the realm of the observer as to that of the object observed. This point is central to the issues being discussed here.

Knowledge as objective or literal truth places too much emphasis on the *object* of knowledge and not enough on the paradigms, perspective, assumptions, language games, and frames of reference of the observer. The challenge before us now is to achieve a better balance, by recognizing that all knowledge is the product of an interpretive process. To achieve this, we need fresh metaphors for thinking about the process through which knowledge is generated. Instead of placing emphasis on the need for "solid," "literal," "foundational," "objective Truth," we need more dynamic modes of understanding that show how knowledge results from some kind of implicit or explicit "conversation," "dialogue," "engagement," or interaction between the interests of people and the world in which they live (Bernstein 1983; Checkland 1981; Checkland and Scholes 1990; Gergen 1982; Morgan 1983a; Rorty 1979, 1985). Instead of seeing knowledge as an objective, known "thing," we need to see it as a capacity and potential that can be developed in the "knower"—hence my interest in imaginization as a process through which, metaphorically, we "read" and "write" the world of organization and management.

Imaginization, as a way of knowing and as a way of acting, seeks to advance the power of the "everyday knower" and the power of the "everyday writer" of social life!

IMAGES OF ORGANIZATION

My first attempt at exploring this process was presented in my book *Images of Organization* (1986), where I demonstrated the metaphorical basis of organization theory and showed how different perspectives could generate different insights. In essence, the book explored a series of *"what if . . . ?"* questions:
What if we think about organizations as machines?
What if we think about them as organisms?
    . . . as brains?
    . . . as cultures?
    . . . as political systems?
    . . . as psychic prisons?
    . . . as flux and transformation?
    . . . as instruments of domination?
As I developed the implications of each perspective, I showed how they created complementary and competing insights, each of which possesses inherent strengths and limitations. For example, while a "machine view" of organization focuses on organization as the relationship between structures, roles, and technology, the "culture view" shows how organization rests in shared meanings. The psychic prison metaphor shows how structures and shared meanings can become conscious and unconscious traps. The political perspective shows how these characteristics are often shaped by clashes of interest and power plays—and so on. I showed how all the different perspectives could be used to "read" the nature and significance of different aspects of organizational life as well as how the injunctions or implications of each metaphor offered specific ideas for the design and management of organizations in practice. Though the book restricted itself to using eight broad metaphorical frameworks to illustrate its message, it developed the idea that organization ultimately rests in ways of thinking and acting and that, in principle, there are no limits to number of images and metaphors that can be used to enrich this process.

My aim in all this was to show how managers and others interested in the world of organization can become more effective in understanding and shaping the realities with which they have to deal. Throughout, I was at pains to avoid asserting the supremacy of any given metaphor or theoretical perspective, because I wanted to encourage "the reader" to realize that there is no one theory, metaphor, synthesis, or perspective that is going to provide all the answers. Hence, in using the book, one is left with many insights about the nature of organization but with no single theory saying that "this is the best way of seeing or thinking about organization." Instead of trying to offer an authoritative statement on "the way organizations are," it throws the problem of interpretation right back onto each and every one of us—on "the knowers" rather than "the known." Or, as I put it in earlier chapters of this book, it obliges and encourages us to become "our own theorists," forging our own understandings and interpretations of the situations we face.

This is what distinguishes *Images of Organization* from the majority of books on organization and management. Most of these offer a specific theory for understanding and managing organizations or try to develop an integrated framework that highlights certain dimensions over others. They reduce our understanding of organization to a particular way of seeing. My approach, on the other hand, was to suggest that, because any *particular* way of seeing is limited (including the one being advocated!), the challenge is to become skilled in the "art of seeing," in the art of "understanding," in the art of "interpreting" and "reading" the situations we face.

In many respects, the approach fits what is known as a postmodern approach to understanding organizational life. The postmodernist movement has grown in strength and significance over the last few decades, suggesting that the search for universal, authoritative, "true" explanations of social reality are always problematic and incomplete because they end up elevating the priority of a particular perspective while downplaying others. As it is sometimes put, "the presence" of the ideas and insights highlighted by a particular theory or perspective always creates "an absence": the insights, ideas, and perspectives that are pushed from view. This creates a problem for anyone who wishes to interpret and explain something, particularly in science and the humanities, where explanations are expected to carry some weight and authority.

For the most part, postmodernism has only resulted in critiques of modes of writing and social processes that elevate one view over another: to disrupt what is typically viewed as "normal" and self-evident so that the problematic nature of "normality" becomes clear. This critical stance has done much to help us understand how biases and blind spots can accompany and sometimes dominate ways of seeing and how all "explanations" are only forms of rhetoric that seek to persuade people to join or accept a particular point of view (see, for example, Berman 1988; Calas and Smircich 1988; Cooper 1989; Cooper and Burrell 1988; Harvey 1989; Linstead and Grafton-Small 1992; Martin 1990; Reed and Hughes 1992).

But, in my view, there is another way in which the postmodern perspective can be developed: by recognizing that, because partiality, incompleteness, and distortion are ever present in explanations of how we see and understand the world, perhaps we need to develop ways of theorizing and explaining the world that explicitly recognize and deal with the distorting nature of knowledge.

My approach to understanding organization and management discussed in *Images of Organization* began to address this task. It is continued in the current book in my general attempt to develop the process of imaginization, as a mode of theorizing and an approach to social change that seeks to help people mobilize highly relativistic, open-ended, evolving interpretive frameworks for guiding understanding and action. The aim is to help people develop ways of seeing, thinking, and theorizing that can improve their ability to understand and manage the highly relativistic, paradoxical, and changing character of the world with which they have to deal.

The old mechanistic worldview, on which so much organization and management theory—and, indeed, science—has been based, encouraged a search for fixed theories and linear methods and techniques of understanding and practice. The postmodern worldview, which, of interest, is paralleled in aspects of the new science emphasizing the chaotic, paradoxical, and transient nature of order and disorder (see, for example, the work of writers like Gleick 1987; Hampden-Turner

1990; Jantsch 1980; Nonaka 1988; Prigogine and Stengers 1984; Quinn 1990; Smith and Berg 1987), requires an approach that allows the theory and practice of organization and management to acquire a more fluid form.

This is precisely what my approach to imaginization sets out to achieve. It develops the implications of the basic methodology offered in *Images of Organization* to create a relativistic, self-organizing approach to management and management theory capable of contributing to the challenges of the Einsteinian world in which we now find ourselves.

IMAGINIZATION AS THE ART OF CREATIVE MANAGEMENT

In terms of specifics, the current book starts where *Images* left off, inviting you to become your own theorist, using images and metaphors to engage in a continuous construction and deconstruction of meaning in your encounters with everyday reality. It offers a highly personalized method for understanding organizations using the metaphor of reading and writing organizational life as its dominant frame. Like *Images*, it treats organizational reality as a kind of "living text" that is simultaneously "written" and "read." Some of the chapters (especially 5 to 8) pay particular attention to illustrating "reading in practice," developing the themes introduced in *Images* and showing how innovative "readings" can lay the basis for innovative "writing." Others, especially Chapters 2 to 4 and 9 to 12, give specific attention to ways in which we can "author" or "write" new organizational realities through a range of processes that mobilize imaginative ways of thinking and acting. The whole book demonstrates the "become your own author-reader- theorist" theme in practice and pursues the no-limits-to-metaphor principle. It shows how traditional concepts of organization can be radically transformed through imaginative processes whereby new images and metaphors are used to create evocative and energizing patterns of shared meaning. It invites us to unleash our powers of creative thought, interpretation, and insight to broaden the possibilities for creative action.

In terms of specific practice, the process of imaginization illustrated in these chapters builds on a number of key principles. These are addressed below under three headings:

1. the interconnection between "reading" and "writing,"
2. how images can be used as "mirrors" and "windows," and
3. imaginization as personal empowerment.

The Interconnection Between "Reading" and "Writing"

At various points in this book, I have used the ideas of "reading" and "writing" as metaphors for capturing the challenge of interpreting and shaping organizational life. As noted above, this builds on the underlying metaphor of reality as a kind of living text.

At first glance, the image seems far-fetched. But, if one thinks about it, the language, images, ideas, and actions through which we write daily life parallel how a book uses words to fix and communicate meaning. Readers, whether of books or life, in turn create their own meaning; in effect, they add their own authoring to the text. In this way, the whole of life can be seen as a living "real time" process of simultaneous reading and writing, producing evolving and diverse patterns of meaning.

This metaphorical frame has provided the basis for a hermeneutic school of social theory specializing in the art of interpretation (see, for example, Boland 1989; Gadamer 1975, 1976; Hollinger 1985; Rorty 1979, 1985; Shotter 1990; Turner 1983). It recognizes that, as readers and authors of our everyday realities, we all have limited horizons, shaped by the values, assumptions, worldviews, interests, and perspectives that we possess as individuals and as members of social groups. Hence our readings and subsequent authorings tend to be partial and one sided, committing us to live realities reflecting all kinds of conscious and unconscious social constructions associated with class, gender, culture, and the daily context in which we live. The hermeneutic perspective focuses on understanding the never-ending circle of relations underlying this social construction of reality.

My theory of reading and writing organizational life builds on these core ideas, but in a loose way. My primary aim has been to develop the metaphor as a *method* for exploring the multidimensional nature of organizations, showing how the horizons generated by different metaphors can be used to create new insights and action possibilities. Richard Boland (1989) has provided an outstanding critique of my approach from this point of view. At its simplest, the approach involves developing a "diagnostic reading" and "story line," using different metaphors as frames for highlighting and ordering different aspects of the reality with which we are dealing. For illustrations, turn to the readings produced in relation to Teleserve (Chapter 5, Exhibits 5.1, 5.2), Network (Chapter 6, Exhibits 6.1, 6.3), and Stereotype (Chapter 7, Exhibits 7.1, 7.2). They illustrate how I try to remain open to multiple and evolving interpretations of a situation, picking up key cues and signals as I go along, to develop a "story line" that evaluates and integrates the various insights into an overall understanding of the situation. The evolving story lines in the above cases are reflected in the progressive development of the "readings," often captured through new images or metaphors of the moment that helped to make sense of the overall situation.

For example, in Teleserve (Chapter 5), my diagnostic reading developed from the multiple dimensions illustrated in Exhibit 5.1, to the interconnection between the political, cultural, and domination metaphors highlighted in Exhibit 5.2, to the story line that "we're engaged in a game of 'political football.' "

For any given situation, it's always possible to generate multiple authentic readings and story lines, because readings are just orderings of reality and are always shaped by the horizon of the reader and the interests to be served (Gadamer 1975, 1976; Habermas 1972). The analysis and story lines that emerge are really forms of rhetoric through which the "author-reader" produces an understanding that serves the interests and agenda that he or she brings to the situation at hand.

For example, the readings that I produced in the interventions discussed in Chapters 5 to 7 were shaped by my use of the framework developed in *Images of Organization* as an analytical tool and by my ability (or inability) to detect the nuances with which I was dealing. And the story lines that I eventually produced were influenced by the nature of the assignments and the interventionist role that I was being asked to play. For example, as I discuss at the very end of the Teleserve case (Chapter 5), the nature and outcome of this intervention would probably have been very different if the assignment had been shaped from "labor" or "gender" perspectives. These would have created different horizons, leading to different readings and to "story lines" and action strategies with different interests and aims in mind—hence the emphasis that I have placed throughout the text on how the process of imaginization can serve different and, indeed, competing interests. It depends on the perspective or horizon from which it is used!

This view on the essential relativity of imaginization links back to the point made earlier regarding "foundational" versus "conversational" approaches to knowledge. A foundational view leads one to look for authoritative, "this is the way it is!" interpretations of a situation. Imaginization, on the other hand, builds around the paradox that any given situation may have multiple dimensions and multiple meanings, which acquire significance in the context of interpretation. None of these is necessarily absolute or "true." The challenge is to recognize that as interpreters and constructors of reality we face many options and that, just like scientists studying light as waves or particles, we can't study all dimensions at the same time. Our challenge is to dialogue and converse with the situations with which we are involved, to "real-ize" meaningful knowledge, knowledge that will allow us to be edified or to act in a personally significant way. That doesn't necessarily satisfy those who are looking for an absolute meaning or "truth" in a situation. But it does capture what seems to be the nature of the human condition: that, as humans, we can only ever acquire limited, partial, *personally significant* ways of knowing the world.

Viewed in this way, we are encouraged to see the "reading" and knowledge generation process in terms of what Donald Schön (1983) has described as "reflective practice," as the product of a craft shaped by assumptions and perspectives of all kinds. Imaginization is a form of "reflective practice" encouraging us to become skilled interpreters of the situations with which we have to deal. It encourages us to develop our skills of framing and reframing, so that we can learn to see the same situation in different ways, so that we can remain open and flexible to multiple meanings, so that we can generate new insights and become comfortable with the paradox that the same situation can mean many things at the same time. It encourages us to become reflective, creative, and expansive in understanding the situations with which we have to deal. A reflective practitioner is someone who is aware of how implicit images, ideas, theories, frames, metaphors, and ideas guide and shape his or her practice and how they can be used to create new possibilities.

In this context, and in terms of my own reflective practice, it is appropriate to recognize that the concept of imaginization is itself a metaphor and, as such, has inherent strengths and limitations. In fusing the concepts of imagination and organization, it seeks to open the process of organizing to an expansive, creative mode of thinking, as opposed to the reductive mode that has dominated the development of mechanistic thought. It highlights and stresses creative possibility. But, at the same time, as critics may rush to point out, it can gloss and downplay the importance of existing power relations, a point addressed in the following pages, and may underestimate some of the deep structural rigidities in patterns of both thought and action. It thus suffers the fate of all metaphors, and indeed of all paradigms, concepts, and modes of understanding, in that it elevates the importance of certain aspects of reality over others.

In this regard, in presenting my approach to imaginization, I have tended to emphasize how new images can help to create new realities, perhaps at the expense of underestimating how new actions can also be used to create new realms of meaning. This is one of the limitations of the particular horizon that I have brought to the writing of this book. Chapter 12 stands as an exception, but much more could be said on the issue.

Images Can Provide "Mirrors" and "Windows"

At one level, the process of imaginization is about the art of framing and reframing (Schön 1963, 1979; Watzlawick, Weakland, and Fisch 1974). It uses images, metaphors, readings, and story lines to cast situations in new perspective and open possibilities for creative action. But there's another dimension to the process, involving a theory about the relationship between a system's sense of identity and its ability to change. More specifically, imaginization builds on the principle that people and organizations tend to get trapped by the images that they hold of themselves and that genuine change requires an ability to see and challenge these self-images in some way. The previous chapters have demonstrated the process, showing how images and metaphors can be used as "mirrors" through which people and groups can see themselves and their situations in fresh light, creating an opportunity for reflection and change.

I like to talk about the process as one involving "mirrors" and "windows." If one can look in the mirror and see oneself in a new way, the mirror can become a "window," because it allows one to see the rest of the world with a fresh perspective. Or, in terms of the imagery introduced earlier, it opens new "horizons," creating opportunities for new actions.

Hence, in the Teleserve case (Chapter 5), I used the image of "political football" to help the human resource management team *see themselves* in a new light so that they could reflect on the need for a new direction. In Network (Chapter 6) and Nursing Services (Chapter 8), I used the method of getting staff to describe the current organization and its problems through animal imagery so that they could see and express their problems and situations in an unconventional way. In Chapters 2 to 4, I tried to create similar leverage on the way we think about management styles, organization structures, and approaches to change.

The aim throughout is to disrupt normal ways of seeing so that people can ask constructive questions about what they are seeing and what they should do. I find the use of metaphor particularly powerful in this activity, because it creates distance and space from conventional ways of thinking: space in which people can feel free to think and act creatively. This is vital in trying to unlock new understandings or a new sense of identity, because one cannot create the new in terms of the old.

Several aspects of the process through which I generate and use metaphorical imagery seem particularly important in this regard.

1. Metaphor always involves a sense of paradox and the absurd, because, as illustrated in Exhibit A.1, it invites the users to think about themselves or their situations in ways that are patently false.

Shared features are emphasized

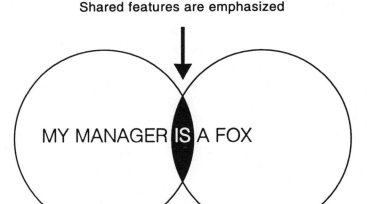

Differences are downplayed

The "injunction of the metaphor" is to:
   See the fox-like aspects of the manager: his cunning, guile, craftiness, smooth image.

But:

   Ignore that he doesn't have a black pointed nose, fur, four legs, or tail!

EXHIBIT A.1 The Nature of Metaphor

   "My manager is a fox."
   "I'm a strategic termite."
   "We're a spider-plant organization."
   "We're playing political football."
   "We're on the Yellow Brick Road."

Metaphor works by playing on a pattern of similarity and difference. Its user seeks to evoke the similarities while downplaying the differences. It involves the generation of a "constructive falsehood" that helps to break the bounds of normal discourse. This plays a crucial role in creating space for change.

2. Metaphor requires its users to *find* and *create* meaning. They have to *find* the similarities between the manager and the fox, to *find* the relevance of the spider plant, to *find* the precise way in which an image can create relevant insights. This helps to create distance and space from conventional understandings and also helps to create *ownership* of the insights. There is nothing self-evident in the meaning of metaphor; meaning has to be created by those involved. Meaning is thus immediate and personal, not distant or abstract.

3. Metaphors only have an impact when they "ring true," "hit a chord," and "resonate" around fundamental insights. One cannot force a metaphor to work, because the process soon becomes an empty ritual where everyone realizes there is little substance. The process thus has a self-regulating quality; there has to be a resonance and authenticity to create energy and involvement. When different people generate different metaphors that have a great deal in common (for example, Charlotte's spiders or the dandelion seeds and supernova in Network, Chapter 6), one knows that one is dealing with highly resonant insights.

4. Metaphors that are generated by the participants in a change project are often more powerful than those generated from outside, because they are directly owned and have immediate meaning. The facilitator of a process can, however, play a powerful role in finding resonant metaphors for capturing insights that others may not see or for recovering and synthesizing key insights that have gotten lost from view. In either case, resonance is key. The metaphor must energize and "take hold."

5. When metaphors are introduced from the outside, it's crucial that people be encouraged to find and elaborate meaning for themselves. When the implications of a metaphor are

laid out in detail, its evocative power is often lost. Metaphors invite a conversational style where meaning and significance emerge through dialogue; resonant meaning cannot be imposed, it has to be evoked.

6. The tentative nature of metaphorical insights means that they cannot be taken too seriously or made too concrete. This has the advantage of helping to create open modes of understanding that have a capacity to self-organize and evolve as one goes along.

When used with these principles in mind, metaphorical images can provide powerful tools for helping people look at themselves and their situations in new ways and, as a result, see and act in the world somewhat differently. The process operates by creating a tension between existing and potential understandings, creating space for the new to emerge. As I have illustrated in several chapters, however, new images do not result in new actions, unless there is an appropriate degree of shared understanding and a will to act on the insights thus generated.

This, I believe, defines an important frontier for development. People writing on the theory of change (e.g., Argyris and Schön 1974; Watzlawick et al. 1974) have made important distinctions between superficial change where the context remains invariant (called single-loop learning or first order change) and change where the context is also transformed (called double-loop learning or second order change). This has important implications for the practice of imaginization, because it highlights how one may be able to generate hundreds of new insights without substantial impact. The challenge of imaginization is to create insights that allow one to reframe contexts substantially rather than superficially. It's the old problem of rearranging the deck chairs on the Titanic! Superficially, one can create the impression of making a lot of changes; but, at base level, nothing of significance may have really changed.

This issue brings us back to the point made earlier about the role of imaginization in transforming horizons. Horizons define contexts. The challenge of imaginization is to help people see and understand the horizons that shape their context, to appreciate their limits, and to open up other horizons when necessary. Or, to change the metaphor, again, the challenge is to open new windows on the world, to create new ways of seeing that can lay the basis for new ways of acting.

Imaginization as Personal Empowerment

Large-scale transformation and change tend to occur when developments acquire the critical mass represented by the "hundredth monkey." But the process usually begins at a more modest level, with individuals or small groups of people taking the initiative.

This, I believe, is where imaginization has to begin.

Imaginization starts with ourselves and, in its broadest sense, invites us to assume our personal power in rethinking and reshaping the world around us. Against the background of the rigidities and resilience of old organizational structures and mind-sets, and the immense social problems that the universe now faces, this may seem like a call to spit into the wind. But, if modern theories of chaos and self-organization have anything to say, a lot of spitting can make a difference. It's a question of critical mass.

We have all probably experienced situations where individuals or groups have tried to imaginize and act on a new reality only to find the process reversed by those exercising power over their lives. We have all probably experienced situations where the gulfs and divides between rival stakeholders are so deep that those involved would rather continue occupying entrenched battle lines than find a shared way forward. We have all read stories of *successful* individuals, communities, and organizations that suffer dramatic reversals in fortune, perhaps being more or less eliminated overnight as the result of uncontrollable changes in the world economy. These are some of the harsh, all-too-real aspects of the socioeconomic context with which we have to deal. They point to what is happening in the infrastructure of the "Titanic," and at times it may seem overwhelming.

Yet, if we dwell on the enormity of the problems, our powerlessness soon becomes a self-fulfilling prophesy. For everyone, at every level, can see themselves as being hemmed in by processes and situations over which they feel they have no control. Employees often feel constrained by the perspectives, biases, and interests of their managers. The managers, in turn, feel constrained by "the culture" of the organization and the expectations that they feel *their* managers are imposing. These more senior managers, in turn, feel hemmed in by the dictates of HQ, stock analysts reports, and general corporate policy. Even the chief executive or chairman of the board can point to her powerlessness as she sees forces of global change buffeting and reshaping the economic context with which she has to deal. If we pursue the logic of this kind of thinking, we quickly find that no one seems to have any real power to do anything of any real significance.

But we do!

And that's why I bring the core challenge of imaginization right down to the issue of personal empowerment.

There are, no doubt, deep structures of power shaping the structure and logic of the global economy. We are, no doubt, caught up in all kinds of sedimented patterns of culture, ideology, and social practice that inhibit capacities for change. The power of macro global forces do encourage a sense of inevitability and powerlessness when it comes to having a significant impact on our world. Indeed, even the leaders of major countries sometimes feel that they have no power to shape things and have no option but to swim with the prevailing tide.

That's why we have to bring it all back down to the level of the individual and individual capacities for change—for change is an individual affair! Individuals can form groups, and groups can become social movements. But the process begins and ends with the commitments and actions of individuals. Certainly, it makes a big difference if one is the head of a large corporation as opposed to the average man or woman in the street. But it is the individual involved who has to move.

That's why I present imaginization as an attitude of mind that encourages people to become their own personal theorists, playing an active role in "writing" the realities that they would like to realize. I believe that our innate imaginizing capacities can serve us well in tackling some of the major social and organizational problems of the current time. We are reaching the end of a line of development associated with the mechanistic thinking of the industrial age and are in need of an alternative. We need new metaphors that can help us *remake* ourselves, our society, and our relations with planet Earth.

In short, we need to imaginize as never before!

APPENDIX B

A Note on Research Method

The purpose of this appendix is to take you "behind the scenes" and offer a perspective on the research philosophy and detailed methods that have guided the work leading to this book. It will appeal to readers interested in the potential of imaginization as an approach to research and as a methodology for making future contributions to organization and management theory.

To position my approach, I would like you to consider the following quotations.

First, from Marshall McLuhan (1978):

> Our new environment is electrical and resonant rather than visual, evoking a sense of primal involvement and touch, rather than the visual sense of objective spectatorship. In the new acoustic ground we naturally tend to relate by pattern-recognition of *figures in a ground,* rather than by the matching of objects according to verisimilitude.

Second, from Kurt Lewin (1949):

> To proceed beyond the limitations of a given level of knowledge, the researcher, as a rule, has to break down methodological taboos which condemn as "unscientific" or "illogical" the very methods or concepts which later on prove to be basic for the next major progress.

These views speak to significant elements of my research philosophy. Along with McLuhan, I believe that we are living in a new environment that calls for new ways of generating insight and knowledge. And, along with Lewin, I believe that certain methodological "taboos" have to be broken if we are to make progress toward this end.

Most of the case studies described in previous chapters are products of an action-learning style of research that has evolved as a result of my attempts to develop imaginization in practice. In this note on methodology, I wish to describe the basic principles as well as the status of the ideas and knowledge generated.

ACTION LEARNING

Action-learning approaches to research build on the idea that it is possible for the research process to have a dual objective in (a) trying to produce useful research knowledge while (b) using a process that can help the people involved in the research gain a better understanding of their situations. As the term suggests, it seeks to combine action and learning, to create a situation whereby everyone involved in the research learns while doing. As such, it provides an ideal style of research for people, such as myself, who are concerned to fuse the development of theory and practice and who wish to understand more about organizations through some kind of direct involvement and problem-solving activity rather than as more detached academic observers. The approach is most often used in problem-oriented contexts where the "researcher" is asked to help explore a problem or set of issues or to unlock some kind of new initiative.

Over the years, the approach has been applied in a wide range of situations. For example:

1. It has been used to develop processes of individual and group learning, as in Revans's (1982) approach to management education and problem solving whereby managers come together to tackle each other's problems. The aim is to create a learning setting where different perspectives are brought to a common problem so that the problem can be solved and, in the process, everyone can improve their problem-solving skills.

2. It has been used to generate organizational change and development initiatives through individual and group-based

processes of inquiry, as in Argyris and Schön's (1978) approach to the development of individual and organizational learning and in "Tavistock-style" approaches to action research (Baburoglu and Ravn 1992; Susman 1983; Susman and Evered 1978; Trist 1976, 1982).

3. It has been used to create initiatives in relation to complex, "domain-level" clusters of problems that reach beyond the boundaries of a single organization and demand interorganizational attention and action, through, for example, search-conferencing methodologies (Emery and Emery 1976; Morley and Ramirez 1983; Morley and Wright 1989; Trist 1982, 1985; Williams 1982).

4. It has also been developed through modes of "participatory research" and "participatory action research" (Elden and Levin 1991; Fals-Borda 1987; Freire 1970; Hall 1981; Harries-Jones 1991; Whyte 1989, 1991) used in group settings and designed to empower those involved to gain better understandings of their realities and to develop strategies for change. It has been used in this context as a tool for social activism and social change, particularly in mobilizing the interests of disadvantaged groups.

As a research methodology, "action learning" is closely linked with what others describe as "action research" (Lewin 1948, 1951; Rapoport 1970; Susman 1983; Susman and Evered 1978) and "action science" (Argyris, Putnam, and Smith 1985). All three approaches build on the pragmatist tradition of finding ways of linking theory and practice so that knowledge can be action based and derived from practice in the real world as opposed to being generated in scientific laboratories or through abstract survey methods. The tradition has been most fully developed through the work of John Dewey (1929, 1933), Kurt Lewin (1948, 1951), and Chris Argyris (1985) in North America and by members of the Tavistock Institute in England (Trist 1976, 1982; Trist and Murray 1990).

"Action research" and "action science" in the Lewinian tradition, as described and practiced, for example, by Argyris et al. (1985), Argyris and Schön (1974, 1978), and Susman and Evered (1978), places a great deal of emphasis on integrating theory and practice within a scientific framework. For example, Chris Argyris and his colleagues (1985: 4) see the key features of action science as involving the development of "(1) empirically disconfirmable propositions that are organized into a theory; (2) knowledge that human beings can implement in an action context; and (3) alternatives to the status quo that both illuminate what exists and inform fundamental change, in light of values freely chosen by social actors." Their action science seeks to develop a "science of practice." The aim, again using the words of Argyris et al. (1985: x), is to develop theory and knowledge that is "useful, valid, descriptive of the world, and informative of how we might change it."

Looser forms of action research have adopted more of a problem-solving approach, often with an emphasis on *action* rather than on research and theory building. Actions, or potential solutions to problems, are treated as "hypotheses" that can be subjected to empirical test and refinement. The aim is to find successful ways of solving problems and to disseminate the case studies so that people can learn from the experience and apply the methods in similar settings.

My style of action learning falls somewhere between these two approaches. It is less systematic and "scientific" than the experimental approach of action science advocated by Argyris and his colleagues, for, as I will explain below, it proceeds in a free-flowing mode that cannot always be carefully controlled. Also, the primary aim is not to produce valid *descriptions* of the world but accounts or "stories" of interventions that may create what I call "generalizable insights" that are relevant for understanding more about the intervention process and the key organizational dynamics, issues, or problems being addressed.

In more specific terms, the accounts or "stories" of my research seek to generate (a) useful knowledge about the process of imaginization in practice and how it can be used in other settings, (b) useful knowledge about its role and potential contributions as a method for guiding processes of organizational change, (c) insights about the role of the interventionist and the strategies and tactics that may contribute to success or failure, (d) insights about the ability of people to create their own personal images or theories of their situations and what they would like to see changed, and (e) an understanding of key organizational patterns and pathologies that can be of help in managing similar situations elsewhere.

I am most comfortable describing the research approach as a form of "action *learning*" because this is the image that seems to capture the nature of the endeavor. The research is conducted in a mode that seeks to generate learning on the part of myself and the client group with a view to helping the people involved to gain a better understanding of *their* problems and to initiate appropriate actions.

As in all action research and action-learning processes facilitated by "outsiders," the process demands many trade-offs and balances. For example, there are often conflicts between the demands of "good research," on the one hand, and of "practical relevance," on the other. Also, there's the dilemma of whether the learning process and definitions of "problems," situations, and potential solutions will be driven by the researcher, by the individuals or groups involved, or by some combination. In some modes of action learning, the researcher can take strong control, shaping the process to an enormous degree. In others, much more of a partnership relationship can be struck. For example, in certain modes of participatory research (see, for example, Elden and Levin 1991), considerable emphasis is placed on creating democratic processes of "co-learning," with clearly defined processes that help to ensure that the researcher's views and agenda don't have undue influence on the process. In some applications of this approach, the research is completely participant controlled, with the researcher-facilitator focusing entirely on *process*, avoiding any contributions that have an influence on content.

As will be clear from the case studies presented in earlier chapters, my approach builds on an active facilitation role through which I have an influence on both process and content. I am keenly aware, however, that learning cannot be imposed on a situation but must evolve in a collaborative mode. As I engage in an action-learning process, I thus try to be conscious of how my agendas and views may be shaping the process and strive to maintain a balance that allows participants to shape as much of the content as possible. As discussed in Appendix A, one of the principles guiding my practice is to "mirror" what people are telling me and to create every opportunity to work through their ideas and images rather than mine. This does not, however, stop me from taking an active role in shaping content when necessary, especially in trying to create crucial reframings that will allow new initiatives to emerge. Consider, for example, my use of the image of "political football" in Chapter 5. My aim throughout an intervention is to help people develop *their* personal theories and insights about a situation, so that they can be empowered to engage in new actions if they so choose. I also try to enhance the empowerment dimension by modeling processes through which they can achieve similar breakthroughs after the intervention in question has ended. In other words, the medium is part of the message; in engaging in the action-learning process, they can acquire insights on how they can use the process themselves at some future time.

THE METHOD IN PRACTICE

As I have described in most of the preceding chapters, my action-learning initiatives usually begin when I receive an invitation to help with a problematic situation. From the first moment, the project simultaneously becomes a data gathering process and an intervention that will lead to some kind of action. At the moment it begins, I have absolutely no concrete idea where it will lead or what specific methods or tactics will be used. My approach is to adopt the role of an "active listener" and observer. I become like "a sponge" or "blotting paper," absorbing as much of a situation as I possibly can—with a minimum of judgment.

The Basic Protocol

In terms of research protocol, I guide my overall research activities using a loose quasi-ethnographic style of research based on the principles described by Morgan and Smircich (1980) and Smircich (1983). For convenience and as a way of shaping a concrete protocol, I think about what I am doing in terms of the following five injunctions:

1. "Get inside"

2. Adopt the role of a learner

3. "Map the terrain"

4. Identify key themes and interpretations (to produce an evolving "reading" of the situation)

5. Confirm, refute, and reformulate throughout

One can think of these as five steps in the research process, but, in reality, they are iterative and overlap.

Point 1 captures the basic rule that an ethnographic researcher must strive to get inside a situation and understand it as far as possible on its own terms. As I like to put it, the researcher has to find a way of getting the situation "to speak for itself." He or she has to find a way of generating as much data as possible while exerting as little influence as possible.

Point 2 reinforces this, emphasizing that the researcher comes to the situation as a learner rather than an expert. Unlike a more conventional academic researcher, he or she tries to leave all hypotheses behind, suspending judgment so that room is created for new insights to emerge, as the situation "speaks." (This, of course, can be difficult to do, a point that I will address in more detail below.)

Point 3 captures the documentation process. The ethnographic researcher seeks to create a rich description of what is said and happening and of his or her experience of the situation. These data then provide the raw material for developing an evolving "reading" of what is happening by identifying the key themes and interpretations that can be drawn (Point 4). These are verified or reformulated on a continuous basis (Point 5) as the research process unfolds.

In this way, I strive to document and develop an understanding of the overall situation with which I'm being confronted, using the readings thus produced to frame and guide an appropriate intervention. As I have noted, the ideal situation is one where the researcher minimizes his or her influence, so that the situation can be understood on its own terms as far as possible. The ultimate aim would be to create understandings and explanations that are entirely "grounded" in the words, concepts, images, ideas, and theories of the participants involved (Glaser and Strauss 1967) and to mobilize actions generated from within the situation. This can be problematic, especially if the action-learning process is being conducted under constraints imposed by short time frames, by emerging crises, or by the inability of people to devote significant blocks of time to the project. Even though the researcher tries to "get inside," adopts the role of a learner, and tries to let the situation "speak for itself," flashes of insight and broad interpretations inevitably come to mind. Even though there may be no predetermined hypotheses to test, the researcher-facilitator inevitably brings frames of reference to the research and formulates broad ideas or "readings" of what is happening.

To deal with the above problems, I have developed the convention of drawing a somewhat arbitrary distinction between three classes of data.

Class 1 data represent the so-called objective facts of a situation, for example, historical data, numbers of people employed, finances, specific events, furnishings, wall coverings, and what's done and said in meetings. I say "so-called objective facts" because "facts" are socially constructed. In any situation, however, there are usually details on which more or less everyone will agree that are pertinent to understanding the situation and its history.

Class 2 data represent all social constructions of reality other than the above. These are the data collected through conversations and interviews and what people *say* about situations, about other people, and about how they interpret what is happening. This is the normal means through which the day-to-day reality of an organization is constructed; it also shapes how the reality of a situation is constructed *for the researcher.* Different people often have different constructions and interpretations of a situation, and it's important to build a rich picture of what these are because they define the multifaceted aspects of the "reality" with which one is dealing.

Class 3 data represent *the researcher's* social constructions of reality. These influence how he or she "maps the terrain" (Point 3)—because of selective attention, filtering, and other enactment processes—and shape the key themes and interpretations that emerge from the research (Point 4). They are the basis of the researcher's reading of a situation and, as illustrated in my case studies, ultimately shape how he or she understands and acts in relation to that situation.

As I have noted, the distinction between the three classes of data is somewhat arbitrary, but they can provide a powerful way of helping to minimize researcher bias and premature interpretation. For example, in my own practice, I try to absorb all the Class 1 and Class 2 data that I can. I observe, I listen, and I take copious notes. I try to produce as rich an account as possible. When I can't make notes in a situation, I reconstruct situations, meetings, interviews, and conversations as accurately as possible, recalling conversations, describing events, and noting details that may require further verification. I record my own interpretations (Class 3 data)—perhaps in the margin of Class 2 notes as a thought or idea crosses my mind or in a working note on its own, carefully dated to show exactly where and when the idea occurred. My aim is to produce a rich description of the situation that I have encountered together with an accurate record of my own thoughts and interpretations so that I can always trace my influence throughout the course of the whole intervention. This helps me to be conscious of the distinctions between my view of the situation and the interpretations of others and to understand when and why I am exerting an influence in one direction or another.

The stories that I have told about my projects in previous chapters draw on this kind of data base, weaving a story that shows the interplay between Class 1 and 2 data, on the one hand, and my Class 3 "diagnostic readings," on the other. As I have shown, the readings that emerge from a project can take many shapes and forms as events unfold.

Some Qualifications on the Nature of the Data Collected

I have described this approach to research as "quasi ethnographic" because, while it tries to document and understand the situations being encountered as fully and richly as possible, it is not always able to produce the "thick descriptions" on which pure ethnography is based (Geertz 1973). Ethnographers can

usually adopt a much lower profile than an action-based researcher, because, when interviewing or engaging in participant observation, the expectations and pressures to intervene,
facilitate, and shape a situation are less pronounced. The action
learner has to wear two distinct hats at once, one serving the
research agenda and the other oriented toward creating an
appropriate learning environment for those involved.

Because of these constraints, the data generated by the
action learner are often much rougher than those of the ethnog-
rapher, though tape recordings and team-based research can
do much to offset the problems here. This is one of the reasons
that I claimed earlier that my research differs from the "action
science" of Chris Argyris and his colleagues, in that it does not
seek to produce useful, valid *descriptions of the world* as a primary
aim. It seeks generalizable knowledge of a different kind.

Generalizability of the Knowledge Produced

Traditional science has drawn a distinction between the
scientist as observer, on the one hand, and the situation being
studied, on the other. It has built its foundations on the quest
for accurate, representational, replicable knowledge of the situations studied. The quest is to find generalizable laws, regularities, relationships, and facts in one situation that can be
extended to understanding others.

More interpretive forms of research, such as those found in
ethnography and action learning, do not necessarily search for
this kind of knowledge and, even if they do so, could never
claim such generalizability because they are usually restricted
by the nature of their methods to studying very small numbers
of subjects, often working with single individuals, single groups,
or single organizations.

To understand the significance and value of this approach
to knowledge, one has to reframe the whole issue of generalizability and approach it in a different way. I like to think of this
in the following terms. While the focus and priority of traditional science is to generalize "laws," "regularities," "relationships," and "facts," ethnographic and action-based approaches
to research seek to generalize *insights about the pattern* of one

situation that *may* have relevance for understanding a similar pattern elsewhere.

Hence, in my approach to action-learning research, my primary aim is not to produce a set of facts or statements on "the way things are" with a view to asserting an empirical correspondence with situations elsewhere. Rather, it is to render the rich texture of a situation in a way that will allow the reader to gain some experience of the situation and understand the patterns and processes involved so that he or she may use them as key insights or key learnings that may have relevance in understanding similar situations in other contexts. Specifically, through the stories produced as a result of my research, I seek to create two types of generalizability: (a) *generalizable* insights that capture the pattern of events and problems revealed in my case studies and (b) *generalizable strategies and tactics* through which similar problems or situations can be tackled elsewhere.

The first kind of generalization is similar to that sought by ethnographic researchers who engage in an in-depth study of a group, organization, or subculture with a view to helping the reader of the research understand the phenomenon studied. The generalizability here rests in the ability of the reader to achieve *insights* that he or she can use in understanding the same group or groups in other settings. It's to create what I call an "Ah ha! experience"—the feeling that "Ah ha! . . . that's an interesting insight that can help me in my problems or dealings with group x." Hence people reading my accounts of Teleserve (Chapter 5), Network (Chapter 6), Stereotype (Chapter 7), or Nursing Services (Chapter 8) may find themselves seeing and understanding other related situations through the patterns revealed through these cases. In doing so, they are taking away the generalizable insights and understandings that the ethnographic style of research seeks to create. But note that the generalizability rests in the resonance and relevance of the case *as constructed by the reader*; there is no direct claim or assertion, as in more conventional social science research, of any direct empirical correspondence.

The second kind of generalization—of strategies and tactics that may contribute to the development of problem-solving techniques or learning processes—is an objective of most action-learning initiatives. It reflects action learning's aim of creating opportunities for people to experience and see the relevance of a learning process that they can incorporate into their normal activities on an ongoing basis. Hence all the stories of my interventions seek to model and show the process of imaginization in practice, so that readers can develop and use the approach themselves. It is for this reason that I have given such detailed personal accounts of how my process of imaginization unfolds.

Hence, as you read my research stories, you will find that I am trying to enhance the generalizability of my research experience by blending several messages at once: messages about the process of imaginization, messages about the pattern of organizational events being described, messages about potential ways of dealing with them, messages about how one can create new forms of organizational design, messages about how one can reshape one's managerial style, and so on. Each research story can be read in many different ways; the kind of generalization it produces depends on *you*, the reader, as *you* use and interpret it as a reference point for understanding and acting in other situations sharing a common pattern.

Clearly, the generalizability does not rest in the "story" itself, as it usually does in a scientific paper offering a series of generalizable facts or relationships, so much as in the resonance the story *creates* in the reader's mind. It seeks to convey a very different kind of knowledge and insight than that sought in more traditional approaches to organizational research and should not be judged in conventional terms. In fact, I see the knowledge generated as being much closer to that developed through art and literature than science. Just as a painting, sculpture, or a historical novel may evoke some pattern of meaning in its "reader" or "observer," I hope that my studies will resonate and evoke ideas and personal responses in a wide variety of situations. This, ultimately, is what I mean by my research creating a resonant "Ah ha!" For example:

"Ah ha! I know this pattern . . . I've experienced 'The Gulf' in my organization."

"Ah ha! A spider plant! Maybe that will help our board of education's attempt to implement school-based management."

"Ah ha! . . . *I'm* a strategic termite! I can use that image to get a much better handle on what I'm doing, and why it works."

The *research* side of my approach to action learning tries to create generalizable understandings and insights that will create "Ah ha!" experiences for readers of my stories, just as my interventions try to create them for the participants directly involved with my projects.

Validity and "Resonance"

The above discussion of the status and generalizability of the knowledge produced through my research leads us to a related issue concerning the validity of ongoing interpretations and the conclusions that can be drawn from an action-learning project. This must be a concern for any researcher who wishes to get beyond the limits of his or her subjective experience and test the validity of emerging themes, interpretations, understandings, and overall reading of the situation with reference to the wider setting. I try to take this into account through Point 5 of my research protocol, which emphasizes the importance of seeking confirmations, refutations, and reformulations throughout the course of a project.

This is a key feature of all good scientific research, whether one adopts experimental, survey, or ethnographic methodologies. For example, good ethnography requires that insights, interpretations, and conclusions emerging from research be checked in as many ways as possible (Lincoln and Guba 1985)— so too with action-based methodologies. But, as in ethnographic research, there are limitations on the extent to which the kind of validation sought in conventional science can be achieved.

For example, in ethnographic and action research, it has to be recognized that the knowledge generated is always context based, so claims to any universal or broad-based validity are always problematic. For example, in such projects, "the true nature of a situation" can only be verified through the perceptions and interpretations of people whose perspectives are *always* shaped and bounded by the particular horizon of interests and biases that they bring to the interpretation. Thus, in trying to validate that one is producing an accurate description or interpretation of a situation or drawing an appropriate conclusion, one's views may be contested in different ways by the parties involved. There may be no single "valid" interpretation that commands agreement. Hence, in the context of ethnographic and action research, *validity* has an interesting meaning. In conventional science, *validity* carries the notion of truth and reliability. From an ethnographic and action standpoint, such "truth" and "reliability" are relative.

Just as we have to reframe the meaning and significance of "generalizability" as an aspect of ethnographic and action research, so too with the concept of "validity."

This said and done, however, it is important that the ethnographic and action researcher strive to get beyond the limits of his or her own personal understanding of a situation to ensure that there is some wider validation of what is being seen, thought, or done.

The most obvious way in which this can be done is by testing and verifying interpretations as one goes along, through discussions with research participants and coresearchers and by seeking reactions to written descriptions and the conclusions that are finally drawn. But, in the course of an action-learning project, this can be problematic because of the role one is playing. One is present in the situation as a researcher; but one's primary responsibility at any given moment may be to the "action learners" involved and the need to create an effective learning environment. This can create all kinds of conflicts. For, as one draws "Class 3" interpretations and "readings" of what is happening, it may not be possible or productive to share and verify them with others directly involved in the setting, at least at that moment. Such interpretations may be shaping one's interventions as facilitator, and there may be no way that they can be verified to the extent that a more pure research agenda might require. The ethnographic participant observer is at an advantage here, in that he or she may be able to make "verifying probes" by asking a specific question, or for more clarification of an issue, with minimal impact. But, if one is leading or facilitating a group process, such probes may destroy the climate or momentum that is developing. The research agenda may subvert the action agenda.

To deal with this problem, I have developed various tactics that lead to loose and indirect forms of validation. I think of these in terms of testing "resonance": the extent to which one is "in tune" or "in touch" with the evolving nature of a situation; the extent to which images, interpretations, and actions "vibrate" and create some kind of "echo" or response, either negative or positive, in the situation with which one is dealing. Anyone involved in an action-learning process quickly learns the living reality of resonance, vague though it may seem on paper, because, unless one is developing resonant interpretations of what is happening and finding appropriate responses and actions, one cannot stay in meaningful contact with members of the group with which one is working. Energy, interest, and enthusiasm soon wind down, and influence, control, and credibility are soon lost. This experience, and the associated patterns of energy, anger, denial, and overt conflicts within the group, and in relations with the action-learning facilitator-researcher, can be used as an important source of validation as to where things stand.

The difficulty, however, is that there are no clear guidelines to be followed here, and the typical situation is one where validity and "resonance" have to be tested on an ongoing and intuitive basis.

As I have shown in all my case studies of change interventions (Chapters 5-8), no situation ever reveals itself in its entirety from the beginning of an intervention. The interventionist often steps into existing situations that have a long history. Briefings are often biased. To understand the situation, the interventionist has to learn to "peel the onion" and move to progressively deeper levels of understanding. I have illustrated this in my case studies by showing how one reading of a situation leads to another as new pieces of information emerge or as a situation becomes significantly reframed through a combination of insights and events. This process of finding resonant readings or interpretations requires an attitude on the part of the researcher that is open and evolving. He or she has to be ready to change an interpretation as new information or insights emerge, validating or reformulating the unfolding "story" as the process goes along, using whatever information or opportunities present themselves. This is why I like to use metaphors such as those of "mirroring," "reading," or "having a conversation with a situation" to describe my approach, because they communicate the open-ended learning stance that is required in this kind of research.

Resonant images, "readings," interpretations, and conclusions "hit a chord" with those involved; they generate a response; they become "owned"; they become vehemently rejected; they become a focus of attention as people elaborate the meaning, implications, and further interpretations that are evoked; they tap or deflate the energy of a group; heads nod or shake; eyes light up; side conversations erupt. One learns to know when one is hitting this kind of chord and when one is dealing with significantly "valid" insights that can offer the new understandings and action opportunities that the action-learning approach ultimately seeks.

This kind of resonance can provide an important yardstick for judging how a project and one's interpretations are developing. But there are times when it is also necessary to look beyond the resonance, or its absence, because, to return to the "iceberg" image discussed in Chapter 7, a lot of issues may be lying beneath the surface. For example, resonance and excitement around an issue may be serving a diversionary function, displacing attention from more problematic issues.

For an example of a situation in which this can occur, return to consider "The Gulf" phenomenon discussed in Chapter 7. In organizations such as Stereotype, the very processes producing "The Gulf" may serve to cut off initiatives for dealing with it. If you find yourself in an action-learning intervention under such circumstances, you may find yourself producing a "reading" that you, as a researcher and interventionist, may believe to be a very accurate one, but one that cannot be verified directly with those most involved, at least in a safe way.

For example, try testing the idea that the top management team is projecting its internal problems onto the rest of the organization! One may be able to marshall a great deal of supporting evidence in the form of patterns of behavior in the top team that are reproduced lower down the organization. One's fellow researchers may also fully agree with the interpretation. But how does one test the opinion or obtain reactions from those most involved? Certainly, the top team may not wish to hear explanations of this kind!

In such situations, it may be necessary for the researcher to hang on to unpopular interpretations and find indirect means of testing them. Direct forms of validation could unleash all kinds of punitive consequences, especially if the problems are largely unconscious or are leaked and communicated along the organizational grapevine.

The whole process of interpretation and validation can prove to be an ethical mine field and require much creativity on the part of the interventionist-researcher. With hindsight, it's usually quite easy to see the interpretations or interventions that could or should have been made, but, in the real time flow of a project, decisions have to be made on the spur of the moment, and it can be difficult to see the forest for the trees. The only way in which the action-learning researcher can protect against these problems is by building an ethical stance into virtually everything he or she does: by being guided by a commitment to develop a full understanding of issues and by having the courage to do whatever is necessary to realize the agreed mandate of the project in which he or she is engaged.

SOME CLOSING COMMENTS

How can I understand what is happening in this project?

How can I validate my interpretations as I go?

How can I present my insights in a constructive manner?

How can I realize my mandate in a way that is ethical and that respects the competing interests shaping a situation?

What are the insights and ideas that can be generalized from this situation to others?

What can I and others learn from the project in which I am engaged?

These are the kinds of implicit questions that guide my research approach. As I have tried to indicate above, there are often strains and tensions because of the real time decisions that have to be made and the delicate balances that have to be struck between research and action agendas.

As I have shown, there are systematic principles associated with the action-learning style of research, but the approach cannot be reduced to a simple recipe. Rather, it rests in an attitude of mind and a set of skills that help one to keep in close contact with the situations with which one is involved. One of the primary requirements is that the interventionist-researcher

become fully engaged in an open-ended way and seek to contribute to the dual mandate of producing well-documented
research output and a practical contribution to the situation at
hand. I hope that the principles discussed above provide a
useful orientation for anyone interested in embarking on this
kind of research and help to explain the distinctive epistemo-
logical stance that is required.

I began this appendix on research methodology by linking
two quotations, one from Marshall McLuhan and the other
from Kurt Lewin. And this is where I'd like to end.

McLuhan's point is that our electronic culture is being accompanied by a new shift in awareness "from sight to insight";
from an emphasis on representation, matching, and a sense of
the objective to one built on "resonance," meaning in context,
and pattern recognition. This cultural shift underlies the birth
of abstract art and a concern for phenomenology, ethnography,
and the rich texture of things. The same transition is under way
in social science, as phenomenological, ethnographic, and action-based approaches to research emerge alongside the representational. As I have tried to show, an understanding of the
logic and practice of my approach to action learning requires
a reframing of how we view knowledge and the protocol
through which it is generated. This I take to be the essence of
Lewin's injunction to go beyond the limitations of a given level
of knowledge, even if this means breaking methodological
taboos that condemn it as "illogical" or "unscientific." Traditional social science builds on principles of observation, representation, and verification; action learning builds on principles
of involvement, innovative flair, and resonance. It's a different
way of generating knowledge, but one that offers the promise
of considerable *insight*.

Reflections
and
Connections

The following pages provide a guide to the ideas discussed in each chapter, cite some key sources, and offer some suggestions for further reading.

CHAPTER 1: INTRODUCTION

The approach to organization and management developed in Chapter 1 draws on a range of ideas about processes of self-organization and the social construction of reality, discussed and referenced in Appendix A, and links them with the emerging challenge of developing an approach to organization and management that can evolve with change. As a book on management, *Imaginization* has close links with other work exploring the challenges facing modern organizations as we move from a mechanistic to an information-based world (e.g., Beer 1975; Davis 1987; Hawken 1983; Kanter 1983; Morgan 1988; Peters 1987, 1992; Reich 1983; Stacey 1992) and with research on the need for more creative, intuitive, empowered approaches to management (e.g., Agor 1989; Block 1987; DeBono 1970; Russell and Evans 1992; Schön 1963, 1979). Collectively, these writings challenge us to recognize that we are leaving the age of organized organizations and are moving into an era where we need to learn how to facilitate and encourage processes of self-organization that allow "organized" activity to evolve and flow with change. This is what imaginization as an approach to organization and management theory, and as an approach to social and organizational change, helps us to do.

In terms of specific sources and ideas cited in Chapter 1, the story about the Alpine travelers who got lost in the snowstorm can be found in Weick (1987). For further discussion and references on holographic organization see the notes to Chapter 4. For further insights on self-organizing systems see Gleick (1987), Morgan (1986), Nonaka (1988), and Stacey (1992).

CHAPTER 2: LOOKING IN THE MIRROR

The ideas developed in this chapter are a logical development of the imaginization theme. If we can rethink organization and management through metaphor, why not ourselves? Parallel developments can be found in psychotherapy, medicine, and the growing field of personal renewal and development, where images and metaphors are often used to help people gain insights about their current reality and how it can be reshaped (see, for example, Gordon 1978; Hunt 1992; Siegel 1988). In the field of organization and management research, Beck and Moore (1985) and Krefting and Frost (1985) have used a similar methodology to explore aspects of corporate culture and the images managers hold of themselves and their organizations.

CHAPTER 3: STRATEGIC TERMITES

The process of drawing parallels between humans and the insect world has a long history but still remains controversial. Many people wish to reject the whole idea that there can be any meaningful parallels between what they see as the zombielike world of the anthill, beehive, or termite colony and human society. As Lewis Thomas (1974: 11) observes:

> It is quite bad form in biological circles . . . to imply that the operation of insect societies has any relation at all to human affairs. The writers of books on insect behavior generally take pains, in their prefaces, to caution that insects are like creatures from another planet, that their behavior is absolutely foreign, totally unhuman, unearthly, almost unbiological. They are more like perfectly tooled but crazy little machines, and we violate science when we try to read human meanings in their arrangements.

But, as Thomas and the emerging discipline of sociobiology are beginning to show, the evidence is overwhelming. Obviously, there are major differences between the social organization of ants, bees, termites, and humans. But there are similarities as well. Images of the insect world thus provide excellent platforms for creating new reflections on our own.

It is in this spirit that I evoke and use the metaphor of the termite colony, recognizing that many issues are still open to debate and that there's still a great deal of mystery as to how and why termites are so skilled and how they organize and develop their colonies. Is there a genetic blueprint unfolding here? Is the colony governed by invisible systems of chemical or hormonal communication? Or, as Rupert Sheldrake (1981, 1988) has suggested, is the termite colony analogous to a television receiver attracting signals and assuming form and pattern from what he calls a morphic field? Is the termite colony the manifestation of a collective brain with many bodies or, as Lewis Thomas (1974: 12) has put it, "an intelligence, a kind of live computer, with crawling bits for its wits"?

Readers interested in pursuing these ideas and exploring the intricacies of the insect world will find writings in the new biology of great value. My favorites are Howse (1970), Marais (1973), Sheldrake (1981, 1988), Thomas (1974), Wilson (1971), and Wilson and Holldolber (1990). For those interested in observing a termite colony at work, I recommend the film *Castles of Clay* by Alan Root (Benchmark Films, 1978).

The links between the organization of insect colonies and emerging processes of self-organization have been highlighted by Prigogine and Stengers (1984) and presented as an illustration of their theory of how order can emerge from chaos. The termite strategy is a metaphorical way of grasping some of the implications of chaos theory and ideas about self-organization. Developments of this theoretical perspective are likely to prove very important for organization and management theory. Initial explorations and contributions have already begun to be made by Nonaka (1988), Smith (1986), Smith and Gemmill (1991), Stacey (1991, 1992), Wheatley (1992), Zimmerman (1992), and Zimmerman and Hurst (forthcoming).

The "termite strategy" has much in common with the work of management writers like Henry Mintzberg and James Waters (1985), who emphasize the emergent as opposed to rational, preplanned aspects of strategic management, and of Beer, Eisenstat, and Spector (1990), who have demonstrated the advantages of decentralized approaches to change. It also links with Pava's (1980) concept of normative incrementalism, which stresses how coherent strategy can evolve from systematic small steps.

The discussion of Honda's motorcycle strategy, referred to in the text, can be found in Pascale (1983, 1984). Mintzberg (1974) offers key insights on the relatively haphazard nature of managerial work.

CHAPTER 4: ON SPIDER PLANTS

The story behind the spider plant provides an interesting example of how the process of imaginization can evolve.

In *Images of Organization* (1986), I wrote a chapter sketching the relationship between organizations and brains. Many writers on management have talked about "the brain of the organization" as a way of depicting strategic and other top management activities (e.g., Beer 1972). Their message: The organization needs a brainlike function to be effective.

But there is another way of pursuing the metaphor: by asking whether it's possible to design organizations as if they *are* brains and whether we can use the findings of modern brain research to develop new insights on organizational functioning. My chapter in *Images* addressed this task and gave particular attention to the parallels being drawn between brains and holographic systems. Brain researchers are using holographic imagery to create novel insights about the brain, and, extending the metaphor, I posed and tried to answer the question of whether it would be possible to develop holographic styles of organization.

As discussed in Chapter 1, the hologram provides a powerful image for thinking about organization and for exploring the possibilities of creating systems where the whole is contained in the parts. (See, for example, Morgan 1986 and MacKenzie 1991.) But it's a rather abstract image. For example, in talking with practicing managers, I find that ideas about holographic organization often generate a great deal of interest and excitement. But the metaphor gives no concrete indication of what a holographic organization would look like. A holographic plate smashed into 100 pieces doesn't provide much inspiration! Given this problem, I thus decided to try and find a more evocative way of communicating what a holographic organization would look like. Building on the idea that it comprised wholes within wholes, and had the capacity to reproduce itself, the first image that came to mind was a strawberry patch. But the image was confusing rather than evocative. It didn't resonate or add any useful insight or value.

Then the spider plant came to mind.

It seemed a perfect metaphor that could be used to capture the differentiated yet integrated character of a holographic organization.

As I pursued the implications of the metaphor in my management seminars and organizational change projects, all the features that I have discussed in Chapter 4 came into play— from umbilical cords to hybrid variations.

I now use the metaphor to help managers find creative ways of thinking about organizational design, for developing styles of "remote management" (Morgan 1988) that are simultaneously "hands on" yet "hands off," and for thinking about problems of organizational differentiation and integration following the seminal ideas offered by Lawrence and Lorsch (1967). Although the metaphor is powerful in illustrating holographic principles, I also find it powerful for communicating other key management principles as well.

I have chosen to tell the story of the spider plant in detail, because I believe that it provides a powerful illustration of the basic message of this book. We find in the story a progression of images leading from the idea that organizations can be designed as brains, to the images of the hologram and holographic plates broken into 100 pieces, to a strawberry patch and a spider plant. And from there, the image has been developed to focus on umbilical cords, hybrid flowers, and bumblebees.

There is nothing sacred or special about this progression of images. It simply illustrates imaginization at work as well as how one can move from image to image as one tries to wrestle with the basic problems and limitations of the ideas being generated.

I find the hologram an incredibly powerful image for thinking about organization. But it was the *limitations* of the image that led to the spider plant.

My chapter has been about spider plants, but the main message is that there may be many new metaphors through which the management process can be enriched. For further illustrations, one only has to look at the way management writers promote their basic ideas by building around resonant metaphors. Consider, for example, how Henry Mintzberg (1979, 1987) talks about different organizational configurations and encourages us to think about "crafting" strategy or promoting corporate innovation through the development of "hothouses" or "weed patches." Consider how David Hurst (1984) encourages us to replace organizational boxes with bubbles; how Mills (1991) invites us to think of his "cluster organization" as a bunch of grapes linked to a strong central vine; how Charles Handy (1989) evokes the images of an Irish shamrock and a "federal system" to capture aspects of the new organizational structures emerging in the global economy. All these authors are inviting us to build on resonant metaphors as a way of creating new thinking so that we can shape new patterns of action. They provide us with other examples of imaginization in practice.

CHAPTER 5: "POLITICAL FOOTBALL"

The story presented in the text provides an ideal illustration of what imaginization is all about. A simple telephone request to conduct a management seminar unfolds into a project involving significant organizational change. In the process, the problem being addressed gets framed and reframed in numerous ways as those involved attempt to grasp the nature of the situation being faced.

The work of Emery and Williams on Repetition Strain Injury can be found in Emery (1984) and Williams (1985).

Readers interested in exploring the literature on the socio-technical approach to organization should consult Cherns (1976), Emery (1969), Emery and Trist (1973), Herbst (1974), and Trist (1982). Those interested in exploring some of the social and organizational consequences of the new technology will find it useful to consult Zuboff (1988).

Discussions of self-organizing approaches to management and organizational designs based on autonomous work groups can be found in Hirschhorn (1991) and Mohrman and Cummings (1989).

There is a strong body of sociological literature on power, politics, and exploitation in the workplace, particularly as this relates to the use of technology as a form of control. (See, for example, Alvesson and Wilmott 1992; Braverman 1974; Burroway 1979; Clegg and Dunkerley 1980; Edwards 1979; Knights and Willmott 1986.)

CHAPTER 6: "WE'RE A BLOB OUT OF WATER"

As a case study, the Network story is particularly interesting in highlighting the kind of imagery that is necessary to shape and energize free-flowing organizations that build around a networking style. As has been suggested, these can't usually be managed through old models, where systems and rules are in control. When the energy and motivations of people are the driving forces behind an organization, they are usually best sustained through a "values-driven" approach to management.

Organization theorists have been talking for some years now about the importance of encouraging network styles of organization to meet the challenges of changing environments. The idea of creating a network conjures an image of crisscrossing patterns of communications and interconnections, linking people, institutions, or nodes of activity. It encourages outreach and exchange as well as collaborative endeavors that often allow significant new initiatives and patterns of connections to emerge. It provides a means of helping organizations think about alternatives to hierarchy and about how we can create more democratic, latticed forms.

But, despite all this, there is something missing. The image conjures an impression of a new structure; it places a lot of emphasis on process and on how networks are ultimately created and sustained by networking; and it encourages outreach and an expansive focus. But little is said about the networker or the qualities that people need to make networks come alive.

This, I believe, is where the likes of Charlotte's spiders and dandelion seeds should come to mind. The fundamental message of this chapter is that innovative approaches to organization may require us to think of our activities through such images and the holographic, self-organizing properties and potentials they imply. It also shows us how the images needed to help us articulate new organizational forms are probably already present in our organizations: in the imaginative capacities of staff and those who know the organization well.

The Network story is also interesting in showing how unusual metaphors can be used to identify and grasp core organizational problems in an evocative way. As noted, the image of the octopus as a "blob out of water" captures the failure of the organization to differentiate itself to meet the needs of different environments. As such, it addresses one of the key issues in Lawrence and Lorsch's (1967) theory of differentiation and integration.

CHAPTER 7: "FUTUREBLOCK"

So many organizations encounter "Futureblock." They are engaged in change after change after change but are not really doing anything very differently. One of the most powerful ways of understanding this phenomenon is through the concepts of "first" and "second order change" offered by Paul Watzlawick and his colleagues (Watzlawick et al. 1974) and the concepts of single- and double-loop learning (Argyris and Schön 1974, 1978). In essence, these concepts suggest that change can occur within an existing frame or paradigm (first order change/single-loop learning) or through the development of new frames or paradigms (second order change/double-loop learning). The first order changes that we see in Stereotype are changes occurring in a set context that don't really challenge that context—hence the "stuckness." To tackle "Futureblock," we need to become more skilled at second order change, which involves changing the basic context. Miller (1990) also provides a fascinating analysis of the "stuckness" problem, showing how success leads to failure as organizations get trapped by the patterns creating success.

The Stereotype story illustrates a common pattern found in many organizations. Indeed, I believe that the tendency of "Model 3" organizations to get stuck in their existing mode of practice is one of the major organizational pathologies of our times. Change efforts in these organizations frequently get trapped by the existing culture and politics of the organization. Though the organization may be formally committed to change, people and systems interact in ways that prevent change! I have tried to highlight key dimensions of this process in Chapter 7, but much more could be said. For example, readers interested in explaining the interconnection between structural, cultural, and political elements of change are referred to Tichy (1983) and Tichy and Devanna (1987). Readers interested in probing some of the deep psychological aspects of "Futureblock" are referred to the excellent discussions now available on the psychoanalysis of organizations. See, for example, Baum (1987), Denhardt (1981), Gemmill and Oakley (1992), Hirschhorn (1988), Jaques (1955), Kets de Vries (1991), Kets de Vries and Miller (1984), Menzies (1960), Morgan (1986), and Schwartz (1990).

In these texts, you will find comprehensive discussions of how unconscious processes subvert the pursuit of formal goals and objectives; how insecurities, projections, introspections, fears, narcissism, and other aspects of human psychology can shape leadership and interpersonal relations; how formal organizational structures, rules and routines, and aspects of corporate culture can be used as defenses against anxiety; how significant change often requires the use of "transitional objects" to help people take steps into the unknown; and how organizations may develop "neurotic personalities." I described these processes in *Images of Organization* as forces that often serve to create "psychic prisons" shaping and constraining possibilities for action and change. The psychic prison metaphor provides a powerful means of identifying and unraveling the intricacies of corporate life and hidden blocks to change.

All these issues have relevance for understanding phenomena such as "The Gulf" and the hidden dimensions of our organizational "icebergs," and I recommend this whole area as a veritable gold mine for developing new insights on conventional aspects of organization and for learning how to deal with personal and social resistance to change. In addition, the work of Argyris and Schön (1974, 1978) is important in showing how discrepancies arise between espoused theories and the theories in use that actually shape action, creating dilemmas and false foundations for change.

The contingency analysis offered in Exhibit 7.2, and related discussion, draws on a method for analyzing relations between organizations and their environment developed in Morgan (1986: 60-65, 1989a: 76-79). I find this a very simple yet powerful diagnostic scheme for gaining an initial grasp on an organization's internal and external alignments.

The basic assumption underlying a contingency approach to organization is that effective organizations succeed in achieving a "good fit" *internally*—in terms of relations between organizational structure, managerial styles, technology, and the needs, values, and "culture" of employees—and *externally*—in relation to the environment (Lawrence and Lorsch 1967). One of the main strategic challenges facing management is to create an appropriate internal and external balance while allowing for appropriate internal differentiation to meet the requirements of subunit tasks. Using Exhibit 7.2 as a rough frame for capturing key organizational relationships, the main point that needs to be emphasized here is that organizations like Stereo-type often get caught in malalignments because their internal configurations cannot keep pace with external changes.

My discussion of the six models of organization is based on a statement first offered in Morgan (1989a: 64-67). Readers interested in exploring these issues further are referred to the work of Burns and Stalker (1961) and Lawrence and Lorsch (1967) on the links between organizations and environment, and to the typologies of organization drawing distinctions between mechanistic and more flexible, adaptive, "adhocratic" approaches, for example, Mintzberg (1979). For a discussion of matrix organizations, see Davis and Lawrence (1977) and Kolodny (1981). For a discussion of emerging network-style organiza-tions similar to Model 6, see Handy (1989), Nadler, Gerstein, and Shaw (1992), and Peters (1992).

CHAPTER 8: "BOILING DRY"

References on the holographic approach to organization were provided earlier in these notes in relation to Chapter 4 and in *Images of Organization* (1986), where I sketch some of the key principles underlying capacities for self-organization. They are the cybernetic principles of redundant functions, requisite variety, learning to learn, and minimum critical specification. In Morgan (1989b), I show how they apply to use of the new technology, which stands as one of the most powerful means of spreading holographic organization in practice. Microcom-puters create powerful opportunities for developing decentral-ized systems of management where important elements of the whole can be built into the decentralized parts. They allow for the development of interconnected work units that are simul-taneously connected and separate.

CHAPTER 9: IMAGINIZING TEAMWORK

It's difficult to open a book on teamwork nowadays without reading about the great coach or player, or the team "on a roll," "playing above itself" game after game. The implication is that exactly the same kind of performance can be produced in everyday organizations. Usually, it's possible to find isolated examples that support the case. But, more often than not, the metaphor is overused. My aim in this chapter has been to put some of the issues in perspective and to warn against some of the dangers of trying to drop teamwork "from a helicopter."

There is a great deal of literature on teamwork in organizations and on how team-based organizations can provide a basis for creative, flexible modes of organization. See, for example, Hackman (1990), Hirschhorn (1991), Larson and LaFasto (1989), and Stewart (1989). My discussion on the nature of sports metaphors owes much to the work of Robert Keidel (1988), who provides an excellent analysis of the implications of games like football, baseball, and basketball for the process of organizing. They have different implications for the definition of roles and accountabilities, managerial styles, and systems of communication, monitoring, and evaluation. They have a major impact on the fluidity of operations, on the empowerment of team members, and on the intuitive and other informal connections that can bind a team together. Consistent with the theme of Chapter 9, Keidel believes that many organizations play too much football and too little basketball. The challenge is to move away from the bureaucratic style encouraged by the former and to facilitate the self-organizing activity found in the latter. It also provides a means of breaking the rather "macho" gender bias, which has tended to dominate thinking about teamwork up until now, by tapping more "female" images of teamwork in practice.

CHAPTER 10: PICTURE POWER

Techniques of visual imaging are making an important impact in many fields of human inquiry. In medicine and health care, patients are being encouraged to generate images and pictures of their personal well-being as a means of aiding recovery (Achterberg 1985; Gordon 1978; Siegel 1988). In sports, the power of visual imaging has been shown to be an important ingredient in successful performance, and, in psychotherapy and family therapy, the technique has a long history.

The ideas on "picture power" discussed in this chapter are an extension of this kind of practice. They apply to the world of organization techniques that have already begun to prove their worth in many ways.

CHAPTER 11: LIVING THE MESSAGE

The basic idea in this chapter builds on Marshall McLuhan's (1964) notion that the "medium is the message"; it provides an extremely powerful means of developing action-based approaches to change.

CHAPTER 12: RETHINKING PRODUCTS AND SERVICES

The ideas developed in this chapter are based on the work of Davis (1987) and have links with other writing on the nature of creativity. See, for example, the work of Koestler (1969) and Schön (1963, 1979) on the role of metaphorical processes in creative thought and of DeBono (1970) on lateral thinking.

Readers interested in pursuing the implications of the Einsteinian metaphor for organizational functioning are referred to the excellent work of Stanley Davis on this subject. His book *Future Perfect* (1987) provides a splendid example of imaginization using Einstein's insights as a launchpad. Paul Hawken's (1983) book *The Next Economy* will also prove valuable to readers who wish to explore how the "mass economy" is giving way to an "information economy." Readers interested in a more theoretical view of the role of information in society at large will find the work of cyberneticians like Gregory Bateson (1972, 1979) a provocative source of ideas.

Stalk and Hout (1990) have recently published an excellent analysis of the significance and role of time in developing competitive advantage in business contexts.

My account of Moller's "skycar" is based on Gooderham (1991).

CHAPTER 13: IF YOU ONLY HAVE A HAMMER

The story of the wasp is taken from Lewis Thomas (1974).

For a discussion of Donald Schön's concept of "reflective practice," see Schön (1983).

For an overview of the ecologically minded philosophy that is challenging us to rethink relations with our planet, see Berry (1988) and the writings on global mind change (e.g., Harman 1988).

APPENDIX A: THE THEORY BEHIND THE PRACTICE

Most of the detailed references relating to the ideas presented in this appendix are provided directly in the text. For convenience, some of the general references are reproduced below, together with other citations that will be helpful to readers interested in pursuing the general ideas.

On the debate about the social construction of reality, and the socially constructed nature of knowledge, see Berger and Luckmann (1966), Bernstein (1983), Burrell and Morgan (1979), Kuhn (1970), Morgan (1983), and Weick (1979).

On the relationship between knowledge and power, see Dreyfus and Rainbow (1982), Flax (1990), Foucault (1973, 1980), Freire (1970), Habermas (1972), and Rainbow (1984).

On the hermeneutic approach to social analysis, see Boland (1989), Gadamer (1975, 1976), and Rorty (1979, 1985). Boland (1989) provides a particularly clear exposition of basic principles.

On the role of images and metaphors in the social construction of reality, see Lakoff and Johnson (1980), Morgan (1983b), Ortony (1979), and White (1978).

On the links between knowledge, dialogue, and conversation, and the connection between knowledge and human interests, see Bernstein (1983), Bohr (1958a, 1958b), Heisenberg (1958, 1971), Morgan (1983), and Rorty (1979, 1985).

On the role of "reflective practice" and the art of framing and reframing, see Schön (1983) and Watzlawick et al. (1974).

On the relationship between understandings and actions in shaping reality, see Weick (1979).

On the postmodern approach to social theory and its relevance for organization and management theory, see Berman (1988), Calas and Smircich (1988), Cooper (1989), Cooper and Burrell (1988), Harvey (1989), Linstead and Grafton-Small (1992), Martin (1990), and Reed and Hughes (1992).

On the new science, cybernetics, and emerging theories of chaos and self-organization and their implications for management, see Gleick (1987), Jantsch (1980), Nonaka (1988), Prigogine and Stengers (1984), Stacey (1992), and Zimmerman (1992).

On the role of self-identity in processes of change, see Morgan (1986: 249-246), which links this issue, and by implication the idea of mirroring discussed in Appendix A, with writings on the theory of autopoiesis (Maturana and Varela 1980; Smith 1984; Varela, Maturana, and Uribe 1974). This theory seeks to explain how systems are able to produce and reproduce themselves and acquire enduring structure over time. The theory is very abstract and has been developed primarily to understand biological and cognitive systems. Its main proponents disclaim any direct relevance for understanding social systems. But, despite this, I find myself intrigued with one of the key autopoietic ideas: that the *identity* of a system is its most important product. This is an interesting notion, because most applications of systems theory emphasize how social systems like organizations are guided by goals and objectives and that relationships with the environment are shaped and structured to achieve these ends. The theory of autopoiesis seems to suggest otherwise: that systems structure their relationships with the environment to sustain a sense of identity, that they enact their environments as extensions of themselves. This has important implications, suggesting that, if you wish to change a system, it may be more important to work on its sense of identity than on the goals it is trying to achieve. If one can affect a system's basic sense of identity, one creates a potential for the system to reorganize its understanding of its environment. If you only try to change goals and objectives, the system's understanding of the environment may remain unchanged. These are some of the basic ideas underpinning the mirroring methodology discussed in Appendix A.

APPENDIX B: A NOTE ON RESEARCH METHOD

Appendix B provides a full discussion of the ideas underlying the action-learning methodology used in my research, together with lists of appropriate references.

Bibliography

Achterberg, J. *Imagery in Healing.* Boston: Shambala, 1985.

Agor, W. H. (ed.). *Intuition in Organizations: Leading and Managing Productively.* Newbury Park, CA: Sage, 1989.

Alvesson, M. and H. Willmott. *Critical Management Studies.* London: Sage, 1992.

Argyris, C., R. Putnam, and D. M. Smith. *Action Science: Concepts, Methods, and Skills for Research and Intervention.* San Francisco: Jossey-Bass, 1985.

Argyris C. and D. Schön. *Theory in Practice.* Reading, MA: Addison-Wesley, 1974.

Argyris, C. and D. Schön. *Organizational Learning: A Theory of Action Perspective.* Reading, MA: Addison-Wesley, 1978.

Astley, W. G. "Administrative Science as Socially Constructed Truth." *Administrative Science Quarterly,* 30: 497-513, 1985.

Baburoglu, O. N. and I. Ravn. "Normative Action Research." *Organization Studies,* 13: 229-295, 1992.

Bateson, G. *Steps to an Ecology of Mind.* New York: Ballantine, 1972.

Bateson, G. *Mind and Nature.* New York: Bantam, 1979.

Baum, H. *The Invisible Bureaucracy: The Unconscious in Organizational Problem Solving.* New York: Oxford University Press, 1987.

Beck, B. and L. Moore. "Linking the Host Culture to Organizational Variables," in P. J. Frost et al. (eds.), *Organizational Culture.* Beverly Hills, CA: Sage, 1985.

Beer, M., R. Eisenstat, and B. Spector. "Why Change Programs Don't Produce Change." *Harvard Business Review,* 67: 158-166, 1990.

Beer, S. *Brain of the Firm.* New York: Herder and Herder, 1972.

Beer, S. *Platform for Change.* Sussex, UK: John Wiley, 1975.

Berger P. and T. Luckmann. *The Social Construction of Reality.* Garden City, NY: Doubleday, 1966.

Berkeley, G. *A Treatise Concerning the Principles of Human Knowledge.* New York: Everyman (reprint), 1910a.

Berkeley, G. *A New Theory of Vision.* New York: Everyman (reprint), 1910b.

Berman, A. *From the New Criticism to Deconstruction.* Urbana: University of Illinois Press, 1988.

Bernstein, R. J. *Beyond Objectivism and Relativism: Science, Hermeneutics and Praxis.* Philadelphia: University of Pennsylvania Press, 1983.

Berry, T. *The Dream of the Earth.* San Francisco: Sierra Club Books, 1988.

Block, P. *The Empowered Manager.* San Francisco: Jossey-Bass, 1987.

Bohr, N. *Atomic Theory and the Description of Nature.* Cambridge, UK: Cambridge University Press, 1958a.

Bohr, N. *Atomic Theory and Human Knowledge.* New York: John Wiley, 1958b.

Boland, R. J. "Beyond the Objectivist and the Subjectivist: Learning to Read Accounting as Text." *Accounting, Organizations and Society,* 14: 591-604, 1989.

Bradley, R. T. *Charisma and Social Structure.* New York: Paragon, 1987.

Braverman, H. *Labor and Monopoly Capital.* New York: Monthly Review Press, 1974.

Brown, R. H. *A Poetic for Society.* New York: Cambridge University Press, 1977.

Burns, T. and G. M. Stalker. *The Management of Innovation.* London: Tavistock, 1961.

Burrell, G. and G. Morgan. *Sociological Paradigms and Organizational Analysis.* London: Heinemann, 1979.

Burroway, M. *Manufacturing Consent.* Chicago: University of Chicago Press, 1979.

Calas, M. and L. Smircich. "Reading Leadership as a Form of Cultural Analysis," in J. G. Hunt, R. D. Belliga, H. P. Dachler, and C. A. Schriesheim (eds.), *Emerging Leadership Vistas,* 201-226. Lexington, MA: Lexington, 1988.

Checkland, P. *Systems Thinking, Systems Practice.* Chichester, UK: John Wiley, 1981.

Checkland, P. and J. Scholes. *Soft Systems Methodology in Action.* Chichester, UK: John Wiley, 1990.

Cherns, A. "The Principles of Sociotechnical Design." *Human Relations,* 29: 783-792, 1976.

Clegg, S. and D. Dunkerly. *Organization, Class and Control.* London: Routledge & Kegan Paul, 1980.

Cooper, R. "The Other: A Model of Human Structuring," in G. Morgan (ed.), *Beyond Method,* 202-218. Beverly Hills, CA: Sage, 1983.

Cooper, R. "Modernism, Postmodernism, and Organizational Analysis 3: The Contribution of Jacques Derrida." *Organization Studies,* 10/4: 479-502, 1989.

Cooper, R. and G. Burrell. "Modernism, Postmodernism and Organizational Analysis: An Introduction." *Organization Studies,* 9: 91-112, 1988.

Davis, S. *Future Perfect.* Reading, MA: Addison-Wesley, 1987.

Davis, S. M. and P. R. Lawrence. *Matrix.* Reading, MA: Addison-Wesley, 1977.

DeBono, E. *Lateral Thinking.* Harmondsworth, UK: Penguin, 1970.

Denhardt, R. B. *In the Shadow of Organization.* Lawrence, KA: Regents Press, 1981.

Derrida, J. *Writing and Difference.* Chicago: University of Chicago Press, 1978.

Dewey, J. *The Quest for Certainty.* New York: Minton, Balch, 1929.

Dewey, J. *How We Think* (rev. ed.). Lexington, MA: D. C. Heath, 1933.

Dreyfus, H. F. and P. Rainbow. *Michel Foucault: Beyond Structuralism and Hermeneutics.* Brighton, UK: Harvester, 1982.

Edwards, R. C. *Contested Terrain.* New York: Basic Books, 1979.

Elden, M. and M. Levin. "Co-generative Learning: Bringing Participation into Action Research," in W. F. Whyte (ed.), *Participative Action Research.* Newbury Park, CA: Sage, 1991.

Emery, F. E. (ed.). *Systems Thinking.* Harmondsworth, UK: Penguin, 1969.

Emery, F. E. *Tenosynovitis or Repetition Strain Injuries.* Submission to Task Force on Repetition Strain Injury in the Australian Public Service, Canberra, Australia, 1984.

Emery, F. E. and M. Emery. *A Choice of Futures.* Leiden, the Netherlands: Nijhoff, 1976.

Emery, F. E. and E. L. Trist. *Toward a Social Ecology.* London: Tavistock, 1973.

Fals-Borda, O. "The Application of Participatory Action-Research in Latin-America." *International Sociology,* 2: 329-347, 1987.

Flax, J. *Thinking Fragments: Psychoanalysis, Feminism and Postmodernism in the Contemporary West.* Berkeley: University of California Press, 1990.

Foucault, M. *The Order of Things: The Archeology of the Human Sciences.* New York: Vintage, 1973.

Foucault, M. *Power/Knowledge,* C. Gordon (ed.). Brighton, UK: Harvester, 1980.

Frankl, V. *Man's Search for Meaning.* New York: Simon & Schuster, 1984.

Freire, P. *Pedagogy of the Oppressed.* New York: Seabury, 1970.

Frost, P. J. and C. P. Egri. "The Political Process of Innovation." *Research in Organizational Behavior,* 13: 229-295 (Greenwich, CT: JAI), 1991.

Frost, P. L., L. Moore, M. R. Louis, C. Lundberg, and J. Martin (eds.). *Organizational Culture.* Beverly Hills, CA: Sage, 1985.

Frost, P. L., L. Moore, M. R. Lovis, C. Lundberg, and J. Martin (eds.). *Reframing Organizational Culture.* Newbury Park, CA: Sage, 1991.

Gadamer, H. G. *Truth and Method.* New York: Seabury, 1975.

Gadamer, H. G. *Philosophical Hermeneutics.* Berkeley: University of California Press, 1976.

Geertz, C. *The Interpretation of Cultures.* New York: Basic Books, 1973.

Gemmill, G. and J. Oakley. "Leadership: An Alienating Social Myth?" *Human Relations,* 45: 113-129, 1992.

Gergen, K. J. *Toward Transformation in Social Knowledge.* New York: Springer-Verlag, 1982.

Gergen, K. J. "The Social Constructionist Movement in Modern Psychology." *American Psychologist,* 40/3: 266-275, 1985.

Glaser, B. G. and A. L. Strauss. *The Discovery of Grounded Theory.* Chicago: Aldine, 1967.

Gleick, J. *Chaos.* New York: Viking, 1987.

Gooderham, M. "Daring Young Man's Dream Is About to Take Off." *Globe and Mail* (Toronto), February 23, 1991, p. 10.

Gordon, D. *Therapeutic Metaphors: Helping Others Through the Looking Glass.*
     Cupertino, CA: Meta Publications, 1978.
Habermas, J. *Knowledge and Human Interests.* London: Heinemann, 1972.
Hackman, J. R. (ed.). *Groups That Work (and Those That Don't).* San Francisco:
     Jossey-Bass, 1990.
Hall, B. L. "Participatory Research, Popular Knowledge and Power: A Per-
     sonal Reflection." *Convergence,* 14: 6-17, 1981.
Hampden-Turner, C. *Charting the Corporate Mind.* New York: Free Press, 1990.
Handy, C. *The Age of Unreason.* Boston: Harvard Business School Press, 1989.
Harman, W. *Global Mind Change.* Indianapolis: Knowledge Systems Inc., 1988.
Harries-Jones, P. (ed.). *Making Knowledge Count.* Montreal: McGill-Queen's
     University Press, 1991.
Harvey, D. *The Condition of Postmodernity.* Oxford, UK: Basil Blackwell, 1989.
Hawken, P. *The Next Economy.* New York: Ballantine, 1983.
Heisenberg, W. *Physics and Philosophy.* New York: Harper, 1958.
Heisenberg, W. *Physics and Beyond: Encounters and Conversations.* New York:
     Harper & Row, 1971.
Herbst, P. G. *Socio-Technical Design.* London: Tavistock, 1974.
Hirschhorn, L. *The Workplace Within: The Psychodynamics of Organizational Life.*
     Cambridge: MIT Press, 1988.
Hirschhorn, L. *Managing in the New Team Environment.* Reading, MA: Addi-
     son-Wesley, 1991.
Hollinger, R. (ed.). *Hermeneutics and Practice.* Notre Dame: University of
     Notre Dame Press, 1985.
Howse, P. E. *Termites.* London: Hutchinson, 1970.
Hughes, H. S. *Consciousness and Society.* New York: Knopf, 1958.
Hunt, D. E. *The Renewal of Personal Energy.* Toronto: Institute for Studies in
     Education Press, 1992.
Hurst, D. K. "Of Boxes, Bubbles and Effective Management." *Harvard Business
     Review,* 62: 78-88, 1984.
Jantsch, E. *The Self Organizing Universe.* Oxford, UK: Pergamon, 1980.
Jaques, E. "Social Systems as a Defence Against Persecutory and Depressive
     Anxiety," in M. Klein (ed.), *New Directions in Psycho-Analysis,* 478-498.
     London: Tavistock, 1955.
Kanter, R. M. *The Change Masters.* New York: Simon & Schuster, 1983.
Kass, H. D. and B. R. Catron (eds.). *Images and Identities in Public Administra-
     tion.* Newbury Park, CA: Sage, 1990.
Keidel, R. *Corporate Players.* New York: John Wiley, 1988.
Kets de Vries, M. (ed.). *Organizations on the Couch.* San Francisco: Jossey-Bass,
     1991.
Kets de Vries, M. and D. Miller. *The Neurotic Organization.* San Francisco:
     Jossey-Bass, 1984.
Knights, D. and H. C. Willmott (eds.). *Managing the Labor Process.* Aldershot,
     UK: Gower, 1986.
Koestler, A. *The Act of Creation.* London: Hutchinson, 1969.
Kolodny, H. "Managing in a Matrix." *Business Horizons,* March: 17-24, 1981.

Krefting, L. A. and P. J. Frost. "Untangling Webs, Surfing Waves and Wild-catting," in P. J. Frost et al. (eds.), *Organizational Culture*. Beverly Hills, CA: Sage, 1985.

Kuhn, T. S. *The Structure of Scientific Revolution*. Chicago: University of Chicago Press, 1970.

Lakoff, G. and M. Johnson. *Metaphors We Live By*. Chicago: University of Chicago Press, 1980.

Larson, C. E. and F. M. J. LaFasto. *Teamwork*. Newbury Park, CA: Sage, 1989.

Lawrence, P. R. and J. W. Lorsch. *Organization and Environment*. Cambridge, MA: Harvard Graduate School of Business Administration, 1967.

Lewin, G. (ed.). *Resolving Social Conflicts*. New York: Harper & Row, 1948.

Lewin, K. "Cassirer's Philosophy of Science and Social Science," in P. A. Schlipp (ed.), *The Philosophy of Ernst Cassirer*. New York: Tudor, 1949.

Lewin, K. *Field Theory in Social Science*. New York: Harper & Row, 1951.

Lincoln, Y. S. and E. G. Guba. *Naturalistic Inquiry*. Beverly Hills, CA: Sage, 1985.

Linstead, S. and R. Grafton-Small. "On Reading Organizational Culture." *Organization Studies*, 13: 331-356, 1992.

Mackenzie, K. D. *The Organizational Hologram: The Effective Management of Organizational Change*. London: Kluer, 1991.

Marais, E. N. *The Soul of the White Ant*. Harmondsworth, UK: Penguin, 1973.

Martin, J. "Deconstructing Organizational Taboos: The Suppression of Gender Conflict in Organizations." *Organization Science*, 1: 339-359, 1990.

Maturana, H. and F. Varela. *Autopoiesis and Cognition: The Realization of the Living*. London: Reidl, 1980.

McLuhan, M. *Understanding Media*. New York: New American Library, 1964.

McLuhan, M. "Foreword," in *York Wilson* by Paul Duval. Ottawa: Nallack Galleries, 1978: 9-11.

Menzies, I. "A Case Study in Functioning of Social Systems as a Defence Against Anxiety." *Human Relations*, 13: 95-121, 1960.

Miller, D. *The Icarus Paradox*. New York: Harper & Row, 1990.

Mills, D. Q. *Rebirth of the Corporation*. New York: John Wiley, 1991.

Mintzberg, H. *The Nature of Managerial Work*. New York: Harper & Row, 1974.

Mintzberg, H. *The Structuring of Organizations*. Englewood Cliffs, NJ: Prentice-Hall, 1979.

Mintzberg, H. "Crafting Strategy." *Harvard Business Review*, 64: 66-75, 1987.

Mintzberg, H. and J. Waters. "Of Strategies, Deliberate and Emergent." *Strategic Management Journal*, 6: 257-272, 1985.

Mohrman, S. A. and T. G. Cummings. *Self Designing Organizations: Learning How to Create High Performance*. Reading, MA: Addison-Wesley, 1989.

Morgan, G. "Paradigms, Metaphors and Puzzle-Solving in Organization Theory." *Administrative Science Quarterly*, 25: 605-622, 1980.

Morgan, G. (ed.). *Beyond Method: Strategies for Social Research*. Beverly Hills, CA: Sage, 1983a.

Morgan, G. "More on Metaphor: Why We Cannot Control Tropes in Administrative Science." *Administrative Science Quarterly*, 28: 601-607, 1983b.

Morgan, G. *Images of Organization*. Newbury Park, CA: Sage, 1986.

Morgan, G. *Riding the Waves of Change: Developing Managerial Competencies for a Turbulent World.* San Francisco: Jossey-Bass, 1988.

Morgan, G. *Creative Organization Theory: A Resourcebook.* Newbury Park, CA: Sage, 1989a.

Morgan, G. "Organizational Choice and the New Technology," in D. Morley and S. Wright (eds.), *Learning Works.* Toronto: York University, ABL Publications, 1989b.

Morgan, G. and R. Ramirez. "Action Learning: A Holographic Metaphor for Guiding Social Change." *Human Relations,* 37: 1-28, 1984.

Morgan, G. and L. Smircich. "The Case for Qualitative Research." *Academy of Management Review,* 5: 491-500, 1980.

Morley, D. and R. Ramirez. "Food for the Future of Mexico." Occasional Paper. Toronto: York University Action Learning Group, 1983.

Morley, D. and S. Wright (eds.). *Learning Works.* Toronto: York University, ABL Publications, 1989.

Nadler, D., M. Gerstein, and R. Shaw (eds.). *Organizational Architecture.* San Francisco: Jossey-Bass, 1992.

Nonaka, I. "Creating Organizational Order out of Chaos: Self Renewal in Japanese Firms." *California Management Review,* Spring: 57-73, 1988.

Ortony, A. (ed.). *Metaphor and Thought.* Cambridge, MA: Cambridge University Press, 1979.

Pascale, R. T. "Honda B." Harvard Business School Case No. 384-050, 1983.

Pascale, R. T. "Perspectives on Strategy: The Real Story Behind Honda's Success." *California Management Review,* 26: 47-72, 1984.

Pava, C. *Normative Incrementalism.* Ph.D. Dissertation. Philadelphia: University of Pennsylvania, Wharton School, 1980.

Peat, D. *The Philosopher's Stone: Chaos, Synchronicity and the Hidden Order of the World.* New York: Bantam, 1991.

Peters, T. *Thriving on Chaos: Handbook for a Managerial Revolution.* New York: Knopf, 1987.

Peters, T. *Liberation Management.* New York: Knopf, 1992.

Pinder, C. C. and V. W. Bourgeois. "Controlling Tropes in Administrative Science." *Administrative Science Quarterly,* 27: 641-652, 1982.

Prigogine, I. and I. Stengers. *Order out of Chaos.* New York: Bantam, 1984.

Quinn, R. E. *Beyond Rational Management: Mastering the Paradoxes and Competing Demands of High Performance.* San Francisco: Jossey-Bass, 1990.

Rainbow, P. (ed.). *The Foucault Reader.* Harmondsworth, UK: Penguin, 1984.

Rapoport, R. N. "Three Dilemmas in Action Research." *Human Relations,* 23: 499-513, 1970.

Reason, P. *Human Inquiry in Action.* Newbury Park, CA: Sage, 1988.

Reed, M. and M. Hughes (eds.). *Rethinking Organization.* London: Sage, 1992.

Reich, R. *The Next American Frontier.* New York: Times Books, 1983.

Revans, R. *Action Learning.* Bromley, UK: Chartwell Bratt, 1982.

Rorty, R. *Philosophy and the Mirror of Nature.* Princeton, NJ: Princeton University Press, 1979.

Rorty, R. *Consequences of Pragmatism.* Minneapolis: University of Minneapolis Press, 1985.

Russell, P. and R. Evans. *The Creative Manager: Finding Inner Vision and Wisdom in Uncertain Times*. San Francisco: Jossey-Bass, 1992.

Saussure, F. de. *Course in General Linguistics*. New York: McGraw-Hill, 1955.

Schön, D. A. *Invention and the Evolution of Ideas*. London: Tavistock, 1963.

Schön, D. A. "Generative Metaphor: A Perspective on Problem Setting in Social Policy," in A. Ortony (ed.), *Metaphor and Thought*, 254-283. Cambridge, MA: Cambridge University Press, 1979.

Schön, D. A. *The Reflective Practitioner*. New York: Basic Books, 1983.

Schwartz, H. *Narcissistic Process and Corporate Decay*. New York: New York University Press, 1990.

Sheldrake, R. *A New Science of Life*. London: Bland and Briggs, 1981.

Sheldrake, R. *The Presence of the Past*. New York: Vintage, 1988.

Shotter, J. "The Manager as Author." A paper prepared for the Conference on Social-Organizational Theory, St. Gallen, Switzerland, August 1990.

Siegel, B. *Love, Medicine and Miracles*. New York: Harper & Row, 1988.

Smircich, L. "Studying Organizations as Cultures," in G. Morgan (ed.), *Beyond Method*, 160-172. Beverly Hills, CA: Sage, 1983.

Smircich, L. and M. Calas. "Organizational Culture: A Critical Assessment," in F. Jablin, L. Putnam, K. Roberts, and L. Porter (eds.), *Handbook of Organizational Communication*. Newbury Park, CA: Sage, 1987.

Smith, C. "Transformation and Regeneration in Social Systems: A Dissipative Structure Perspective." *Systems Research*, 3: 203-213, 1986.

Smith, C. and G. Gemmill. "Change in Small Groups: A Dissipative Structure Perspective." *Human Relations*, 44: 697-716, 1991.

Smith, K. K. "Rabbits, Lynxes and Organizational Transitions," in J. R. Kimberley and R. E. Quinn (eds.), *New Futures: The Challenge of Managing Corporate Transitions*, 267-294. Homewood, IL: Irwin, 1984.

Smith, K. K. and D. N. Berg. *Paradoxes of Group Life*. San Francisco: Jossey-Bass, 1987.

Stacey, R. D. *The Chaos Frontier: Creative Strategic Control for Business*. Oxford, UK: Butterworth-Heinemann, 1991.

Stacey, R. D. *Managing the Unknowable: Strategic Boundaries Between Order and Chaos in Organizations*. San Francisco: Jossey-Bass, 1992.

Stalk, G. and T. Hout. *Competing Against Time*. New York: Free Press, 1990.

Stewart, A. *Team Entrepreneurship*. Newbury Park, CA: Sage, 1989.

Susman, G. I. "Action Research: A Socio Technical Systems Perspective," in G. Morgan (ed.), *Beyond Method*, 95-113. Beverly Hills, CA: Sage, 1983.

Susman, G. I. and R. D. Evered. "An Assessment of the Scientific Merits of Action Research." *Administrative Science Quarterly*, 23: 582-603, 1978.

Taylor, F. W. *Principles of Scientific Management*. New York: Harper & Row, 1911.

Taylor, G. R. *The Natural History of the Mind*. New York: Dutton, 1979.

Thomas, L. *The Lives of a Cell*. New York: Penguin, 1974.

Tichy, N. *Managing Strategic Change*. New York: John Wiley, 1983.

Tichy, N. and M. Devanna. *The Transformational Leader*. New York: John Wiley, 1987.

Trist, E. L. "Action Research and Adaptive Planning," in A. W. Clark (ed.), *Experimenting with Organizational Life.* New York: Plenum, 1976.

Trist, E. L. "The Evolution of Sociotechnical Systems as a Conceptual Framework and as an Action Research Program," in A. H. Van de Ven and W. F. Joyce (eds.), *Perspectives on Organization Design and Behavior.* New York: John Wiley, 1982.

Trist, E. L. "Intervention Strategies for Interorganizational Domains," in R. Tannenbaum et al. (eds.), *Human Systems Development.* San Francisco: Jossey-Bass, 1985.

Trist, E. L. and H. Murray (eds.). *The Social Engagement of Social Science: A Tavistock Anthology.* Philadelphia: University of Pennsylvania Press.

Tsoukas, H. "The Missing Link: A Transformational View of Metaphors in Organizational Science." *Academy of Management Review,* 16: 566-585, 1991.

Turner, S. "Studying Organization Through Levi-Strauss's Structuralism," in G. Morgan (ed.), *Beyond Method.* Beverly Hills, CA: Sage, 1983.

Varela, F. G., H. R. Maturana, and R. Uribe. "Autopoiesis, The Organization of Living Systems." *Biosystems,* 5: 187-196, 1974.

Watson, L. *Lifetide.* New York: Simon & Schuster, 1979.

Watzlawick, P., J. Weakland, and R. Fisch. *Change: Principles of Problem Formation and Problem Resolution.* New York: Norton, 1974.

Weick, K. E. *The Social Psychology of Organizing.* Reading, MA: Addison-Wesley, 1979.

Weick, K. E. "Substitutes for Strategy," in D. J. Teece (ed.), *The Competitive Challenge.* Cambridge, MA: Ballinger, 1987.

Wheatley, M. *Leadership and the New Science: Learning About Organization from an Orderly Universe.* San Francisco: Berret-Koehler, 1992.

White, E. B. *Charlotte's Web.* New York: Harper, 1952.

White, H. *The Tropics of Discourse.* Baltimore: Johns Hopkins University Press, 1978.

Whyte, W. F. "Introduction," in "Action Research for the Twenty-First Century: Participation, Reflection, and Practice." *American Behavioral Scientist,* 32: 5, 502-512, 1989.

Whyte, W. F. (ed.). *Participative Action Research.* Newbury Park, CA: Sage, 1991.

Williams, T. A. *Learning to Manage Our Futures.* New York: John Wiley, 1982.

Williams, T. A. "Visual Display Technology, Worker Displacement and Work Organization." *Human Relations,* 38: 1065-1084, 1985.

Wilson, E. O. *Social Insects.* Cambridge, MA: Harvard University Press, 1971.

Wilson, E. O. and B. Holldobler. *The Ant.* Cambridge, MA: Harvard University Press, 1990.

Wittgenstein, L. *Tractatus Logico-Philosophicus.* London: Routledge & Kegan Paul, 1922.

Wittgenstein, L. *Philosophical Investigations.* Oxford, UK: Basil Blackwell, 1958.

Zaleznik, A. and M. Kets de Vries. *Power and the Corporate Mind.* Boston: Houghton Mifflin, 1975.

Zimmerman, B. "The Inherent Drive Towards Chaos," in P. Lorange, B. Chakravathy, J. Roos, and A. Van de Ven (eds.), *Strategic Processes for the 1990s*. London: Basil Blackwell, 1992.

Zimmerman, B. and D. K. Hurst. "Breaking the Boundaries: The Fractal Organization." Forthcoming.

Zuboff, S. *The Age of the Smart Machine: The Future of Work and Power*. New York: Basic Books, 1988.

Zweig, C. and J. Abrams (eds.). *Meeting the Shadow*. New York: Jeremy Tarcher, 1991.

Index

339

About
the
Author

Gareth Morgan is well known for his creative contributions to management. He is the author of seven books, including *Images of Organization, Creative Organization Theory* and *Riding the Waves of Change*. He acts as consultant and seminar leader to numerous organizations throughout Europe and North America, and is Distinguished Research Professor at York University in Toronto. He has sat on the editorial boards of the *Academy of Management Review, Administration and Society, The Journal of Management,* and *Organization Studies;* and is a Life Fellow of the International Academy of Management. Born in Wales, he now lives in Toronto with his wife, Karen, and their children Evan and Heather.